MARIJUANA BUSINESS

HOW TO OPEN AND SUCCESSFULLY RUN A MARIJUANA DISPENSARY AND GROW FACILITY

TABLE OF CONTENTS

SECTION IV

Location and Building Structures

SECTION V

Construction of your Dispensary and Grow Facility

SECTION VI

Security

Photos: Inside Your Grow Facility

SECTION VII

Employees

SECTION VIII

The Grow Facility

SECTION I

THE NEW GOLD RUSH

Rushes of Yesterday

IN THE 1800s, HUNDREDS OF THOUSANDS OF AMERICANS CAUGHT "GOLD FEVER" and were richly rewarded for finding caches of the soft, yellow, magical metal. The saying back then was "Thar's gold in them thar hills!" Gold was big business; it involved big dreams and made big money, which helped create cities like San Francisco, Sacramento, and Eureka in California, as well as Leadville, Central City, and Cripple Creek in Colorado.

The discovery of gold near these cities also created an empire for merchants meeting the demand for needed supplies—tools, wagons, burrows, dry and canned goods, to name a few. Gold strikes were *gold* for local businesses too. People moved long distances to get a slice of the golden pie—this business of mining and digging for gold, and selling products and services to assist in that endeavor. Riches were there to be had, and many made fortunes in this new, lucrative business. Hard work, long hours, and sometimes luck made many families wealthy. Today people worldwide still consider investments in gold to be the safest, most enduring investment available.

During Prohibition in the 1920s, beer and alcohol production companies like Coors, Anheuser-Busch, Falstaff Brewing, Berghoff Brewing, Jim Beam Distillery, Jack Daniels Distillery, and Southern Comfort Distillery had to scramble to convert their facilities to produce non-alcoholic beverages. Many of the beer producers altered their facilities to make soft drinks, while the distilleries either went underground or temporarily out of business. They struggled to keep afloat until Prohibition was repealed. After Prohibition, these same companies once again generated hundreds of millions of dollars in sales, which in turn generated millions of dollars in state and federal revenue. Alcohol became the next "gold rush." The breweries and distilleries also created jobs for countless numbers of people, feeding the economy with their spirits.

And now we are in the midst of the next rush: the business of growing and dispensing marijuana.

Beginning in 1996, over twenty states and the District of Columbia have legalized medical marijuana. Revenues from these sales have increased the coffers in those states and allowed them to benefit from the latest "gold rush." Now the saying has become "Thar's weed in them thar hills!"

In 2012, two states, Washington and Colorado, bravely advanced to the next step and legalized marijuana for personal/recreational use. As of this publishing, there are forty-three states that have ballot measures to allow medical marijuana, and four states have put a legalized marijuana proposal on ballots for upcoming elections in 2014.

> **FACT**
>
> **Marijuana is the most common illegal drug used in the United States. Approximately 100 million Americans have tried marijuana at least once, and more than 25 million have smoked it in the last year.**

As of right now, Wall Street doesn't cover the marijuana market as an industry. However, some professional investors have seen many new start-ups begin to influence investors in the emerging market. Todd Harrison, CEO and founder of Internet-based financial media company Minyanville Media, Inc., predicts this will change. Harrison feels that once legalization is more widespread, investing in marijuana businesses will become a more conventional arena. Harrison says the marijuana industry "will be the single best investment idea for the next ten years and more." (Lauren Lyster, February 27, 2014, 12:19 p.m., *Daily Ticker*) For the industrious and savvy entrepreneur—who can certainly be any one of us—the possibilities for making a substantial amount of money investing in marijuana businesses, Harrison believes, will be driven by the broader legalization of marijuana, inspired by states' needs for tax revenue. He points to expectations that legal marijuana use is expected to generate $134 million in tax revenue for the upcoming fiscal year in Colorado, the first state to allow recreational marijuana. That's nothing to sneeze at, and Harrison calls the state the "litmus test" for broader legalization. Harrison also cites the expected decline in crime rates and prison populations as powerful incentives to decriminalize marijuana use.

Is this the new Gold Rush? Will people want to get involved with this industry? What is the potential for earnings . . . millions? Billions? As more states agree to the sale of marijuana, the opportunity to open dispensaries and/or grow facilities will continue to rise. Over the last two decades, large corporations like Monsanto, a sustainable agricultural company, have bought up hundreds of family farms and turned their food harvests into huge profits. It is not a stretch to envision the same tactics being applied to the marijuana industry. The opportunity is here, and it's real, and the possibilities are endless.

This book is a step-by-step guide to help you be on the winning side of this Green Rush. Your journey starts here . . .

Cannabis in History

MENTION MARIJUANA TO THE AVERAGE AMERICAN, and you're likely to conjure images of kids at Woodstock or teenage stoners toking in their parents' basements. But cannabis has been used—as both a recreational drug and medicine—for tens of thousands of years, starting in Central and South Asia. In Romania, charred cannabis seeds were discovered in a ritual brazier (a bowl or box typically used for burning fuel) dating back to the third millennium BCE. Ancient mummies, from China to Egypt, have been found alongside leaf fragments and seeds, showing evidence of cannabis consumption in some. Like many products made from herbs and flowers, the use of cannabis is an age old remedy "for what ails ya."

Cannabis is a flowering plant genus (of three known types) that is known world-wide, and the drug that we know as cannabis or marijuana has many different names, depending on the locale. The ancient Hindus of India and Nepal called it *ganjika*—scholars still dispute whether it's connected with the drug soma, which was mentioned in the *Vedas*, the oldest scriptures of Hinduism. The Aryans introduced it to the Assyrians, who came to know it as *qunubu*, or "way to produce smoke," as well as to the Scythians, Thracians, and Dacians. The shamans in many of these cultures used the drug in their religious ceremonies and to induce trances. Archaeologists at Pazyryk, the Altai Mountain Region of southwestern Siberia, have found evidence of the consumption of hemp seeds as a religious sacrament (which matched reports by ancient Greek historian Herodotus). It also became a staple of some Sufi orders of Islam during the Mamluk period, nearly one thousand years ago.

> **FACT**
>
> **The first two drafts of the United States Declaration of Independence were written on paper made from hemp.**

Curiously enough, a 2001 study published in the *South African Journal of Science* revealed that two dozen clay pipes dug up from the garden of William Shakespeare contained traces of cannabis. It is speculated that Shakespeare's references to "noted weed" and "journey in my head" of Sonnets 76 and 27, respectively, might point to his use of the drug.

Cannabis made its way to North America, where nineteenth-century author John Gregory Bourke noted in The Medicine Men of the Apache the use of *mariguan*—Cannabis indica, or Indian hemp—by the Mexican residents of the Rio Grande Region of Texas. In writings dating back to 1894, he describes the ways in which *mariguan* treated asthma, eased women through childbirth, and kept away witches and evil spirits. It was rolled into cigarettes or

> **FACT**
>
> **From 1850 to 1942, marijuana was listed in the United States Pharmacopoeia as a useful medicine for nausea, rheumatism, and labor pains and was easily obtained at the local general store or pharmacy.**

added to mescal (a colorless alcohol akin to tequila) and was often taken with sugar to supposedly enhance the effects. Bourke also mentioned that *mariguan* was also known as "loco weed," and likened it to hasheesh . . . "one of the greatest curses of the East," which he believed made its users "become maniacs . . . apt to commit all sorts of acts of violence and murder."

Not long afterward, cannabis was criminalized in countries around the world, including the United States. The sale of the drug was first restricted in Washington, DC, in 1906. The Marihuana Tax Act was passed in 1937, prohibiting the production of the drug. Around the same time, the "dangers" of marijuana use were dramatized in the propaganda film *Reefer Madness* (originally titled *Tell Your Children*), in which formerly clean-cut teenagers get high, hit pedestrians with cars, commit suicide, and eventually go mad.

As we all know from pop culture, marijuana was embraced by the counterculture of the late 1960s, and its use became far more widespread. By the 1970s, state laws and local regulations that banned the sale and possession of cannabis were beginning to be abolished, thanks in part to the 1969 ruling in Leary v. United States, which deemed the Marihuana Tax Act unconstitutional. In the 1970s, Nixon declared the War on Drugs—calling drug abuse "public enemy number one"—and labeled cannabis a Schedule I drug, the most restrictive category. By the end of the decade, however, a fifth of the country had already decriminalized possession. Nixon dramatically increased the size and presence of federal drug control agencies, and pushed through measures such as mandatory sentencing and no-knock warrants. Nixon temporarily placed marijuana in Schedule I, the most restrictive category of drugs, pending review by a commission he appointed, led by Republican Pennsylvania Governor, Raymond Shafer. In

FACT

Harry Anslinger, the Commissioner of the Federal Bureau of Narcotics from 1930 until 1962, is responsible for spreading anti-marijuana myths and starting a national movement against weed. He said the only marijuana smokers in the US were mostly Negroes, Hispanics, Filipinos and entertainers . . . their Satanic music, jazz and swing resulted from marijuana use . . . this marijuana caused women to seek sexual relations with Negroes, entertainers and any other types of hoodlums.

1972, the commission unanimously recommended decriminalizing the possession and distribution of marijuana for personal use. He ignored the report and rejected its recommendations.

Between 1973 and 1977, however, eleven states decriminalized marijuana possession. In January 1977, President Jimmy Carter was inaugurated on a campaign platform that included marijuana decriminalization. In October 1977, the Senate Judiciary Committee voted to decriminalize possession of up to an ounce of marijuana for personal use. Nixon's private war on the use of drugs and his obsession with marijuana regulations were quickly losing their foothold amongst other political parties.

All through the 1980s, the comedy duo of Cheech and Chong made a living satirizing the use of marijuana. Their groundbreaking movies helped develop a new public awareness and alter an entire generation's view on "smoking a 'j'," "rolling a joint," "doing a doobie," and the ramifications of the illegality of marijuana. This simple-minded comedy made light of the use of marijuana in a time when many people in the United States viewed marijuana use as a major offense. Succesful beyond their wildest dreams, their hilarious irreverent, satirical, pot-smoking culture, no-holds-barred comedy skits about pot smoking hippies moved nine hit comedy albums and eight films to number one, breaking box office records, shattering comedy album sales and garnering multiple Grammy nominations, mesmerizing fans for over a decade.

The end of the Vietnam conflict brought home many American soldiers looking to self-medicate their post-traumatic stress symptoms with the help of marijuana. For many of these Vets, marijuana meant life. It allowed them to cope, sleep and manage the demons of war. (*For Veterans, Marijuana Can Mean Life*, Tim King, *Salem News*.com, 11/28/2007)

When the Reagans entered the White House, their "Just Say No!" campaign took over the nation; the federal government began to crack down, with more and more marijuana arrests. But as the hysteria wound down, advocates began to speak up for sensible drug reform.

In 1992, then Governor Clinton said he "never denied" smoking marijuana. (*New York Times*, Gwen Ifil, March 30, 1992) "I didn't say I was holier than thou, I said I tried. I never denied that I used marijuana." Of his Rhodes Scholar years, Clinton has said, "When I was in England, I experimented with marijuana a time or two and didn't like it." That became the now infamous statement: "I didn't inhale." This undoubtedly opened the eyes of many Americans—*if the president tried it, then how bad can it be? Why shouldn't I?*

In 1996, Proposition 215—which allowed for medical use of marijuana—passed in California. Since then, twenty different states, as well as Washington, DC, have passed similar laws.

The report from *High Times* magazine, January 2014, also claims that the five-year national market has the potential to balloon to $10.2 billion—a more than 700% increase above the current value. This growth will come from both increased demand in existing state markets and new venues in the fourteen states that are expected to have legalized recreational marijuana sales by then. Specifically, the report predicts that within five years Alaska, Oregon, Rhode Island, New Hampshire, Vermont, Maryland, Hawaii, Maine, Missouri, Massachusetts, Nevada, Arizona, California, and Delaware will have legalized marijuana for adults.

In 2012, the United Nations revealed 2010 statistics in its Global Drug Report: cannabis was the world's most widely produced, trafficked, and consumed drug, with an estimated 119 to 224 million adult users.

In November 2013, Colorado and Washington became the first states to legalize recreational use of marijuana. As of this publishing, legalization efforts are taking place in many other states, including Alaska, Arizona, Maryland, and New York.

President Barack Obama has recently given those who favor marijuana legalization the ammo they need for a battle at the federal level. In an interview with David Remnick of the *New Yorker*, President Obama went on record to defend marijuana use, saying, "I don't think it is more dangerous than alcohol." That quote had immeasurable impact on Americans—for better or for worse—but it definitely cast a new light on the acceptance of marijuana use as not only a medical aid, but a source of recreational enjoyment.

Times are truly changing—and changing fast—for this controversial plant.

What *is* the Controversy?

MARIJUANA CAN BE USED TO HEIGHTEN EUPHORIA, to relax, and to increase one's appetite. Less positive side effects can include a decrease in short-term memory, dry mouth, impaired motor skills, reddened eyes, and increased paranoia or anxiety.

Since the 1950s, drug policy in the United States has followed a simple tenet: use of cannabis leads, almost inevitably, to harder drugs. This "gateway" concept remains difficult to shake, and its validity remains widely debated. Some studies have concluded that there is no proof that marijuana use leads to use of harder drugs, while others indicate that hard drug users are likely to abuse a variety of substances. Proponents of the latter theory believe that interventions must address the use of multiple drugs, not just the hard ones.

FACT

Worldwide, it is estimated that about 162 million adults use marijuana at least once per year, and 22.5 million use the drug daily.

According to a similar hypothesis, users of any illegal substance—including cannabis—are more likely to be involved in situations that introduce them to hard drugs and the people who sell them. This argument allows alcohol and tobacco products to be considered gateway drugs as well. On the other hand, it stands to reason that cannabis is simply more accessible to users, especially younger ones, than harder substances—and alcohol and tobacco, in most cases, are even more accessible than cannabis. Perhaps the curious will experiment with any drug they're offered, regardless of a proper "gateway sequence."

On the medical marijuana front, cannabis has been a blessing to many people worldwide beset with health ailments. Because the drug is known to reduce nausea and vomiting, it is often prescribed to people suffering from AIDS or being treated with chemotherapy. It can also treat pain and muscle spasticity in some forms of epilepsy.

The American Society of Addiction Medicine remains skeptical about the medicinal value of cannabis, as the plant does not meet its standard requirements for approved medicines. The U.S. Food and Drug Administration (FDA) asserts that the side effects of the drug can be harmful, and that its production and supply should remain unregulated. They do, however, approve of small, controlled doses of pure THC (tetrahydrocannabinol), the primary psychoactive element of cannabis. The FDA's announcement is

NEWS FLASH

Effective May 30, 2014, the House GOP voted to prohibit federal agents from busting medical marijuana operations that are legal under state laws.

puzzling at many levels. It makes no mention of any recent FDA analysis or investigation, regulatory filing, or any other activity within the normal scope of the agency's work that led to this policy change.

Currently, the federal government classifies marijuana as a Schedule I substance, but its compounds, like CBD and THC, can be reclassified at a lower level of risk if approved for medical use by the FDA. The agency's approval of the synthetic THC-based drug Marinol in 1985, for example, resulted in THC becoming a Schedule III substance.

The classification of marijuana as Schedule I puts the plant into "the most dangerous" category of illegal substances "with no currently accepted medical use." The Schedule I status is why the FEDS continue to raid medical marijuana dispensaries and prosecute the owners and workers. It's also part of the problem scientists have in obtaining cannabis, and funding, to conduct legal research on the drug in the U.S.

FACT

According to one report, it would take 800 joints to kill a person—but the cause of death would be carbon monoxide poisoning.

If marijuana were reclassified as Schedule III—like THC—it would be officially recognized as having an accepted medical use and presenting less potential for abuse and addiction. (Matt Ferner, *Huffington Post*, March 7, 2014)

Marijuana and Crime

THE U.S. WAR ON DRUGS PLACES GREAT EMPHASIS ON ARRESTING PEOPLE for smoking marijuana. Since 1990, approximately 17 million Americans have been arrested on marijuana charges, a greater number than the entire populations of Alaska, Delaware, the District of Columbia, Montana, North Dakota, South Dakota, Vermont, and Wyoming combined. In 2010, state and local law enforcement arrested 746,000 people for marijuana violations. This is an increase of 800 percent since 1980 and the highest per capita in the world.

As has been the case throughout the 1990s, into the 2000s, and continuing today, the overwhelming majority of marijuana violation charges were for simple possession—around 88%. The remaining 12% were for sale/manufacture, an FBI category that includes marijuana grown for personal use or purely for medical purposes. FBI statistics indicate that one marijuana smoker is arrested every 45 seconds in America. Taken together, the total number of marijuana arrests for 2010 far exceeded the combined number of arrests for violent crimes, including murder, manslaughter, forcible rape, robbery, and aggravated assault.

Like most Americans, people who smoke marijuana also pay taxes, love and support their families, and work hard to make a better life for their children. State agencies frequently step in and declare children of marijuana smokers to be in danger, and many children are placed into foster homes as a result. This causes enormous pain, suffering and financial hardship for millions of American families. It also engenders distrust and disrespect for the law and for the criminal justice system overall.

Legalization is also becoming widely accepted as a social justice issue. Advocates have become increasingly vocal, arguing that it makes no sense for federal authorities to continue treating marijuana as a Schedule I substance, alongside substances like heroin and LSD. (drugwarfacts.org)

FACT

There are currently hundreds of different slang terms used for marijuana, including pot, weed, grass, green, herb, ganja, Mary Jane, dank, chronic, doja, reefer, dope, cheeba, bud, and hydro. You've probably heard most of those, but there's more to marijuana than the laundry list of pseudonyms.

Legalization = Revenue

IN 1996, CALIFORNIA LEGALIZED MEDICAL MARIJUANA. Washington and Alaska soon followed, legalizing medical marijuana in 1998, and Maine legalized medical marijuana in 1999. There are twenty states plus Washington, DC, which have allowed the legalization of medical marijuana.

Then history was made on November 6, 2012.

Marijuana was legalized for recreational use in Colorado and Washington. In those two states, people over the age of 21 can now possess up to an ounce of marijuana for recreational use and grow up to six plants. These states have become the testing grounds for the rest of the country. They will be watched and analyzed as their residents begin to grow and carry "weed" without fear of being arrested.

A recent report in the *Denver Post* reported that sales of recreational marijuana and edible marijuana products generated $1.3 million dollars in sales. This figure covered November and December sales for 2013 and is only the beginning of a very lucrative enterprise for those willing and able to invest now in the Green Rush.

As of February 1, 2014, the Colorado Department of Revenue reported one third of a million dollars had been collected in taxes as a result of sales in recreational marijuana stores in the first thirty days of being officially open. Part of these proceeds will go into the general education fund for Colorado.

The legal/recreational/medical marijuana marketplace is estimated to grow 64 percent to $2.34 billion in 2014 from $1.44 billion, according to a recent report by marijuana investment and research firm Arcview Group. This translates into increasing city and state revenue as well as enabling the general population to benefit from added steady jobs: a potential win-win situation for all.

With favorable revenue results in such a short time after legalizing recreational use in Colorado, the marijuana craze is likely to steamroll across the country, not slowing down anytime soon. In states around the nation, pro-pot legislators, bolstered by public opinion and the examples set by Colorado and Washington, are putting the once-taboo issue before their colleagues, hoping to become the next state to legalize. Activists are also making a push to get the issue before voters as early as 2015 with well-funded campaigns in many states, even some as unlikely as Florida.

The sudden interest by legislators in even the most conservative southern states to consider legalization, or at least get the issue of medical use marijuana in front of voters, is driven by the staggering tax revenue that each state could generate from sales. The Board of Equalization estimates that legalizing marijuana could generate about $1.4 billion in state tax revenue annually. There are also other ways this new industry could benefit states besides an increase in state tax revenue, like increasing consumer purchases of goods and services, creating new job opportunities, and most importantly, helping people with many medical conditions. Legal marijuana business will create job growth, such as construction, labor, technical, marketing, legal, and administrative. These are just a few of the professions that will be needed to build, outfit, open, advertise, and operate these locations around the United States.

Additionally, the significant decrease in minor "marijuana drug" offenses would keep thousands of people out of jail, which would ease the overcrowding in those facilities and save taxpayer dollars and headaches.

Is this the beginning of a multi-state reformation process on the legality of marijuana much like the state-by-state rollback of Prohibition in the early twentieth century?

The parallels are obvious. Like alcohol prohibition before it, the criminalization of cannabis is a failed federal policy that delegates the burden of enforcement to the state and local police. How did America's "Noble Experiment" with alcohol prohibition come to an end? When a sufficient number of states, led by New York in 1923 and ultimately joined by nearly a dozen others, enacted legislation repealing the states' alcohol laws, prohibition effectively discontinued. With state police and prosecutors no longer enforcing the federal government's unpopular law, politicians eventually had no choice but to abandon the policy altogether. History now repeats itself.

It wasn't considered possible to repeal federal alcohol prohibition until states ramped up the pressure by repealing their own prohibition laws from the books. Now that polls are increasingly showing nationwide majority support for marijuana legalization and voters in two states have actually passed legalization measures, expect to see more states jumping on board quickly. We can also expect to see more members of Congress and elected officials who heretofore have only supported us silently behind closed doors, start to speak out and take action publicly. The politicians have been behind the people on this one, but more savvy leaders are starting to realize that there's political opportunity in getting in front of this issue. (Matt Cantor, *Newser Staff*, April 8, 2014)

The momentum is on legalization's side. Since it now has the forces of capitalism behind it—one study has predicted a $10 billion industry by 2018—steps may soon be taken to further normalize the marijuana business. For opponents who believe marijuana is damaging to the mind and body, these financial stats appear to be of less importance. While supporters of marijuana use continually cite the comparative effects of weed and alcohol, or counter anti-pot studies with emerging research that has supported the drug's therapeutic qualities, scientific research into the effects of marijuana will continue to be discouraged until the federal ban on the substance is lifted or relaxed—and maybe not even then. People will always be divided on subjects such as these. Still, the medical marijuana industry is very young, and new studies are just coming out and will continue to emerge to support the drug's therapeutic effects.

The recent legalizations have increased public awareness and have opened new avenues for business opportunities. While debates on marijuana's health effects should and will continue even beyond the next wave of legalizations, it's clear that the floodgates have already opened. More states will legalize marijuana, either for medical or for recreational/personal use, and some will do so relatively soon. Public support for legalization of marijuana is at an all-time high. Nationwide polls range from 44 to 52 percent. In California, 56 percent of the population supports legalization of marijuana. It is an exciting and historical time for California as the battle for legalization is nearing an end, with victory lingering around the corner.

How long before every state in the union legalizes the medical/personal use of marijuana? No crystal ball here, but as Bob Marley once said, "Herb is the healing power of nations."

The American Dream

FOR HUNDREDS OF THOUSANDS OF IMMIGRANTS, the Statue of Liberty was their first view of the United States, signifying a new life filled with unlimited opportunities. The statue is an iconic symbol of the "American Dream."

The "American Dream" is the national ethos of the United States, a set of ideals in which freedom includes the opportunity for prosperity, success, and upward social mobility achieved through hard work. In 1931, James Turslow Adams, an American writer and historian, wrote about the American dream: "Life should be better and richer and fuller for everyone, with opportunity for each according to ability or achievement . . . regardless of the fortuitous circumstances of birth or position."

The idea of the American Dream is rooted in the United States Declaration of Independence, which proclaims that "all men are created equal" and that they are "endowed by their Creator with certain unalienable Rights," including "Life, Liberty and the pursuit of Happiness."

Is the American Dream still possible in today's economic environment? Have the United States and the rest of the world hit a plateau regarding new business ventures and the ability to find wealth? The *New York Times* and the *Wall Street Journal* have recently published articles stating "The American Dream is Dying" and that thirty percent fewer new businesses are opening today than ten years ago. Does this close the window of opportunity for would-be entrepreneurs? If this were the case would no new businesses be developed? Would business in general stop all together? Of course not! Mark Zuckerberg is an American computer programmer, internet entrepreneur, and philanthropist. He is the chairman and chief executive of Facebook, Inc., and his personal wealth, as of April 2014, is estimated to be $25 billion. Together with his college roommates, their "Dream" was launched. Your business dream is up to you. This book will help you get there and put you on the right path to your American Dream ...

Close your eyes and ponder that for a minute. Think about the possibilities of finding that American Dream! Will you be the next Mark Zuckerberg? Why not?

What's more American than baseball and apple pie? Not much, but owning your own slice of the pie and succeeding because of your hard work is the dream come true. What is your American Dream? What does your slice of the pie look like? Is it marriage, two kids, and a big house in the suburbs or a swanking condo overlooking the ocean? Or is it living in the middle of the city, eating fine food, shopping in great boutiques and traveling around the world? Or does it look completely different? Like maybe building a quiet cabin in the woods, meandering along a quiet river, climbing the highest of mountains, or becoming a voice for a subject that tugs at your heart? While millions of people trudge off to work each day for a company that provides the promise of a regular paycheck (if you're lucky), job security (if you're lucky), and a benefits package (if you're lucky), millions more aren't content to have someone else control their destiny and limit access to fulfilling their dreams. If you are among the second group that says, "I want to participate in life on my own terms," then finding your slice of the apple pie and creating your own American Dream is well within your reach.

So how do you get there? Where do you find your American Dream and how much of your time, energy, and money are you willing to invest to find it?

Today the new American Dream is much more entrepreneurial, and it's about shaping one's own destiny: mobility, flexibility to do your own work, and the ability to have a career as an expression of who you are as a person.

And for some, the American Dream will come at the hands of the legal medical/personal use marijuana business. This is cutting edge for entrepreneurs looking to get into a business that will revolutionize the way people view marijuana use today.

SECTION II

IS YOUR HEAD IN THE CLOUDS?

The Marijuana Business: Is it Right for YOU?

MANY PEOPLE ARE LOOKING FOR NEW CAREERS because they are unhappy with their jobs and/or pay scale and they wish for a better way of life. They research new and different opportunities, hoping to ultimately find an occupation or build a business that will eventually make them wealthy and enable them to do all the things they dream about doing in life—and more.

Colorado and Washington legalized pot and now all of a sudden every businessman and entrepreneur is interested in this new industry. I mean, that *is* why you bought this book—to get the facts about opportunities in the marijuana business and determine if this is a viable option for you.

Is this a dream? Is this for real? No, it is not a dream, and YES! It is for real! This is a bright new industry today—owning and operating a marijuana dispensary and/or grow operation—is a real, very real, business prospect.

This opportunity comes at a time in our economy when most new startup businesses struggle when they first open, trying to find their footing. In this case, the marijuana business is so new the competition is not yet as fierce as with many other new businesses. On the other hand, this business is so new that there are not a lot of models to study or experts to follow either. The biggest hurdle ahead of you when starting and running a marijuana business is the uncertainty you will have of what direction to take.

What *will* set your new business apart from your few competitors' operations is the insight you will gain from reading this start-up guide, which can ease up on the many "trials and errors" that many of your competitors have and will go through.

However, *this business is not for everyone*. The next several pages discuss some of the things you will need to think seriously about when making the decision to forge ahead in the marijuana industry. The opportunities are endless, but so are the risks and the uncertainties.

The road to success is there for those who are willing to take it. Life itself is a risk. So when you are confronted with a situation involving a certain degree of chance, educating yourself and putting together a plan will reduce the gamble involved in your investment.

> *"You must take risks, both with your own money or with borrowed money.*
> *Risk taking is essential to business growth."*
>
> — *J. Paul Getty* —

New business is a risk but more risky is being ignorant of the industry you are venturing into. Marijuana, cannabis, pot, weed . . . no matter what the term is, it is not your normal business. Nor is it understood by most common folk. What poses the most risk is being incompetent and lacking the necessary skills, knowledge and capital to build a successful "Marijuana Business." What is risky is a poorly written plan and not being able to analyze your risk to reward ratio. What is risky is not being able to ascertain your risk-bearing capacity to know how much risk you, your family or investors can carry, what's the upside, and the possible reward.

This Ain't No Popsicle Stand

BEFORE YOU START RUBBING YOUR HANDS TOGETHER, ready to dive into the adventure, know this. Owning a marijuana dispensary and/or grow facility is a labor intensive business. It is not easy. The hours are long, as much as twelve to fourteen hours a day—and the garden is operational seven days a week. There are many risks involved with owning and operating this type of business. It can also be dangerous.

For those of you who bought this book thinking the marijuana business would be a way to make a quick buck, have a business you can sit back and run from your living room, and have plenty of weed to smoke and watch it grow (no pun intended), this business is not for you. Yes, it's a great business with endless opportunities. However, any good entrepreneur who has made money with their business, and lots of it, will tell you that they had to work hard to get to those results. The legal marijuana business is no different. You can't expect to make millions of dollars with a minimum-wage work ethic!

That's part of the American dream too, folks. You can't have one (the dream) without the other (hard work).

"Think not of yourself as the architect of your career but as the sculptor.
Expect to have to do a lot of hard hammering and chiseling and scraping and polishing."
— B.C. Forbes —

Legit or Quit

UNTIL RECENTLY, THE SALE AND USE OF MARIJUANA HAVE BEEN ILLEGAL ACTIVITIES. For those of you who would like to continue to lurk on the dark side, set the book down and go about your day. This book is about the legal marijuana business. Legal—enforced by the government with rules and regulations and fees and licenses and paperwork. Part of the equation.

If you are not a detail person willing to put in long hours and follow the rules, if you plan to cut corners, which may veer to the wrong side of the law, then your head is indeed in the clouds.

As states open up to the sale of marijuana, new laws being placed will enforce many mandated requirements on dispensaries and grow facilities.

House Bill 1284(CO), which creates strict new regulations for medical marijuana businesses, generated considerable controversy. The law requires dispensaries be licensed at both the state and local levels, and it allows local governments—or voters—to ban dispensaries and large-scale marijuana growing operations in their communities.

In Colorado, people convicted recently of a felony—or of a drug-related felony ever—will be barred from operating a dispensary or grow business. People thinking about opening a marijuana business must have lived in that state for two years. And all dispensaries must grow at least 70 percent of the marijuana they sell, meaning people currently operating as wholesale growers either have to partner with a dispensary or shut down. Although these are laws specific to Colorado, it is a safe bet that each state will set up their own specific guidelines that you will be expected to follow if you are in this business. As this industry develops, expect new governing laws to take place on the local and state levels.

These laws are not to be overlooked. They are watched closely by law enforcement; one mistake can and will shut you down. All in all, the process of doing business isn't supposed to be easy—otherwise, everyone would be an entrepreneur. Learn the rules, follow them, be a positive participant in this exciting new opportunity in America, and your business will very likely be on a stellar path to success.

Costs to Consider

A MARIJUANA DISPENSARY IS NOT A COMMON BUSINESS that can be started with just a minimum amount of capital and time. First you have to ask yourself how much it costs to start a marijuana dispensary and grow operation. Just like any other ordinary business, you need to consider the cost of the place, whether it's rented or mortgaged, bills, payrolls, necessities and, most importantly, the state and city's mandatory fees, etc. This will be very costly. Listed below are many of the items you will need to think about when opening your business:

- Dispensary furniture and office equipment
- Grow facility equipment
- City and state licenses
- Legal fees
- Gardening supplies
- Architect and engineering plans
- Security deposits for both the grow and the dispensary facilities
- Delays in opening while still paying rents
- Industrial hygienist certification
- Retail display furniture and cabinets
- Employee lounge equipment (tables, chairs, refrigerator, microwave)
- Computer system equipment (desktop, tablets, printer, scanner, fax machine, internet expenses, point of sale system, software and systems, office supplies)
- Alarm systems for both dispensary and grow facility
- Cameras, flat screens and/or monitors for security system
- Signage for exterior of building (dispensary only)
- Website design, logos, and print material
- Business cards
- Advertising and public relations
- Phone systems
- Sound systems

- Lighting (displays, interior, and exterior for safety)
- Reception furniture
- Initial retail products order
- T-shirts, hats, and uniforms
- Insurance
- Miscellaneous equipment and supplies (towels, cleaning supplies, mops, vacuum, toiletries)
- Construction costs for dispensary and grow facility
- Electrical upgrades for grow facility
- All permits for state and city
- Deposits for utilities
- Plus an additional 20% for unforeseen expenses and maintenance expenses.

Still focused on that dream? Okay then, make it a reality.

The Money Hunt

SO YOU'VE DECIDED TO JUMP ON THE LEGAL MARIJUANA TRAIN. In the old days, a gold miner could talk an investor into what was called a "grubstake," where the investor would fund the miner and take a share of the profits. However, that was then and this is now. The normal channels to secure start-up money from financial institutions and the Small Business Administration (SBA) are probably not going to be viable options any time soon. It is highly doubtful the federal government will ever allow the SBA to authorize loans for what they consider an illegal substance business.

In case you were wondering just exactly how much you will need to begin your business, be prepared: you will need $200,000 to $1,000,000+ dollars to get into the legal business of owning and operating a marijuana dispensary and/or grow facility depending on the state. No, that is not a mistake in the zeros. You must consider some of the following necessities your capital will purchase: all of the permits (city and state), retail space rent, electric, water, alarm systems, software, computers, equipment, display cases, inventory, employees, etc.

You may have all the skills, education, drive and personality it takes to create a successful business, but without financing, your dream of owning a legal marijuana business may only be pie in the sky. But where there is a will, there is always a way.

The amount of money you will need will depend on the business you are thinking of starting. To open a marijuana dispensary and/or grow operation, money is essential, and the capital needed to get started is not minimal.

There are many factors to consider when opening either of these operations. The capital needed up front and ongoing for the first year is substantial. The ability to bankroll this business will be one of the largest obstacles to getting started and continuing your new marijuana business.

FIND FUNDING ON THE INTERNET

The Internet has revolutionized how businesses find start-up money. Numerous sites offer advice regarding how to put together a business plan and connect with various sources that can help you find the financing you need. Investigate financial firms that specialize in acquiring investors. The following sites, among others, will give you the information you need to begin the process of finding legitimate investors for your business:

- www.fundingpost.com
- www.newyorkinvestmentnetwork.com
- www.angelinvestmentnetwork.com
- www.go4funding.com
- www.startups.co/Investors

FAMILY & FRIENDS

This is the other most viable source for start-up money. Family and/or friends may consider gifting you the money based upon your business plan. This avenue eliminates bank paperwork, credit approval, and bank fees (although bank loans are not available at this time, they may be in the future). The one major drawback to using money from friends and/or family is that if the business falters, your relationships with these people could be irreparably damaged. Another avenue to consider is speaking with your attorney, dentist, doctors, professional colleagues, college roommate, etc. Don't be afraid to approach or ask for their time, attention and consideration. The worst they can say is, "no thanks." This business opportunity is new, and increasing numbers of people are considering options in the industry. They may not immediately want to jump in, but they will listen to a good sales pitch.

Regardless of who you want to approach with the idea of investing in your business, you need to have a watertight business plan, an itemized expense sheet, a bottom-line amount that you need, and a really good sales pitch backed with figures, statistics and potential for profit. In other words, you need to tell a really good story—one that makes financial sense—if you want your potential investors to believe in your business as much as you do.

Think about forming a co-op with a circle of friends/family/business acquaintances that guarantees a certain percentage of the profits for each investor. If you make the contributions equal and the profit return equal, you will avoid any one investor feeling as though they deserve more because they invested more than the others. This also leaves you in complete control of how you ultimately run your business.

━━

The following alternatives may also enable you to accomplish your dream:

- How much cash do you have in your bank accounts?
- What assets can you sell? (Cars, jewelry, gold, silver, antiques, etc.)
- Do you have a stock portfolio you can leverage?
- Can you draw equity from real estate or a home you own?

CREDIT CARDS

Today over fifty-four percent of businesses use credit cards in some manner to get up and running. They provide instant cash and the interest can be used as a legitimate deduction on your tax return. But realistically, how much of a balance or limit do you have? The downside is the high interest rates most credit cards carry might put you in a hole with no way out. This is not the ideal way to start a business, but it may be the only way to get the money to at least start you on the right path of business ownership.

LIFE INSURANCE POLICY

If you have a whole life insurance policy with at least three years of maturity, you could obtain a loan against the cash value. Most insurance companies will lend up to 90 percent of the policy's cash value at rates generally more reasonable than those charged by credit card companies. Warning: You must continue to make your payments or *poof!*—there goes your money.

RETIREMENT FUNDS/401Ks

If you still have regular employment, check into the possibility of taking money out of your 401k. Rules may vary from company to company but you can generally follow these guidelines:

- If you are older than 59½, you can take out your entire portfolio without any penalties and just pay income tax on the amount you withdraw.
- If you are younger than 59½, you will be charged a ten percent penalty on the amount you withdraw and also have to pay income tax on the amount at well.

This may be one of your only options for raising the money to open your marijuana business. Remember though, this money would have been used for your future retirement. Make sure before you use this you have enough money to complete the process of opening. Taking this money out and not being able to open your business because you didn't raise enough capital would be a painful way to end up with no retirement plan in the future.

HOME EQUITY

If you own your home or income property, you can obtain a home equity loan or a second mortgage. Most financial institutions will allow you to borrow as much as eighty percent of your property's equity. Be mindful though: if you borrow against your home and your business fails, the bank will not hesitate to foreclose on your home.

Many of us don't have the luxury to borrow against our homes due to the downturn in the real estate market. However, if this is an option for you or some of your would-be investors, this is a very good way to obtain the money needed to open your business at a very affordable interest rate. You also may be able to spread out your payments for up to fifteen years.

SOCIAL MEDIA

A large number of people belong to various social media sites and groups. These types of sites have proved to be viable resources for practically everything under the sun. You may have to get very creative in order to find your start-up money, but it is entirely possible that you could create your own consortium of investors via the social media network.

Contact current owners of legal marijuana businesses and pick their brains. If they are willing to reveal to you how they got started, their advice could be invaluable. They might even be willing to invest in your business based on a contract to share a percentage of the profits—the "grubstake" of the 21st century. However, make sure your store would not be in direct competition with their location.

LEASING

Leasing sources can accommodate all applicants for financing, whether you have been in business for twenty years or are just starting. Leasing programs give you flexibility to finance your furniture, equipment and installation. There is usually a seventy-two hour turnaround from application to receiving an answer. The leasing company does not put liens on your assets, so this maybe a worthwhile alternative. The payments are fixed and not subject to fluctuations with an increase in interest rates (as with a loan). Leasing does not require large down payments; you can expect to put down ten percent, or even less, for the equipment as a security deposit. This leaves you with more working capital for other expenses in your business. Leasing also allows you to upgrade your equipment and technology when needed to keep you competitive.

In the event of a default, the lease agreement usually indicates the lessor will repossess the equipment and resell it at a fair market price. There is also a tax benefit to leasing, as your payments can be used as a legitimate deduction on the recently modified IRS Section 179. This section of the tax code allows businesses to write off thousands of dollars in leased equipment every year.

FUTURE FINANCING

One thing to keep in mind: with the legalization of marijuana and the federal government stating they will not prosecute these types of businesses, banks will eventually feel secure enough to start accepting deposits from, and eventually make loans to, pot stores and growers. Once banks recognize the potential profits to be made from loan transactions, they will allow business people to go through the same loan application process just like any other business. Don't hold your breath waiting for that to happen, though. Your best course of action is to fund your business through private resources and investors.

Lions and Sheep

THIS MAYBE A BAD EXAMPLE OF WHAT TO (OR NOT TO) EXPECT in your marijuana business, but there are things that can happen that will be extremely difficult for you to process under normal business conditions. First off, let's not forget: *you are growing and selling marijuana.* That, and all it implies, is something to seriously process and digest.

The marijuana business itself is not yet accepted by the banking community. This will change across the country as pressure begins to build from Uncle Sam to regulate and control all sales of marijuana for taxing and revenue control purposes.

Currently your retail dispensary business will be one hundred percent cash for all transactions from your customers. Cash is king and we all love it, but a copious amount of it at your location is dangerous. The fact that you will always have a large sum of cash on hand and/or in a safe close by makes you a target for thieves, burglars, gangsters, hoodlums—whatever you want to call them. There is a good possibility that they will lurk around and watch your dispensary and/or grow operation. There will always be a chance that at any moment you could be held up or that your dispensary or grow operation could be broken into. Yes, I do mean with guns, knives, Uzis, Tasers, whatever. A holdup is a holdup. They want two things from you: money and marijuana. They will not ask you to count it, they do not want to be your partners, they are not your friends, and they may shoot you and/or your employees to get it. This is no joke. It happens, and it will continue to happen around the country as more states accept the opening of marijuana dispensaries.

You must also be aware of employee theft. Yes, it happens in all retail businesses. But let's face it—the opportunity to steal your marijuana while they are working for you is much easier for them than it would be to lift a pair of sneakers or a blouse at a department store.

You will have growers in your garden, trimmers in your cultivating area, transportation people, front desk, counter help, etc. All of these employees will have access to your marijuana products. The temptation for them will always be there to help themselves and use it or sell it on the secondary market.

So are you a lion or a sheep? Lions eat sheep. That is the natural order of things. Lions hunt, stalk, slaughter and devour. They take no prisoners. Sheep blindly follow their shepherd, even if he is leading them to certain doom. So which are you, a lion or a sheep?

As an owner of a marijuana business, you must always be like a lion. The sheep will not make it in this business. Many things will be thrown at you. In what order you attack them will be up to you, but you can't let your guard down. You must be ready for the attack at all times.

These examples may seem extreme but you must be aware of what could and may happen while owning and operating this type of business.

SECTION III

LEARN TO WALK BEFORE YOU RUN: YOUR FIRST STEPS

Setting Up the Right Business Structure

"Corporation: an ingenious device for obtaining profits
without individual responsibility."
— Ambrose Bierce —

NEW BUSINESS OWNERS WILL NEED TO MAKE AN EDUCATED DECISION about how they want to legally set up their business. Even current dispensary owners need to revisit their business structures, as there are several choices when it comes to the types of legal organizational structures. The type of business entity you decide upon will affect how much you pay in taxes, the amount of paperwork your business is required to do, the personal liability you will face, and your ability to borrow money. It is essential that you have an understanding of the different business structures in order to make the best decision for your circumstances. An accountant or a lawyer can assist you with the choice that would be best for the success of your marijuana business.

The business structure you choose will lay the foundation you will use to conduct a legal business enterprise. It will also protect you in case you or one of your employees causes an accident and/or damages, or if one of your customers or employees should get hurt or disabled in an accident on your landlord's property. If a lawsuit arises from the accident, your home, business, and assets could be at risk if not properly protected. The legal structure you select for your business should protect you in these cases. However, many first-time business owners often overlook or ignore the necessity of choosing a business structure that will give them the greatest protection. The marijuana industry is one with constant change and dangerous possibilities of harm and lawsuits. Your business and personal protection should be at the top of your priority list when deciding which way you legally set up your business entity.

SOLE PROPRIETORSHIP

A sole proprietorship is the most basic and straightforward form of business organization. It is the simplest to establish. It is easy to form and offers complete control to the owner. It is an unincorporated business owned entirely by one individual and does not require massive amounts of complicated tax forms.

An owner who operates with no other employees besides themselves usually chooses a sole proprietorship. This can be a home-based business or one operated out of a retail commercial location. In general, the owner is also personally liable for all financial obligations, legal liability, debts, and obligations of the business.

Every sole proprietor is required to keep sufficient records to comply with federal tax requirements regarding business documents. They do not have taxes withheld from their business income; they will need to make quarterly estimated tax payments. These estimated payments include both income tax and self-employment taxes for Social Security and Medicare.

One advantage of the sole proprietorship is that additional expenses, such as office expenses, property taxes, utilities, and vehicle expenses, may be deducted from the proprietor's income on their taxes.

The liability of a sole proprietorship is the full responsibility for any debt, liability, and/or lawsuit that the company might incur. It means that the individual business owner is held personally responsible for damages, problems, or adverse consequences resulting from the operation of the business.

The likelihood of you choosing this option to set up your marijuana business is highly improbable. The fact is, in order to operate this business successfully, you will need employees and the protection of a corporate veil. Protection in case of business casualties, changing laws, losing your lease, terminating your lease and/or having to close if the state or city changes its policies on marijuana will be key. A sole proprietorship does not offer this safety.

PARTNERSHIP

A partnership is the relationship existing between two or more persons who join each other to carry on a business with one goal—to earn a profit. Each person contributes money, property, labor, or skill and expects to share in the profits and losses of the business.

It is usually assumed, under most states' laws, that all partners will share control over the business equally. You can state in the partnership agreement which partners are responsible for the job description to which they agree. You may also want to establish voting rights based on the percentage of the initial investment, or how the amount of work and hours will be distributed among the partners. Your agreement should spell out all of this prior to opening the business.

In addition, you can specify in your partnership agreement how profits, losses, and salaries will be allocated among partners. This is also usually based on initial investment and time put into the business. If everyone is equal and puts in the same investment, this agreement becomes very easy.

A partnership agreement should also address the eventuality of a partner leaving the business, a partner who is no longer capable of working in the business, the death of a partner, and the addition of new partners.

Like a sole proprietorship, a partnership has one level of taxation. A partnership is a tax-reporting entity, not a tax-paying entity, which means that profits pass through the partnership to the owners and are divided in accordance with what was agreed to and specified in the partnership agreement. There are no restrictions on how profits are allocated among partners as long as there is economic reason. The partners are responsible for good bookkeeping, paying their tax obligation, Social Security, and Medicare.

While there are many benefits to a partnership, one disadvantage is that the owners have unlimited personal liability for their own actions and the actions of their partners. In general, each partner in the business is jointly liable for the partnership obligations. Joint liability means that the partners can be sued as a group. In some states, each partner can be held accountable for the damages from the wrongdoing of other partners and for the debts and obligations of the partnership.

Three rules for liability in a partnership are:

- Every partner is liable for his or her actions.
- Every partner is liable for the actions of the other partners.
- Every partner is liable for the actions of the employees of the business.

CORPORATION

There are many reasons to form a corporation to conduct business. Many entrepreneurs aren't comfortable remaining in a sole proprietorship and want a level of protection not afforded by a sole proprietorship. While some owners think incorporating is only for big companies, the most common form of a business now is to own and operate a business as a corporation.

A corporation is commonly referred to as a limited company, or just "company."

Some of the main advantages of using a corporation to conduct business include the following:

- **LIMITED LIABILITY:** The owners of the corporation are shareholders in the business and are not liable for the debts and obligations of the corporation. Creditors cannot hold the shareholders responsible for the debts of the corporation. If the company cannot pay its debt, the creditors cannot go after the shareholders personally. This is one of the main reasons people form a corporation.

- **OWNERSHIP IS EASILY TRANSFERABLE:** Ownership of a corporation is transferred easily by transferring the shares. It can be as simple as endorsing the back of the share certificate.

- **TAX ADVANTAGES:** If a corporation operates as a small business and has active income, then it can take advantage of small business deductions and pay income taxes at a substantially reduced rate. There can be a significant tax savings compared to doing business outside of a corporation. A corporation files a separate income tax return. If a shareholder is an employee, he pays income tax on his wages, and the corporation and the employee each pay one-half of the Social Security and Medicare taxes and the corporation can deduct half. A corporate shareholder only pays income tax for any dividends received.

NOTE

A corporation is considered to be a person who is completely separate from its owners. Owners are known as shareholders because they own part of the organization. Like a person, corporations may own property and assets, take on debt to finance operations and long term growth, and sell shares to raise money. A marijuana facility is better suited as a corporation because of the size of the operation and its tax advantages.

- **RAISING CAPITAL:** It is easier to raise capital for a corporation than it is for a partnership or sole proprietor. Lenders are more willing to lend capital to a corporation. Though currently borrowing money through a bank is not possible for marijuana businesses in today's banking world, hopefully in years to come having a corporation will speed up the lending process when banks and lenders do decide to jump into the marijuana pool.

LIMITED LIABILITY, OR LLC

A limited liability corporation, also known as an LLC, is a relatively new legal business definition that was formed specifically to provide a host of benefits to new business owners not offered by other entities. Given all the benefits and flexibility of an LLC, business people, lawyers, and accountants now consider the limited liability corporation as the presumptive choice for new business.

- **LIABILITY BENEFITS:** One of the biggest benefits of an LLC is that all owners of a limited liability company are protected from being personally liable for the debts, obligations, and lawsuits of the LLC. The LLC benefit states that a member is not liable just because he or she is a member/owner of the LLC. There are guidelines that need to be followed by the principals and/or the members of the LLC so this protection is not lost. So build your suit of armor before trouble comes your way. And always remember: if you don't have an asset protection plan, you still have a plan—you've simply planned to allow someone to take your hard-earned assets away from you.

- **INFORMAL DECISION MAKING:** In an LLC, the owners determine the ownership structure, the right to the profits, voting rights, and any other aspect of relationships amongst members. An LLC does not require a board of directors, shareholder meetings, and other managerial formalities, which allows the owners to focus more on their business and less on the requirements and maintenance of corporate guidelines and mandates.

- **FLEXIBLE TAX CHOICES:** The tax choices for an LLC are the second biggest benefit of an LLC for small business owners. The single-member LLC (owned by an individual) can take advantage of having simple sole proprietorship federal income taxation, but without the personal liability of the sole proprietorship. What does that mean? As a business owner, you are able to write off all the expenses of a home office, utilities, and car. Usually, you would normally not have the benefit of doing so. Either a single or a multimember LLC can choose to be taxed as a corporation as well. The tax benefits of an LLC provide more choices than other legal entities.

When you finally do decide which legal structure is right for your business, it's important to choose the entity that gives you the most protection from personal liability with the best tax advantages for your specific situation.

Only a good "numbers person" can look at your current situation and long-term goals to give you the kind of sound objective counsel you need to make the best decision. A good CPA may cost you some upfront money, but in the long run it will be money well spent.

Remember, this business is not easy. In order to be successful, you will have employees (hopefully many), and there will always be the threat of robberies, lawsuits, and business disruption. So a word to the wise: make sure protection and tax obligations and consequences are at the top of your list when you decide which way you will legally set up your business.

Business Plan

THE MOST IMPORTANT DUTY YOU HAVE TO PERFORM after you have decided to own a marijuana business is to create a business plan—and a rock solid one at that.

A business plan is the very foundation for your endeavor. If it is sound, you can construct anything you desire from it. The stronger your plan is, the more likely you are to succeed in finding the financial means to fund your business. The plan needs to have certain elements, and this chapter will give you a basic blueprint to follow. Business plans *do not get funded based on the idea* behind the business itself (although your unique business idea and vision are important). They get funded because you give a professional presentation that captivates and impresses your audience.

Creating your business plan will require an investment of your time, talent, and skills. Don't think you can knock this out in an hour or so—not if you want it to succeed. Your business plan has to be the very best thing you have done in your life. You wouldn't buy a house without knowing it had passed every inspection, so do the same thorough inspection with your business plan. Do your homework. Remember, you only have **one** chance to make a first impression.

The example that follows will help you to put your best foot forward. It's not cut in stone; use the sections that apply in order to tell the best story of why you want to open a marijuana dispensary and/ or grow facility.

If you do not feel 100% confident in your ability to create a business plan on your own, there are many websites that will give you all the help you need. Keep in mind that some of the downloads are free, while others charge fees.

Buy a three-ring binder and dividers with tabs for each section. This will allow you to keep every category organized and in the proper sequence.

TABLE OF CONTENTS

1. Executive Summary

Summarize the key points of your business plan. Keep it simple, logical and to the point.

2. Company Summary

Describe your company, who you are, where you want to operate.

2.1. Start-up Summary

Summarize your start-up table numbers, both expenses and assets.

Table: Start-up

REQUIREMENTS	
Start-up Expenses	$0
Expense 1	$0
Expense 2	$0
Expense 3	$0
Expense 4	$0
Expense 5	$0
Expense 6	$0
Total Start-up Expenses	$0
Start-up Assets	
Cash Assets	$0
Other Current Assets	$0
Long-term Assets	$0
Total Assets	$0
Total Requirements	$0

3. Services

Describe the products and/or services you offer, how they are provided and by whom, and plans for future service offerings.

4. Market Analysis Summary

Describe the different groups of target customers included in your market analysis and explain why you are selecting these as targets.

Table: Market Analysis

MARKET ANALYSIS							
		Year 1	Year 2	Year 3	Year 4	Year 5	
Potential Customers	**Growth**						**TPPA***
Area 1	0%	0	0	0	0	0	0.00%
Area 2	0%	0	0	0	0	0	0.00%
Area 3	0%	0	0	0	0	0	0.00%
Total	**0.00%**	**0**	**0**	**0**	**0**	**0**	**0.00%**

* Total People Per Area

5. Strategy and Implementation Summary

Summarize the organizational strategy for target marketing, sales and marketing activities, and product/service development. Build a focused, consistent sales and marketing strategy.

5.1 Sales Forecast

Use this topic to explain the Sales Forecast Table.

SALES FORECAST			
Sales	**Year 1**	**Year 2**	**Year 3**
Row 1	$0	$0	$0
Row 2	$0	0	$0
Row 3	$0	$0	$0
Total Sales	**$0**	**$0**	**$0**
Direct Cost of Sales	**Year 1**	**Year 2**	**Year 3**
Row 1	$0	$0	$0
Row 2	$0	$0	$0
Row 3	$0	$0	$0
Total Direct Cost of Sales	**$0**	**$0**	**$0**

6. Milestones

Describe the milestones (measurable activities) laid out in the Milestones Table.

Table: Milestones

MILESTONES					
Milestone	**Start Date**	**End Date**	**Budget**	**Manager**	**Department**
Name 1	0/0/00	0/0/00	$0		Department
Name 2	0/0/00	0/0/00	$0		Department
Name 3	0/0/00	0/0/00	$0		Department
Name 4	0/0/00	0/0/00	$0		Department
Name 5	0/0/00	0/0/00	$0		Department
Total			$0		

7. Management Summary

Describe the management and personnel structure of the company, including any gaps that need to be filled.

8. Financial Plan

Summarize the financial aspects of your business plan.

8.1 Start-up Funding

Explain where your funding will come from, in what form (investments and/or loans), and how this funding will cover the start-up requirements outlined in the start-up table.

Table: Start-up Funding

START-UP FUNDING	
Start-up Expenses to Fund	$0
Start-up Assets to Fund	$0
Total Funding Required	$0
ASSETS	
Non-cash Assets from Start-up	$0
Cash Requirements from Start-up	$0
Additional Cash Raised	$0
Cash Balance on Starting Date	$0
Total Assets	**$0**
LIABILITIES	
Current Borrowing	$0
Long-term Liabilites	$0
Accounts Payable (Outstanding Bills)	$0
Other Current Liabilities (Interest Free)	$0
Total Liabilities	$0
CAPITAL	
Planned Investment	$0
Owner	$0
Investor	$0
Additional Investment Requirement	$0
Total Planned Investment	**$0**
Loss at Start-up (Start-up Expenses)	$0
Total Capital	**$0**
Total Capital and Liabilities	**$0**
Total Funding	**$0**

8.2. Projected Profit and Loss

Explain the important points of your profit and loss projections, such as percentage increase in sales and profits, your gross margins, and key budget items.

Table: Profit and Loss

PROFIT AND LOSS			
	Year 1	Year 2	Year 3
SALES	$0	$0	$0
Direct Cost of Sales	$0	$0	$0
Other Costs of Sales	$0	$0	$0
Total Cost of Sales	$0	$0	$0
Gross Margin	$0	$0	$0
Gross Margin %	0.00%	0.00%	0.00%
EXPENSES			
Expense 1	$0	$0	$0
Expense 2	$0	$0	$0
Depreciation	$0	$0	$0
Rent	$0	$0	$0
Utilities	$0	$0	$0
Insurance	$0	$0	$0
Payroll Taxes	$0	$0	$0
Other	$0	$0	$0
Total Operating Expenses	**$0**	**$0**	**$0**
Profit Before Interest and Taxes	$0	$0	$0
EBITDA*	$0	$0	$0
Interest Expense	$0	$0	$0
Taxes Incurred	$0	$0	$0
Net Profit	**$0**	**$0**	**$0**
Net Profit / Sales	**0.00%**	**0.00%**	**0.00%**

* Earnings before interest, taxes, depreciation and amortization

Licenses, Permits, Regulations for Your Business

WHEN YOU'RE CAUGHT UP IN THE EXCITEMENT of starting a new business, it's easy to ignore the need for license and permits. However, license and permits are mandatory, and before you can legally begin to put a seed in a soil pot or try and sell marijuana you will need to have licenses and permits in place. Additionally, if your business has employees and will sell taxable goods (hopefully plenty of marijuana), you need to register with the taxing authorities and regulatory agencies.

Businesses licenses, permits, and tax registrations are issued and administered by all levels of government, federal, state, and local, including county and municipal government. Your state/municipality will require licenses and permits for your dispensary/grow facility. We have used the State of Colorado as an example of what you are likely to be expected to obtain. Other states/municipalities may have different requirements, so, make sure you have everything before you submit the forms and write the checks for submission. **Do not fill out these forms incorrectly!**

This section is designed to walk you through the business licensing process which will help eliminate the possibility of errors, costly re-filing fees, lost time and aggravation.

Medical Marijuana Establishment License Procedures for Business Seeking Licensing

Licensing Technicians must be provided with the following information in order to move to the production system licensing procedures. The following information will create both the electronic and hard file documents for the establishment. A business seeking licensing for A Medical Marijuana Establishment must first do the following:

1. Submit all required documentation to Department of Excise and Licenses
Required Documents:

- Application

- Lease or Deed-if property is leased, written consent from the owner of the property to the licensing of the premises for a Medical Marijuana Establishment is required.

- Certificate of Good Standing from the Colorado Secretary of State Office, along with Articles or partnership and any trade name filing.

- Description of products and services to be provided.

- Floor plan-drawn to scale on 8 ½" x 11" paper, showing the layout of the establishment and the principal uses of the floor area, including where any services other than dispensing of medical marijuana are proposed to occur.

- Security plan indicating how applicant will comply with security provisions listed in the ordinance.

- An area map-drawn to scale on 8½" x 11" paper, indicating the radius of one-quarter mile from the boundaries of the property upon which the establishment is located, the proximity to any school, pre-school or child care establishment.

- Zone Use Permit

- Copy of City Sales Tax license

- Copy of Burglar Alarm Permit

- Copy of contract with alarm monitoring company

- Affidavit of Lawful Presences

FEES

Sec. 32-93. Medical marijuana licensing.
Application and license fees for medical marijuana centers, medical marijuana-infused products manufacturing, and medical marijuana optional premises, cultivation licenses are as follows:

1. Application fees:

Medical marijuana center	$2,000.00

Provided, however, that a business currently licensed in Denver as a medical marijuana dispensary, applying for a license as a medical marijuana center at the same location as the dispensary, shall not be required to pay an application fee.

Medical marijuana-infused products manufacturer	$2,000.00

2. Criminal background check fee, per person checked	Actual costs
3. License fee, per year, for all classes of licenses	$3,000.00
4. Transfer of ownership, plus cost of background check	$100.00
5. Transfer of location	$750.00
6. Modification of premises	$150.00

(Ord. No. 39-10, § 2, 1-11-10; Ord. No. 688-10, § 2, 12-13-10; Ord. No. 105-11, § 2, 2-22-11; Ord. No. 464-11, § 3, 9-16-11)
Cross reference-Medical marijuana dispensaries, § 24-401 et seq.
Fees will change and vary from state to state. Most fees will go up as this industry develops.

2. Applications will be date and time stamped when submitted at front counter and will be reviewed for completeness and accuracy.

3. The application, floor plan, area map, and use permit will be scanned and sent to Development Services for review. Zoning regulations limit floor area to be used for cultivation to 10% of the gross floor except in industrial zone districts. Detailed floor plans must include any area proposed for cultivation.

4. Excise and License Inspectors will measure those facilities that must meet the spacing requirements.

5. Applicants will be given an Inspection Card from Excise and Licenses. The applicant is responsible for contacting the agencies listed on the card and securing all approvals. Once all inspections are complete, the applicant should contact Excise and Licenses for the final inspection.

6. The applicant will be notified, in writing, if the application is disqualified or the license is denied for any of the following reasons:

- Incomplete application
- False information
- Lack of possession of the premises
- Failure to pass inspection by any agency inspecting the premises
- Failure to comply with spacing requirements.

Applicants whose application has been denied shall be entitled to a hearing on the application upon written request to the director. Any application that contains incomplete information shall be denied. Any application denied merely because the application was incomplete may be resubmitted.

7. Excise and License Business Inspectors will conduct physical measurements at all locations that received their sales tax license and/or commenced operation after December 15, 2009.

Forms may be found at:
http://denvergov.org/businesslicensing/DenverBusinessLicensingCenter/BusinessLicenses/
MedicalMarijuanaCenters/tabid/441765/Default

Occupational License Information

THIS CHAPTER WILL WALK YOU STEP BY STEP through the occupational license process. These types of licenses are required by your state/municipality for all employees of Medical Marijuana/Personal Use Marijuana dispensaries and grow facilities. We have used the State of Colorado as an example; check with your state and obtain the correct forms. Make several copies and practice filling them out. Any mistake will void this process and you will have to resubmit a correct form and probably have to pay a new filing fee as well. **Do not fill out these forms incorrectly!**

Occupational License Applications are accepted Monday - Friday
Between the hours of 8:00 AM and 12:00 PM and 1:00 and 2:30 PM
at MED Headquarter Office
455 Sherman Street, Suite 390
Denver, CO 80203

"We make every effort to accommodate all applicants on the day of their arrival.
Occupational License Applicants will NOT be processed after 2:30 p.m."

State statute and rule mandates that anyone working within the Medical Marijuana industry be licensed by the MED (Marijuana Enforcement Division) in order to ensure that they meet specific statutory requirements (C.R.S § 12-43.3-307; C.R.S. § 12-43.3-202 (2) (VIII) and C.R.S. § 12-43.3-401 (1) (d)). These statutory requirements include:

- Applicants must be age twenty-one or older,
- Applicants may not have any Controlled Substance Felony Convictions or any other felony convictions that have not been fully discharged for five years prior to applying,
- Applicants may not have any delinquent governmental or child support debt, AND
- Applicants must be a Colorado resident at the time of application.

Therefore, all occupational license applicants must undergo a background check, the depth of which is dictated by the level of the individual's involvement in the business. The two types of Occupational Licenses available are for "Key Employees," and for "Support Employees."

KEY EMPLOYEES

This license is for employees who make operational or management decisions that directly impact the business. An example of such an employee is a master grower who determines what or how much of a particular strain to produce or an individual whose decisions have a significant impact on the business and its operations, but does not have an ownership interest in the business. Note that two years of tax information is required for this type of occupational license.

SUPPORT EMPLOYEES

This license is for employees who work within the business but do not make operational decisions. An example of such an employee would be a budtender. The majority of occupational license holders are in this category.

DENVER MED OFFICE

Colorado Department of Revenue
Marijuana Enforcement Division
455 Sherman Street
Suite 390
Denver, CO 80203

All applicants initially applying for an occupational license must come into a MED office to submit their application, have their fingerprints taken and pose for a photo that will be placed on their occupational license badge - if they pass the background check and are approved for an occupational license. The information provided on the application is used to conduct a background check to determine if the applicant meets the statutory criteria. Key Occupational Licenses cost $250 and Support Occupational Licenses cost $75; this cost reflects the level of scrutiny necessary to obtain the license.

COME PREPARED

When applying for your license be sure to bring your *completed* application (Key or Support), all supporting documentation (such as tax documents, proof of residency or court dispositions), *and* the full amount of your application fee. They cannot accept credit cards so the fee must be paid in cash or with a check made out to the MED or the Colorado Department of Revenue.

The application fee covers the cost of conducting the necessary background check and is based on the amount of investigation necessary; Key Occupational Licenses cost $250 and Support Occupational The license costs $75.

Once you have received your occupational license, keep in mind that by completing the application you have entered into an agreement to advise the MED, in writing, of any criminal conviction or charge pending within ten days of any arrest, summons or conviction. Additionally, you must advise the MED of any change in your home address should the MED need to contact you—this is especially important when the time comes to renew, as the MED will send any renewal information to this address.

OCCUPATIONAL LICENSE RENEWAL

Sixty days prior to the expiration date of your occupational license badge the MED will notify you via First Class mail, sent to the home mailing address of record with the MED—the home address *you* provided at the time you applied for the license or any updated address you have provided to the MED. This notification will consist of a renewal packet intended to provide the MED with the necessary information to confirm that you still meet the statutory criteria allowing you to hold an MED Occupational License. Complete and sign the application, attach any necessary supporting documentation requested and mail the completed packet and your renewal fee to the MED office.

If your application is approved the MED will mail you a renewal sticker to place on your badge.

If you fail to pass the background check you will have an opportunity to request a meeting to resolve any issues that arise. If you choose not to pursue this option you must return your expired badge to the MED and discontinue your employment within the Medical Marijuana industry.

PLEASE NOTE

If your mailing address has changed it is *your* responsibility to notify the MED of your address change—you can do this by letter or email. Provide your full name, badge number, your previous address and your current address, along with the date you moved. You may email this information to dor_mmedaddresschange@state. co.us. If you do not keep your address of record current and therefore do not receive or complete the renewal packet prior to the expiration date on your badge, it will expire and you will be required to apply for a new badge.

IF YOUR MAILING ADDRESS CHANGES

You are responsible for notifying the MED. You can email this change to: dor_mmedaddresschange@state.co.us

Individuals wishing to upgrade a Support Occupational License to a Key Occupational License will need to complete a Key Occupational License Application and come into the MED Office in order to complete the in-depth background check necessary. Support badges cannot be upgraded to Key badges via the mail-in renewal process.

Business Insurance

BUSINESS INSURANCE PROTECTS YOU AND YOUR BUSINESS from liability, accidents, or damage. Most new business owners trying to save a few dollars when opening up their business make the crucial mistake of foregoing business insurance. Good luck and positive thinking will not protect you, your staff, your crop and/or your clients from losses. Unfortunately, bad things happen, even to the most conscientious owners.

Most of us going into business for the first time don't realize how many things can go wrong. Now compound that ten times for being in a business that is not only dangerous but highly susceptible to robbery or fire. Yes, the marijuana business can be extremely profitable, but you do need insurance right from the day you open your doors. Understand that when in business, Murphy's Law tends to strike when you least expect it. Being prepared for this is an important part of owning any business.

WHY YOU NEED BUSINESS INSURANCE

Do I really need insurance to protect my medical marijuana corporation? Is it necessary? What are the advantages of having insurance? Is it worth it to pay for insurance? Most people ask these questions when they first open. The expense to open a marijuana business is not cheap. As a matter of fact, it's extremely expensive. Covering your equipment and investment is one of the most important aspects of longevity in the business.

If something were to happen to your business or your product, such as a fire or theft, would you be ready to pick things back up and get your business started again without monetary stress? Assuredly, without insurance the answer would be "no."

Thinking about it realistically, you should keep in mind that anything can happen at any time. People don't usually believe that any of those things are likely—until something actually happens to them or their businesses. That's why you need medical/recreational marijuana dispensary insurance. You need to protect yourself and your business from losing money in the event of a misfortune.

———

Possible scenarios that may happen to you, your employees, your dispensary, or your grow facility:

- You arrive at work to find the grow facility was broken into; half of your plants were stolen as well as the safe containing your harvested product.

- You arrive at work to find the grow facility's roof caved in due to a heavy rain. Your entire crop is destroyed and the roof will take weeks to fix. Also, all your equipment was destroyed due to the water damage.

- A client slips in your dispensary and falls, breaking his ankle.

- An employee standing on a step stool falls on one of your glass display cases and severely cuts her hand.

- A trimmer accidently cuts the tip off of his finger while trimming your plants.

- One of your clients has a heart attack while exiting your dispensary.

- One of your employees leaves the coffee maker on and it burns down your dispensary and everything in it.

- A member of your staff crashes his car into your dispensary while trying to park his car.

- Your dispensary is robbed at gunpoint. All of your merchandise and money is taken, plus one of your employees is hurt in the altercation.

As you can see, there are many different reasons why you will need insurance for your marijuana business. Different types of insurance can cover the contents of your business, your health, liability, and your property. Having insurance for everything can be expensive. Let's focus on what will suit your needs when first opening your marijuana business.

MARIJUANA BUSINESS INSURANCE PRICING

Many people assume that medical marijuana dispensary insurance is very expensive and unattainable. This is a very common misconception. Medical marijuana industry insurance is actually very reasonably priced. Companies that do insure marijuana businesses can provide you with general liability and property coverage for your furniture, fixtures, equipment, inventory and tenant improvements for an affordable price. All of these make your medical marijuana dispensary insurance coverage comprehensive. This will help your business stay on its feet should some type of calamity or unfortunate event arise.

LIABILITY INSURANCE

America may be the "promised land," but it's also the "land of lawsuits." Lawsuits are like baseball, apple pie, and hamburgers—it's the American way. You need to protect your business from legal expenses, settlements or judgments, and lawsuits. Liability policies cover business losses for payments to victims of bodily injury or property damage caused by your business. This insurance will also cover medical expenses to victims, attorney fees, and expenses associated with legal proceedings. General liability is a must-have for your daily business operation.

BUSINESS PROPERTY INSURANCE

Business property insurance covers your business in case of unforeseen damage or loss to your building, inventory, or equipment. That means even if the neon sign hanging out in front of your dispensary shorts out in a storm, you would be covered to have it fixed or replaced. Business property insurance coverage extends to items such as laptops, phones, furniture, and valuable documents.

PRODUCT COVERAGE

Insurance companies can provide your cannabis dispensary with coverage for your inventory/product/

weed/edibles/juices/extracts against risks such as fire or theft. They can also provide you with insurance coverage while your product is in transit from the cultivation facility to your dispensary.

BUSINESS INCOME / EXTRA EXPENSE INSURANCE

Insurance companies can also provide coverage for general liability, your inventory/product/weed/edibles/juices/extracts and property. With medical marijuana dispensary insurance, coverage can also cover insurance for your business' income and additional expenditures. This is similar to insurance for all other businesses, not just those that deal with medical marijuana.

When we talk about business income, we mean the net income that wouldn't have been interrupted if your business hadn't suffered fire, theft or another covered claim. This can also include the losses faced by your business in the event that you have to move it to another venue.

Edible marijuana, vaporizing tools, smoking devices and dispensaries are all covered by product liability insurance.

TYPES OF BUSINESS PROPERTY INSURANCE

According to the National Association of Insurance Commissioners, there are three kinds of business property insurance:

- **Basic**—covers damages from natural advert disasters such as fire, storms, floods, volcanic eruptions, earthquakes, tsunamis and avalanches.
- **Broad**—covers the basic damages, plus other unforeseen events, such as a riot, that leaves the dispensary or garden in shambles.
- **Special**—the most comprehensive form of business insurance. It covers basic and broad, plus all the direct physical loss that is included in your policy.

BUSINESS PROPERTY INSURANCE FOR OWNERS WHO RENT THEIR STORE

If you rent your store, don't assume that the landlord is responsible for losses to your business and property. While the building itself is most likely covered, your inventory, computers, equipment, and other property related to your business are not. You must have business property insurance to cover the contents of your dispensary or grow facility.

KEY PERSON INSURANCE

Most small businesses, and almost all start-up businesses, depend on the talents or abilities of a few key people. If you are a "one-man band" or rely on just a few people for the success of your business, your business could fail if something should happen to you or any of your key people. Key person insurance is a way for businesses to insure against business interruption if a key person becomes injured or ill. This is important coverage to have for your dispensary manager or your main gardener in your grow operation.

WORKER'S COMPENSATION INSURANCE

Worker's Compensation coverage is required by state, local, and federal law. If you have employees, you will have no choice about it. The fact of the matter is, if one of your employees gets hurt at work, whether it's your fault or not, you want to be prepared for a lawsuit. Workers' compensation insurance will cover hospital bills, attorney fees, lawsuit awards, and lost wages.

This is extremely important coverage in the marijuana business. The grow facility, although very peaceful, can be dangerous. Lights and water are necessary to yield a great crop, but we all know they don't mix well and could put your employees at risk.

Armed robbery is a possibility in your dispensary. Fact: your employees are at risk. They can get hurt, shot, stabbed or worse. Being insured for this with workman's compensation coverage is common sense. Make sure you are overprotected in this area.

BUYING INSURANCE

Start by finding three insurance companies in the marijuana industry. Explain exactly what kind of business you will be opening and how many employees you will have. You will also need to have a list of the contents (equipment) that will be used in your place of business. Explain to the agent or broker what types of services you will offer. If they are primarily in the marijuana insurance business, they will understand your equipment and the coverage needed. They may feel you need additional coverage. There are a few variables to consider when purchasing your insurance, such as: price, coverage offered, specialization of insurance company, reputation of the insurance company, and the size of the deductible.

- **Price**: Settling on the lowest price is not always the best choice. If one company is much cheaper than another, they may be leaving out a large portion of your coverage. Ask questions, read the policies, and compare.

- **Coverage:** Negotiate more coverage in all aspects. No policy is cast in stone. The worst they can say is no. When it comes to insurance, it doesn't hurt to be over-insured.

- **Specialization of the company:** Each industry and business has its own risk. When picking an insurance company, make sure they specialize in small businesses and have insured other dispensaries and grow operations.

- **Reputation of the insurance company:** Try to work with an insurance company in your area. They may be on "Main Street" in your town. It also makes sense to look online to see if they are in good financial shape. You can check with "Best Insurance Reports." If the company is not rated from an A+ to a B, you should look elsewhere for your insurance.

- **Deductible:** The deductible is one of the most important parts of your policy. A higher deductible will mean lower insurance costs, but it will also increase how much you have to pay out of pocket for any losses you may have.

———

Whatever you do, remember that whoever is writing your insurance policies is doing so because he or she earns commissions on these policies. Your interests and theirs may not always agree. This means that you should shop around, negotiate, and always be on the lookout for a better deal.

As a business owner, you know the value of protecting yourself, your family, your staff, and your clients. Be sure to purchase an insurance policy that will safeguard all aspects of your investment.

Credit Card Processing: Selecting the Right Partner
(If You Can Find One)

THE U.S. JUSTICE DEPARTMENT'S DECISION TO TURN A BLIND EYE to the enforcement of federal marijuana laws in states that authorize use of the drug may eventually make it easier to use credit cards for such transactions, but a banking ban on legal pot sellers remains intact for now. Is change coming soon?

Twenty states and the District of Columbia now allow marijuana to be used for medicinal purposes, and Colorado and the state of Washington have legalized its recreational use. But nearly all banks and credit card companies, reluctant to run afoul of federal drug and banking laws that remain on the books, refuse to do business with even state-licensed sellers of marijuana. This forces business owners and pot buyers to deal only in cash, which carries its own risks.

THINGS ARE LOOSENING UP!

Dozens of recreational marijuana stores in Colorado are allowing customers to purchase cannabis with credit cards or debit cards. So how are they doing this? Is it illegal? Will their customers get in trouble? Will the dispensaries lose their licenses to sell marijuana?

The news has sparked discussion within the industry, as credit card companies have previously maintained a hard line against working with cannabis businesses.

The reason for the rise in credit card usage could be because Visa and MasterCard have quietly decided not to enforce their own rules. Credit card companies are witnessing that the marijuana business is no longer monkey business—it's big business and growing every day, no pun intended. This is a good thing for dispensary owners who are stuck with being able to only take cash. Yes, cash is king, but when you have tens of thousands of dollars onsite, security issues rise exponentially.

UNDERSTANDING THE CREDIT CARD PROCESS

Understanding credit card processing and knowing how to leverage its advantages can have a dramatic and profitable impact for dispensary owners. Choosing the wrong credit card processor or not understanding the best way to structure your processor agreement can be a constant monthly drain on your business.

Most businesses—no matter how large or small—make very small profits on a percentage basis. Knowing how to increase your profits—even by a percentage point or two—can provide the difference between "getting by" and enjoying an income that provides you with the lifestyle you want. Accepting credit cards can change the face of your business by allowing you to expand your sales potential to a population that was not available before.

Following is an overview of the reasons to accept credit cards, the costs and benefits of credit card processing, how to select the right processor, and what questions to ask before signing any agreement. At the time of this writing, credit card processing companies are opening up for Colorado dispensaries as long as they have had an active checking account for at least twelve months. These dispensaries also require that when customers check in to make purchases, they must show two forms of ID to include proof of age (minimum 21).

WHY ACCEPT CREDIT CARDS?

For some dispensary owners, operating on a strictly cash basis seems like the least costly way to operate. No processing fees, no equipment to buy, and it seems clean and simple. In fact, in the early 1990s, more than eighty percent of the money coming into all businesses was in the form of cash. Now, however, that number has flipped and more than eighty percent of the money comes in through credit or checking/debit cards. Why the switch? It's all about convenience for your clients and the potential additional profits for your dispensary. Let's face it—how many people today carry cash? If you have the ability to process credit cards at your dispensary, will your customers buy more? More than likely, yes.

Everything has a cost. Identifying the cost of credit card processing on the balance sheet is easy to do. What is not easy is identifying the cost of NOT accepting credit cards in your business. Several studies have shown that clients are willing to spend more when paying with credit than when paying with cash. In fact, when most businesses start to accept credit cards in its stores, they find that the average transaction for credit clients was $50 compared to cash transactions of only $20. People are not carrying cash these days; instead, they want the convenience of paying with credit or debit cards. It just makes the process of buying your products that much easier for them.

Dispensary owners can capitalize on this by offering products to their clients as well as add-on discounts if they spend more. When paying with credit, clients are much more likely to purchase items like edibles or concentrates, or other items that are far more expensive than their weekly supply of marijuana. Walk-in clients are also likely to prefer paying with credit by the same 60/40 ratio. Referring these clients to a nearby ATM machine to get cash sends the message that you are more concerned about your convenience rather than making it easier for your clients to do business with you. Many will not come back to an establishment that does not accept payment via credit/debit card. The cost of NOT accepting credit may be the loss of sales in additional products and services over months and years, and you could lose the 40 percent of clients who no longer prefer to pay with cash.

If it makes sense to accept credit and debit card payments in your dispensary, how do you make sure you do this in a way that is best for you, rather than best for your bank or a third-party processor?

CHOOSING THE RIGHT PROCESSOR

Your local bank may provide credit card processing, either directly or through a third-party processor. You can also contract directly with a processor like Integrity Payment Systems. Who you choose for this important process can make a huge difference in your bottom line profits.

Most local banks outsource this service to a third party that has an agreement or arrangement with the bank. A few national banks process credit transactions themselves. Regardless, you need to ask several key questions in order to make sure you have the best program for your business.

If the processing is outsourced, it is likely the customer service will also be outsourced. That can create a very frustrating situation should you have a problem or question. Look for a full-service credit card processor that handles not only the sales, but also the back-end processing, customer service, and other functions. They will be the most secure when it comes to protecting your clients' sensitive credit card information. They will also be the most responsive should you ever have an issue.

IS THE LOWEST RATE ALWAYS BEST?

Most processors will quote a rate for processing transactions and position a rate that is one of the lowest rates available. What they do not tell you about are the additional fees involved, including a substantial cancellation or early-termination fee designed to keep you locked into the contract even after you find a better provider. Low rates can be deceiving. Be sure you understand all the terms in the contract.

You want to get to a number called "total cost" or "effective rate." That number includes not only the low rate, but all of the add-on charges, fees, and other costs. The effective rate is the number that matters, not the initial rate.

Card companies such as Visa, MasterCard, Discover, and American Express set different rates for different cards, industries, and customers. These rates are called interchange, and they are numerous. To further complicate the picture, these rates range anywhere from a zero percentage rate with a small per-item fee, to levels that include a percentage rate greater than three percent with large per-item fees.

With a marijuana business, you may not have many options on choosing a processor. Just be happy that you are able to take credit cards at all!

Banking Guidance

THE FEDERAL GOVERNMENT CLEARED THE WAY for banks to work with marijuana businesses, removing a major hurdle that has tripped up the cannabis industry in recent years. Up until now, it has been almost hopeless to open and operate as a regular business entity with a bank.

The U.S. Justice Department and U.S. Treasury Department now provide banks with outlines for how to work with the marijuana industry. Under the guidelines, banks must verify that marijuana companies are properly licensed by their state and local municipalities when considering them for a business relationship.

The Obama administration has given banks the go-ahead to make loans or open accounts for marijuana dispensaries in states where they're legal without running afoul of federal laws, which still consider cannabis an illegal substance.

Banks must then monitor these businesses for any financial wrongdoing and report suspicious activity to regulators. They must comply with a slew of anti-money-laundering rules enforced by bank regulators, and the risk of violations could be big for banks that choose to do business with companies that are breaking federal laws.

Although the Obama Administration and the U.S. Justice Department have given banks the green light to work with marijuana businesses, banks are cautious, holding back to see what the near future holds. The next administration could also change its stance on marijuana and begin a campaign to shut the industry down, creating havoc with the banks. All it would take is one U.S. attorney to file criminal charges, and a bank could lose its charter and be forced to shut down. None of those potential pitfalls are encouraging banks who might otherwise be willing to take a gamble on doing banking business with marijuana dispensaries.

Banks face new challenges and tough decisions as the legalization of marijuana for both medicinal and recreational purposes increases. Meanwhile, legal marijuana sellers look for safe places to park their proceeds.

For now, banks and credit unions in states where sales are legal are in the awkward position of having to turn away business. The reality is that as more states adopt the marijuana laws and enable businesses to open and sell medicinal and recreational marijuana, the banks will eventually start to realize that this business isn't going away and they will begin to get involved. However, the process will be slow. In the meantime, many dispensaries struggle with no banking source—running around gathering money orders, allocating cash to vendors and employees, and creating a massive amount of bookkeeping so they can prove they're doing everything right.

SOME POTENTIAL SOLUTIONS

- Go to a bank that you currently have a relationship with. Most people have a bank where they have their personal accounts or even accounts for another business.

- Look for a new branch that is opening up. They are more aggressive for new accounts.

- Go to a state bank or local credit union. They may be easier to work with and are more sympathetic to a new state business.

- Open up an account for your business like any other business account, but keep the nature of the business nonspecific. Use a "dba" that is nondescript. Maybe something like Healthy Alternatives, for example. Make deposits with tellers that you know.

- Try to attach credit cards to your dba. This reduces the amount of cash going into the bank.

- Make sure *you* and *your* clothes don't smell. Spending all day in the garden or the dispensary and then walking into a bank . . . bad idea. The smell permeates off of you. Be aware. Your senses get dull because you are always around it.

- The smell of your money is important too. Your cashier is exchanging money all day. That money has the smell of marijuana from being touched by employees and from just being in the dispensary. When you take it to the bank, it will smell. Don't question it . . . it will smell! It is a good idea to buy a case of "Febreze" and spray the money before each deposit. It's okay for money to smell—just not like marijuana!

- If your bank finds out your business, most times they will close the account. You may want to open accounts with two different banks, so if one shuts you down, the other is up and running. You can use the second bank account for a sales tax account to handle your tax obligations.

Your Legal and Financial Team

SOMETIMES BUSINESS OWNERS TRY TO RESEARCH AND MANAGE all the legal and financial situations on their own. However, going at it alone can be a costly mistake. While educating yourself on the legal and financial aspects of business and marijuana ownership is always a good idea, don't undervalue or disregard the importance of a good legal and financial team. Educating yourself will make it easier to talk to and understand your lawyer, accountant, and bookkeeper. You should always learn as much as you can about operating your business. However, from a legal and financial standpoint, each business property lease and business model is different, and having the skilled expertise of your lawyer or accountant looking at the finer details will pay off—big time.

Do what you do best—your forte may be marketing or harvesting the best crop in the world, but trying to navigate through one of the fastest growing businesses that is seeing radical changes daily will almost be impossible without a good legal and financial team! Hiring and surrounding yourself with a good professional team will enable you to spend more time running your business.

When you put together your legal and financial team, look for professionals who represent small business owners. It would be extremely helpful if they have assisted with other dispensaries, or are at least familiar with the current legal and accounting operations needed to be in this type of business today. Lawyers and accountants can be costly, but paying for their services and expertise will save you from the financial losses you could face from poorly negotiated lease agreements, unnecessary lawsuits, and late or incorrect tax payments. They should keep you current on city, state and federal regulations, notify you of new laws, and keep you up to date on new requirements and changes.

Just like everything else in this business venture, you will need to do your research to find good people to fill these roles—the ones who will do their best for you. When you need them, you want to know they are there for you and that they understand your business needs! In this chapter, you will find helpful tips about hiring the right lawyer, accountant, and bookkeeper for your business.

HIRING A LAWYER

Having a good business lawyer is essential to negotiating the best lease and properly setting up your business entity. Many aspects of business require legal advice. Once your business is open, you may have issues with other tenants, your landlord, your clients, or your employees that will require the assistance of a lawyer. When a legal problem arises, not having legal representation can put you in a costly position—a position that could have been easily avoided had you secured a lawyer early on in your business venture.

Hiring an attorney and forming a solid business relationship with him or her can save you money and mitigate risk throughout the course of owning and operating your business.

HERE ARE SOME EXAMPLES OF WHY YOU NEED AN ATTORNEY:

- Forming your business structure.

- Negotiating with the landlord.

- Signing your business property lease.

- Closing on the purchase of real estate.

- Closing on the purchase of an existing business or property.

- Working with city officials.

- Mitigating any lawsuits.

However, if you run into a small problem and you feel it can be handled without the advice of a lawyer, then you can find the right forms or information on legal portals such as AllLaw, found at alllaw.com.

The solution is to have open communication with a lawyer who will be ready to work with you quickly if a situation arises. Get legal advice if you have any questions that will cost you money, whether the legal issue is with your business or personal.

WHAT KIND OF LAWYER DO YOU NEED?

Lawyers typically specialize in one type of law or another. It is best to find a business lawyer who specializes in small businesses. However, a general practice lawyer can handle a wide range of legal matters and may be suited to your business needs.

If a legal matter involves a specialized kind of law like bankruptcy, litigation, taxation, or patent laws, then you need to contact a specialist. Make sure to ask your lawyer whether he or she specializes in a type of law before you decide to hire him or her. If you are lucky enough to find a lawyer who has done legal work for other dispensaries or grow operations in the marijuana field, it would be a strong point in that laywer's favor, and to your benefit. Having an understanding of this business is extremely important. A lawyer with this knowledge can assist you from making some very expensive mistakes.

WHERE DO YOU FIND A LAWYER?

The best way to find a lawyer is through a friend, business acquaintance, or a client referral. You can also use an online directory where information is available about lawyers at their websites. Your state's bar association will also have a referral service that can help put you in touch with a lawyer that best suits your needs. Still, word of mouth and a good old-fashioned phone book are the best methods of finding a lawyer. These are the regular channels to find an attorney. A lawyer that is based in the local municipality and has worked with your city attorney will probably be the most effective. At the end of the day, it's all about relationships.

Find at least three prospective lawyers. Next, make an appointment and interview the lawyer. Ask questions pertaining to your business needs. The lawyer's answers will give you an indication about whether this lawyer is suitable for you and your business.

QUESTIONS TO ASK A PROSPECTIVE LAWYER:

Check off the questions below as you ask them.

- ○ What type of law is your specialty?
- ○ Do you have any dispensaries and/or grow operations for clients?
- ○ What is your experience with negotiating a lease?
- ○ What are the top three things you look to do for a business owner when negotiating a lease?
- ○ What experience do you have with employment law?
- ○ What are your legal fees? Are your fees hourly or do you charge a flat rate?
- ○ Are paralegals or associates available to handle routine matters at lower rates?
- ○ How long have you been practicing law, and what has been your area of focus?
- ○ Do you actively write articles or present at seminars for other professionals?
- ○ What if a matter arises that is outside of your area of expertise?
- ○ What is your availability to take on new clients and how responsive are you?

HOW MUCH DO LAWYERS CHARGE?

Lawyers' fees can sometimes be very expensive. It all depends on what type of legal advice they are giving, and most importantly, how much time they are spending on your needs. There are many different types of fee arrangements. Most lawyers charge hourly fees. Their fees are calculated by multiplying the amount of hours they spend on your case by an hourly rate.

If a lawyer is reviewing your real estate lease, he may charge you a preset amount (a fixed fee). If they are filing your articles of incorporation for your new business, they may also charge you a fixed fee. You should always ask a potential lawyer to explain their fees and billing practices. Don't take things for granted. You might think that the attorney only took a few minutes to help you, then later you receive a bill for a few thousand dollars.

Reading documents, especially your lease for your business, takes more than a few minutes. However, a lawyer can save you thousands over the term of your lease when they find and flag loopholes or clauses that are in favor of your landlord.

Most lawyers require a retainer to get started. In the case of a real estate closing or filing articles of incorporation, the lawyer will send you a bill or you can pay them the day of closing. They usually will have a bill prepared and you will know the detailed breakdown of their fees before the closing. You also have to remember that you are responsible for court fees, services, or any charges to the lawyer while representing you. This includes the time it takes your lawyer to get to and from the courthouse or legal meetings.

Having a good lawyer at hand is one key to having a successful business.

HIRING AN ACCOUNTANT

Just as you need a lawyer to help with the legal matters of your business, you will need an accountant to advise you on the financial aspects. Don't make the mistake of attempting this one on your own.

We tend to think of accountants when it comes to taxes, but there are many other services your accountant will provide. Whether you're deciding if you should incorporate your new business, or trying to decide whether to buy or lease your property and or equipment, a good accountant will be able to tell you how such decisions would affect your taxes and/or your business' growth.

You need to make sure that you feel comfortable with the accountant you hire. The accountant should be sincere and trustworthy. If you are clear about your requirements, then you will be able to choose the right accountant.

HOW TO FIND THE RIGHT ACCOUNTANT

The easiest way to find a good accountant is by asking other business associates who they use for accounting services. You must ask them what type of services their accountant provides, and most importantly, are they satisfied with the services the accountant offers? If you don't get any worthy referrals using this method, use the Internet to find accountants located close to where you will be opening your business. Close proximity to your accountant will make it easier and more manageable for communication and availability. Yes, you can learn QuickBooks; but your time is better spent in other areas—like managing and overseeing your grow operation. The marijuana business is extremely hands-on and time consuming.

THE FACE-TO-FACE MEETING

Face-to-face meetings are imperative because your accountant is someone you will see routinely throughout the year, and this person is going to get to know the most intimate details of your personal and business finances. They will also help you to mold your business for success. You are looking for a long-term partner to advise you on the financial matters of your business. It's a big deal. You are establishing a lasting relationship that must be built on trust.

QUESTIONS TO ASK A PROSPECTIVE ACCOUNTANT:

Check off the questions below as you ask them.

- ○ Are you a CPA? (Don't be afraid to ask him or her about their education.)
- ○ Do you work with any other marijuana businesses? If so, how will you avoid conflict?
- ○ If you have worked with other dispensaries, what do they offer?
- ○ What type of software programs are you familiar with? Will you help me grow my business, or are you going to be more of a bookkeeper?
- ○ Will you help me set up yearly tax planning? (They should be able to advise your business so it functions with peak tax efficiency.)
- ○ Will you offer your personal finance advice? (A key to a good accountant is not just managing your business, but also managing your personal finances as well. Both business and personal finances, when managed correctly, are key to your success.)
- ○ Does this accounting firm have the state-of-the-art technology and software needed to enable me to work and communicate with you efficiently? Describe it. (Technology has improved small business capabilities. Good communication is vital with your accountant, and the Internet has made that easy.)

◯ What organizations do you belong to?

◯ Are you affiliated with a local bank? (You may never know when you need a loan. There is an old saying "It is not how much you know to be successful, but who you know." Don't look at your new accountant as just a bookkeeper; ask them if they have the ability to refer business to your dispensary.)

◯ What type of business advice would you give me right now, before I open, that could help save me money? (Their answer to this question will give you a good idea if this person is right for you.)

◯ Why should I hire you? (The answer they give will paint a clear picture as to whether they fit in your business plan or not.)

FINDING A BOOKKEEPER

Your accountant will probably recommend that you also have a bookkeeper to help keep your finances organized and tracked in a timely manner. Having a bookkeeper on your financial team will help you be better prepared for visits with your accountant and save you money in the long run.

You will find that the daily grind of running your dispensary and/or grow business is extremely time consuming; scheduling staff, dealing with customers, tracking inventory, vendor relationships and dealing with all the new personalities is a lot to manage. Having someone else who is responsible for keeping your finances organized is essential.

Your bookkeeper should be required to:

- Keep track of checks and other income.

- Pay bills and reconcile the business checkbook.

- Pay employees as well as file and pay federal and state payroll taxes.

- Pay quarterly business taxes.

- Keep track of receivables.

- Keep track of inventories and commissions to your staff.

- Help monitor all compliance standards for your dispensary and grow facility.

- Your state and local municipality requires mountains of paperwork and your bookkeeper should help you stay organized with all the regulatory requirements.

SECTION IV

LOCATION AND BUILDING STRUCTURES

Finding the Right Location
For Your Dispensary

IT IS SAID THE THREE MOST IMPORTANT DECISIONS you will make are location, location, and location. If you are creating and building your dispensary, or even relocating or opening a second location, then the details of the location might not be the first thing on your mind, but they should be.

Put location on the top of your list as the single most important factor for your new business. Your amazing concepts, business ideas, services, products and the best marijuana in your area will go unnoticed if you do not take the time to do your homework and pinpoint the perfect location. Your location is a huge factor in how you market your business, determine which products to carry, and set prices. Your location says a lot about you, your business, your brand, and the customers you wish to attract.

Here are several key factors that you should consider when choosing a location for your dispensary and or grow operation. You must keep in mind that once you have met your city and state regulations on areas that have been approved for marijuana, you should follow these principles for best suited locations:

POPULATION & YOUR CUSTOMER

Begin by researching the city and area you have selected for your medical marijuana business thoroughly before making a final decision. Read local papers and speak to the small business owners in the region. Ask them the difficult questions regarding their business:

- What unexpected expenses, like taxes and fees, came up when you started your business here?

- Is the Chamber of Commerce active in promoting new businesses?

- Are they open to a marijuana operation in their area, and will they help promote your new business?

- Is the city or county good at repairing the streets, sidewalks, etc. on which your business will be located?

Obtain location demographics from the library, online, Chamber of Commerce and/or the Census Bureau. The best advice you will receive is from the local coffee shop or restaurants in the neighborhood. Observe the people: how do they dress, where do they shop, when are people shopping, and are they buying or browsing?

ACCESSIBILITY, VISIBILITY, & TRAFFIC

Don't confuse a lot of traffic for a lot of customers. Your marijuana business wants to be in a location where there are many shoppers, but only if the shopper meets the definition of your target market. Small retail stores may benefit from the traffic of nearby larger stores. When considering visibility, look at the location from the customer's viewpoint. In many cases, the better visibility your business has, the less advertising needed. A freestanding building on the outskirts of town will need more marketing dollars than if your business is located in a strip mall or on a main street.

This **CHECKLIST** will give you more insight on picking your location:

How many people walk or drive past the location in a given day, week, or month?

Day _____   Week _____   Month _____

Is the area served by public transportation?	○ Yes	○ No
Is it lit up and safe at night?	○ Yes	○ No
Can clients easily get in and out of the parking lot?	○ Yes	○ No
Is there adequate parking?	○ Yes	○ No
Does this location have 10 parking spots for every 1000 square feet of space?	○ Yes	○ No
If the location is off a busy street or highway, is it easy to get to?	○ Yes	○ No
Is there adequate fire and police presence in the community?	○ Yes	○ No
What is the crime rate in the neighborhood?	_____	
Can the store be seen from the main flow of traffic?	○ Yes	○ No
Will the dispensary's sign be visible?	○ Yes	○ No
Is there easy access to the dispensary?	○ Yes	○ No
If there is a divider on the main street, would clients have to make a U-turn?	○ Yes	○ No

SIGNAGE, ZONING, & PLANNING

Before you enter into a lease or purchase agreement, be sure you understand all the rules, policies, and procedures related to your business location. Contact the local city hall and zoning commission for information on regulations regarding the space you are interested in. The planning board determines the correct use for the location. Although the landlord may love the idea of having a full-service dispensary and grow operation in that location, the planning board will have the final say on whether or not it is allowed.

It also may be a good idea to ask the planning officer about signage and regulations. Many towns are very sensitive about the height and the type of signage allowed.

COMPETITION & NEIGHBORS

When choosing your location, it is a good idea to see how many dispensaries are in the same vicinity as the location you are interested in. If this is a new area opening up for medicinal or recreational marijuana, you most likely may be the only one in that area. Other types of businesses may help or hurt your business. The key is to be next to a retailer that draws other people to the area. Schools and hospitals are out of bounds. You will have a 1,000 square foot red flag on these types of properties. Being next to a busy coffee shop or designer store may be fantastic to give you instant exposure. Being next to a muffler shop or a business that is very loud or uses all the available parking will be a major deterrent, but unfortunately this may be the only area in town approved for marijuana sales or farming.

SMALL TOWN OR BIG CITY?

There aren't many options in small municipalities, because they limit the area and the amount of dispensaries, so take what you can get and hope you don't get taking advantage of. In large cities, there are more opportunities, but you need to do your homework and get in front of the most desirable locations. Marijuana-zoned areas can become as pricey as beachfront real estate.

LOCATION COSTS

Besides the base rent, consider all the costs involved when choosing your marijuana business location. These costs will be your monthly overhead no matter what else arises:

- Lawn care, building maintenance, utilities, and security
- Upkeep and repair of the heating/air conditioning units
- Property taxes (depending on the lease)
- Water and sewer costs
- Insurance on the property and contents

PERSONAL FACTORS

The marijuana business requires you to be there every day. When choosing a location, it is important to think about your personal factors. How far would the business be from your home and other things you do on a daily basis? Do you need to take children to school? How close is your bank? How far is shopping? The commute can easily overshadow the exhilaration of your new business if you are spending a lot of time traveling to and from work. Commuting has the potential to stifle your independence.

QUESTIONS THAT WILL MAKE OR BREAK YOUR LOCATION

Most people focus their energy on the creative side of the new business and neglect some important aspects of choosing a location. Answering these questions for the site you are considering will help you determine if you have chosen the right location for your new business:

CHECKLIST: Check off the questions below as you get answers.

- ◯ Is the facility located in an area that is zoned for a marijuana business?
- ◯ Is the facility large enough for your business?
- ◯ Does it meet your layout requirements?
- ◯ Does the building need repairs?

- ○ Does the building have a crawl space or basement for easy access to utilities?
- ○ Are the lease terms and rent favorable?
- ○ Is the location convenient to where you live?
- ○ Can you find qualified employees in the area?
- ○ Does the location have the customers you are looking for?
- ○ Is this a seasonal community?
- ○ Does the area have the image you are looking for?
- ○ Is this a safe neighborhood?
- ○ Is there exterior lighting on the building?
- ○ Will local businesses attract clients to your business?
- ○ Are there many competitors nearby?
- ○ Can suppliers make deliveries conveniently at this location?
- ○ Is the parking adequate for the dispensary?
- ○ Is the area served by public transportation?
- ○ Can potential clients see the location at night?
- ○ Will there be walk-in business?
- ○ Is the building insulated?
- ○ Is there enough electricity coming into the building?
- ○ In case of robbery or fire is there a police and/or fire department in the area?

Finding the Right Location for Your Grow Facility

HOW TO PICK THE RIGHT LOCATION

If you are successful and able to secure a license to operate in the industry, the first question is, how do I pick the right location? What do I look for?

Picking the right location is extremely important. If you make a mistake with the wrong spot, you may be forced later to move your whole operation at a great expense.

The first step is to approach your local municipality, visit the city clerk's office and ask if any zones have been designated as areas for the cultivation and medical or recreational sales of marijuana. Your city may have a certain part of town where they want your business to be located. There might be restrictions on how many marijuana businesses are able to operate in town and how far apart. Each municipality is different; it's up to the city council to establish what they want in their community, so it's important for you to know what they are thinking. They make the rules that you will need to follow. If they have decided to allow dispensaries to open anywhere, it's up to you to choose the correct location. The federal government enforces a distance requirement, which must be adhered to in looking for a spot.

The most important factor in picking your location is to be at least **one thousand feet** away from any public or private school, university, or day care center. This regulation also applies to certain businesses such as liquor stores and adult bookstores. The federal government still considers marijuana an illegal controlled substance, so stay away from any government-owned buildings. You might also want to stay away from hospitals and places of worship, just to be safe. When I state **one thousand feet, it's one thousand feet at a minimum.** If you think nine hundred ninety-seven feet works, think again. You will be forced to move. It has happened. In most cases, you are looking for two locations; one for the dispensary and the other for the garden or grow (it will be referred to both ways throughout the book).

The best and most efficient way to pick the perfect spot is to have both operations under one roof. Your dispensary is in the front and your cultivation center in the back. This is not easy to find because of the zoning differences for manufacturing/cultivation centers and retail type businesses. Opportunities for this type of operation are more available outside city limits in the county where the building you rent/own has no zoning restrictions. This location makes an ideal business model because of the ease of management in having everything under one roof.

Theoretically speaking, you actually are running two businesses at the same time. Both are open seven days a week, both have different personnel, and both have completely different operating procedures. If your garden is located an hour away from your dispensary, you have more travel time involved in addition to the business itself, which is very time consuming. If you are looking to work forty hours a week in the beginning to start this business, it's not for you. Be prepared to work every day, ten to twelve hours or more, if you want to see true success.

If you aren't able to get everything under one roof, then the next best thing is to have your dispensary and garden as close to one another in the same municipality as possible. Remember, it was mentioned above that both of these operations are open seven days a week. Try to make it easy on yourself to go back and forth between the two facilities to manage your business effectively. Your garden is where the crux of your entire business is, so stay attuned to what's happening with your crop. There have been instances of a garden destroyed by root aphids (insects) in a week's time. If the subtle changes in the plants had gone unnoticed, the whole crop could have been lost. If you have no crop, you will be forced to buy from another dispensary or grower (depending on your state). Buying from someone else reduces your profit margin dramatically, and depending on the size of the garden, it could mean hundreds of thousands of dollars in lost revenue. As a startup, you can automate your grow and view everything online, but it will dramatically increase your initial financial investment. It all depends on what you want to spend and risk.

Here is what to look for when searching for a **GROW LOCATION**.

- First and foremost, check with your municipality for "zoned" areas. Once that is established, here are some pointers to look for in the garden:

- What is the amount of electricity coming into the space? Most of the time you will have to increase the amount of electricity coming into your location. For example, a 100 light operation needs approximately 800 amps of power to run. The size of the location is about 5000 square feet. In a normal warehouse, you would normally get a 200 amp panel. So look for a warehouse that may have had an industrial tenant in there previously. Hopefully, they increased the electrical service. Inspect it to determine if you need to increase your panel.

- Is there enough power coming into the building? In most cases no, so you will have to look at the transformer designated to your building and see what other parts of the area or buildings are being covered by this. If you check with your electric company you can see how much is dedicated to your building. On experienced business owner in Colorado had to increase his transformer from 150 to 500 KVA, at the cost of $28,000 dollars. Keep this in mind.

- Is there enough air conditioning? This is critical in any indoor operation. Imagine each light is 1000 watts of power, creating a lot of heat, and multiply that by 100. It gets very hot!! The bottom line is that you will need a lot of air to keep your environment right. See if you can find an aggressive landlord that who is willing to rent to a dispensary and grow operations, ask him to increase the air conditioning.

- The rule of thumb is one ton for every three lights unvented. Unvented means that most hooded light systems are vented from the outside with air to cool the bulbs so they aren't creating a lot of heat. If you are venting your lights, it would be one ton for every five lights. If you were putting in a 100 light operation, I would recommend 30-40 tons. If your landlord covers this, it will save you a lot of money.

- Rent a building away from others with little or no foot traffic. Marijuana has a very strong smell and the odor will leak outside the building. If detected, it presents an opportunity for theft and possible air quality violations.

- Make sure that your building is well lit. If not, add lighting where needed.

- A cement or cinder block built warehouse is the preferred style of construction to rent. Buildings constructed of a metal or aluminum siding are less secure and less efficient for indoor environmental conditions.

- Look for a landlord who wants a long-term lease. Space is very limited and real estate is at a premium. Many municipalities ban the industry all together and won't allow you to rent/own and operate gardens in their town. Look for warehouse space that has empty space available next to it. This may become critical later for expansion. Some cities will allow you to expand if there is empty space connected to your existing location tied by a common dividing wall. This would allow you to use your existing license for expansion and not have to apply for a new one, which probably won't be available. Every municipality is different, so this is no guarantee, but something that could help you.

One last thing: don't sign any lease until you have an operating license in hand or a contingency in the lease for if things don't work out. Make sure you are not responsible for the balance of your lease if you are closed by forces out of your control, such as being closed by a state or federal act, a raid (wrongfully conducted) . . . the list goes on.

Building Structures that Make Sense

GETTING INVOLVED IN THE MARIJUANA BUSINESS can be overwhelming. The fact that you decided to do it and have gone through the process with your state and city to find out where you will be able to build and operate your marijuana dispensary and/or grow facility was a big undertaking.

The next step is to narrow down your location options and decide what type of building structure best suits your needs. Many dispensary and grow facility owners in Colorado have gone through a huge learning curve, and it is still happening today.

Due to the fact that your city council basically tells you where you can operate your business, your choice of properties may be limited. The dispensary and grow operations currently open today in Colorado may or may not have had a choice when choosing rental properties. A limited supply of properties to choose from may have caused them to build structures that really weren't designed for growing operations, but at the time that may have been all that was available. With recreational marijuana being approved in the state of Colorado, the landlords that were previously reluctant to rent to marijuana business owners may now see these businesses as good risks and viable tenants, enabling you to better find the building structure that is best suited for your marijuana business needs.

BEST-SUITED STRUCTURES:

BRICK/CINDERBLOCK

The story of the Three Little Pigs is just as true today as it was when it was first told to children long ago. Brick will always win in the end.

Virtually fireproof

Since the primary ingredient in brick is clay, which is fired to around 2000 degrees Fahrenheit, it is a noncombustible material. As such, it is an excellent cladding choice to resist or confine fires. In fact, both the National Institute of Standards and Technology and the Building Industry Association conducted separate one-hour fire tests that conclusively demonstrated that nothing outperforms good old-fashioned brick, and that today's "advanced" materials, such as vinyl, are engulfed by flames within minutes. Brick is such a strong and durable building material that your insurance companies may even offer you a discount on your commercial insurance costs if your building is made of brick.

Shelter from the storm

With weather patterns changing around the world, the threat of different types of catastrophic storms have to be a part of your planning when choosing a building structure. Commercial buildings made out of brick or cinderblock give you added protection and insurance that your business will withstand these types of unusual events.

Superior moisture control

According to a nationally-renowned, independent building products research laboratory, brick veneer wall assemblies control moisture better than wall systems clad with other exterior materials. Therefore, brick veneer wall systems help minimize mold growth, wood rot, infestation by insects, and corrosion of fasteners embedded in wood better than other wall assemblies.

Brick is naturally energy efficient

Brick is a building material that has exceptional "thermal mass" properties. Thermal mass is the ability of a heavy, dense material to store heat and then slowly release it. For you, this means that during the summer months your brick building stays cool during the hottest part of the day. During the winter, brick walls store your buildings heat and radiate it back to you. This means your heater and air conditioner don't have to work as hard to keep the inside of your building warmer in winter and cooler in summer. Vinyl, aluminum, wood, or EIFS (artificial stucco) are all thin, light building materials that do not have good thermal mass properties. The superior thermal mass qualities of brick have been known for centuries.

This may not seem important to you when you are initially looking for rental space, but when the heat of the summer or the arctic air of the winter come into play, the temperature outside will affect many things inside your grow operation. Heating and air conditioning are two of the most intricate parts of your business. A brick building can save you thousands of dollars a month on your utility bill due to the insulating properties of brick. Your first choice when deciding on a property should be brick or masonry. Overall, this will give your growing capabilities an edge and will yield better results, not to mention save you money every month when the utility bills come in.

Better brick than sorry

When building a business you want to make sure that your valuables are in a convenient and secure place when your operation is closed and you and your employees leave for the day. However, while you're at home, your business faces the risk of burglary, fire, and water damage. This can lead to a lot of worry—and yes, all of these things may happen.

The risk is far less in a brick or masonry building. The structure itself is difficult to break into and less inviting to thieves who may be looking to rob a dispensary or grow operation. Going back to the Three Little Pigs, even the Big Bad Wolf couldn't get into the brick building. It will also make your facility as "bullet proof" as you can get.

STEEL OR METAL STRUCTURES

Most of us think of metal as indestructible. Let's face it, the only man who could bend steel was Superman. Of all the types of structures that can be used for outdoor storage and other purposes, almost nothing beats metal buildings. A metal building is versatile for all types of outdoor use due to its strength, durability, versatility, and cost relative to other structures.

What makes metal buildings such a popular option for businesses and homeowners alike? Metal storage buildings, metal garage buildings, and other prefab metal buildings are often used by residential customers who need extra storage space, and they function well as sheds or portable garages. The reasons they are used by homeowners are similar to the reasons that there are so many commercial metal buildings constructed for businesses. There are many pros to metal building construction that make it such a popular option. There are cons as well. Below are the benefits and drawbacks of using metal buildings for your marijuana grow facility.

PROS

Strength - Perhaps one of the largest benefits of metal buildings is their strength. Using metal or steel in construction makes for very strong structures. Metal buildings do not require a great deal of additional support structures or intricate design elements in order to increase the strength of the design, since metal building construction in and of itself offers strength that is unsurpassed by other materials. This is a great benefit with regard to weather disruption or in case of earthquakes; most likely the building would survive. The other good news with this type of structure is that if you decided to expand, it would not be difficult and could be done on site, typically like an erector set.

Durability - In addition to the strength that metal offers, metal building components also have the benefit of durability. Metal lasts longer than other materials such as wood, vinyl or plastic, and requires virtually no maintenance. When constructing metal buildings, you do not have to worry about mold, mildew, rot, insect damage and other issues that often arise with wood buildings.

CONS

Temperature regulation

- It is sometimes difficult to regulate temperature and airflow within a metal building structure. This is because metal building insulation is not as efficient as the insulation qualities of other materials. For this reason, most metal buildings are used for storage or garage purposes, rather than for living purposes—you do not find many metal homes around, because metal is not the best material for constructing residential living structures. Many commercial buildings have a brick or decorative cinderblock front and the rest of the building is metal construction. The front looks aesthetically beautiful and secure; the back and sides are metal. This enables the construction process to move along quickly, and the overall cost is cheaper than constructing a full masonry building.

- The major problem is that these buildings become hothouses during the summer and are typically almost impossible to keep warm during the winter. If you decide to rent or build one of these structures, you will have to insulate the walls and ceilings to adequately prevent temperature fluctuations. You will also find that no matter what you do, your energy cost will be much higher to run your grow operation in this type of building.

Noise

- Metal buildings can also be rather noisy. For the same reasons as the problem of temperature regulation—lack of insulation—the structures can carry noise and there can be a lot of echoing in the open space.

Dents and rusting

- While metal buildings don't have the same issues as wood buildings or other structures with rot, mildew, mold, and insects, one of the issues they may have is rust. Rusting of metal buildings primarily occurs in situations where a dent or large scratch is left unfixed. When the unfinished edges are exposed to the elements, rust can occur. This is easily rectified by quickly fixing any dents or scratches, or covering them with a sealer to prevent rust from forming.

Steel is only as good as the thickness

- Many of us look at a commercial structures made of steel and assume that they must be strong enough to withstand anything. This may be the case with regard to weather related events, but the common thief looks at these types of buildings as targets. Metal is strong, yes, but what makes it impervious to the common thief is the thickness of the steel.

- Most steel-constructed buildings use different thicknesses based on the building cost. Believe it or not, the metal sometimes is only a little bit thicker than the metal of a can of soda. You can imagine how easy it would be to cut a hole or drive a common screw driver through the side of one of these buildings. Thieves carry tools that can easily penetrate and cut through a steel wall. Entering your building could take minutes, and stealing your hard-earned cash or your harvest is very possible.

- In order to prevent this, many dispensaries that house their grow operations in these types of metal buildings use ¾ inch marine plywood on the interior of the buildings on the exterior walls. They also may put a wire mesh first and the plywood on top. Some use clever alarm devices where they wire the interior mesh so that if it is cut an alarm will sound. Not only will this slow down a thief, but the extra plywood acts as a barrier and also insulates the walls. They paint the plywood with a heavy-duty waterproof semi-gloss paint to eliminate moisture and mildew. This can also be washed down if necessary.

Wow! What's that smell?

- Who would have thought that you would have to worry about the smell that emanates from your building? Hey, if you didn't know it, marijuana stinks. Not in the sense that it stinks and you will not make money—no, that's not it. In this case, other businesses may smell your beautiful crop. People walking by your grow facility or dispensary, neighboring tenants, and, yes, thieves. The word will spread that your building is a grow farm. Soon the world knows. The problem with using a steel building once again is ventilation and insulation. If it is not thoroughly insulated and ventilated properly, the smell of marijuana will permeate the air around your building. The only defense you have is to spend the extra money to thoroughly insulate the walls and ceiling.

WOOD AS A COMMERCIAL BUILDING

The use of wood framing in building construction has existed for hundreds of years in the United States. Wood is generally available in all parts of the country and it was used to construct many buildings that exist in towns and cities today. This material has once again become an acceptable method for constructing commercial buildings. With the construction industry more competitive than ever and the cost of concrete and steel increasing, wood has become a popular alternative. The continued development of engineered wood has increased its use as a structural component. Engineered wood, trusses, and beams are now available in lengths that span large distances and have excellent load carrying capabilities.

Many older towns have commercial buildings that are made out of wood. It is possible to find a large old barn or commercial warehouse that is partially brick with the remaining walls and ceilings primarily wood. The rent may be considerably less that other newer buildings, but the cost to renovate and update utilities, ventilation and insulation may or may not be worth it.

CONS

Kindling

Wood buildings can be dangerous for many reasons, depending on how old it is and if it has been taken care of. There will always be the danger of fire. Let me remind you that you will have an enormous amount of electricity going through this building. You will also have a great amount of lighting that throws off extreme heat. The possibility of fire is extremely high. The amount of money invested in equipment in your grow facility will not be insignificant, and having to move it or the risk of it being damaged will be more likely with a wood building structure.

Old innards

Many old buildings have inadequate electrical and plumbing problems. Older buildings may still use fuse boxes, and the cost to upgrade will be thousands of dollars. The plumbing in these buildings is usually comprised of old lead pipes. In many cases, the insides of these pipes rot and get clogged. The cost to upgrade the water supply into the building and run new pipes will also be thousands of dollars. Unless you own the building and/or the landlord is willing to pay, then these costs cannot be justified in your initial budget.

Insulation

Back in the day before most of us were born, most building construction did not include insulation. Coal was cheap and most commercial buildings didn't use much to keep the buildings warm. If they did, they would only heat the offices with a potbelly stove.

Thus, many old wooden commercial buildings have little or no insulation. In order to make this work for your grow operation, the entire building will have to be insulated. This process is not cheap, considering you may have to strip walls to get the insulation into the walls.

Moisture and mold could get ugly

Wood and water don't mix. Older wood absorbs water more quickly than new wood. Let's face it, you're going to have an indoor garden. Water will be used daily to assist in the production of harvesting—without water you have no garden. Water promotes wood rot, insects, mildew, humidity and mold—everything that you do not want in your garden.

YOU CAN'T ALWAYS GET WHAT YOU WANT

Finding the right location in any business can be crucial to survival. In this case, due to your town or city regulations, finding the right location for your grow facility may be more of take what you can get. You also can't forget that many landlords are still reluctant to rent buildings to marijuana grow operations. Until more states continue to approve marijuana from a medical and recreational standpoint, there will always be people who may not want to go along with a marijuana business opportunity. If you are lucky enough to have a choice of properties, make sure you consider the pros and cons for each, based on the guidelines above, then make your move.

Negotiating Your Lease

NOW COULD BE ONE OF THE BEST TIMES EVER to negotiate a great commercial lease for your business. Since the downturn of the economy, we have seen a huge decrease in commercial shopping center occupancy. Some centers are only fifty percent filled with tenants. Landlords are looking for any opportunity to lease their locations and they are giving incredible deals to fill their empty spaces.

This creates a huge opportunity that would normally cost you much more. The key is to know what to look for and what questions to ask. Realize that your rent will be one of the largest fixed expenses you have every month.

The importance of negotiating this lease agreement will help you with your budget and financial outlook. Any miscalculations made on negotiating this lease will be with you the entire term of the lease. That could be very costly and, unfortunately, will not go away once you sign the agreement.

When you are looking for a location for your marijuana business, most will be available for lease only, not to own or buy. Before you agree to the basic terms of the commercial lease that the landlord hands you, you should realize that there is plenty of leeway in commercial leases for negotiations. Here are the most common things to consider when negotiating your lease to get the best deal possible:

- Analyze all costs associated with the potential space (construction, air conditioning, electric upgrades, handicap-access bathrooms).

- Is it a triple net or gross lease? Triple net means there are added expenses such as maintenance and property taxes. Gross is a total lease amount with no add-ons.

- City impact fees (example: one-time water hookup with the city).

- Are there any restrictions on services and or products that you will be selling (marijuana)?

- Deposits and down payments.

- Free rent.

BASIC LEASE COST

The first item of business you and your landlord will need to discuss is how much you will pay to rent the space. Usually, your monthly rent will be determined based on the square footage of the space, which is calculated at a per square foot cost. If you multiply width times the length of the space, then multiply your answer by the dollars per square foot, that will give you your base yearly rent.

Example

25' length x 25' width is 625 square feet. Predetermined square foot price negotiated with landlord is $14 per square foot.

Multiply your 625 (square feet) x 14 (dollars per square foot) = $8750. Now divide $8750 by 12 (months). This will give you your monthly rent: $8750/12 = $729 a month.

ADDITIONAL COSTS

Sometimes you will have additional costs to figure into your monthly rent expense, called CAM (common area maintenance), or triple net. It is often an addition to the monthly rent or an annual assessment per tenant. The CAM includes the maintenance of any common areas, like walkways, landscaped places, parking lots, and, in some cases, restrooms.

It is common for the landlord to concede and include CAM charges in the rent price of your commercial lease if negotiated correctly. Getting the most of your leased space is often determined by the market conditions of your location.

Below are some additional CAM expenses to look for when negotiating your lease:

- Property tax.

- Snow removal, lawn maintenance, landscaping.

- Repairs and maintenance to driveways, sidewalks, or parking lots.

- Utilities (electric, gas, sewer, and water).

- Refuse collection.

- Security

- Insurance—prorated among tenants. Landlord will have additional policy for exterior of building.

- Mechanical system repairs and replacements (such as heating and A/C maintenance and replacement).

- Structural and roof repairs.

- Outside warehouse lighting for nighttime security.

REPAIRS & IMPROVEMENTS

These are a critical part of your lease negotiations. The build-out in your garden can be very expensive. Ideally, if the previous tenant was a cultivation facility, changes could be minimal; however, this usually only occurs after a few years of operating in a state.
Three important factors to consider:

- The amount of electricity coming into your location and the amount of power coming into the whole building.

- The size of the air conditioners and heating units.

- The size of the transformer for the building.

This information will help you determine how much you will need to add to run the operation properly.

Plumbing, electric, handicap-access bathrooms, lighting, flooring, and painting are all part of the move-in process. Be very careful when the landlord says "take it as-is." That means you will pay for all repairs and upgrades. If you can do these repairs or improvements yourself, you may be able to do them inexpensively. But, be careful! You will need to meet code requirements for any changes.

However, in most cases, the landlord will want a licensed contractor to do the work. Some landlords are willing to absorb the cost of reasonable upgrades since you are improving their property.

FINANCING YOUR CONSTRUCTION COSTS

Obtaining financing from your landlord may be the easiest and the most overlooked method of getting financing. Many landlords have already built money into their financial projections that they will use to attract new tenants. These tenant improvement allowances can range from $5 to $25 per square foot. This is normal practice in the commercial rental market. Once the landlord finds out that you want to operate a garden in his warehouse, you may be paying a premium. This is a hot industry and landlords know this. They also will be aware of limited available space. Try to downplay the opportunity and focus the landlord on the huge expenses you will be occurring in the build-out of your garden. With all the limitations and the expenses that would be involved should you have to move your garden, try to strike a long-term lease. Negotiate the tenant improvements upfront and right into the lease.

One other important note THAT MUST BE ADDED to your lease: if for any reason your business is shut down by city, state, or federal circumstances that are out of your control, such as a changing statute, you will be released from any lease obligation.

SIGNING YOUR LIFE AWAY—PERSONAL GUARANTY

Definition:

- A guarantee that the primary owner will assume personal responsibility for repayment of the loan, should the company not repay the loan.

  www.businesstown.com/finance/money-glossary.asp

- An agreement to make oneself liable or responsible to another for the payment of a debt, default, or performance of a duty by a third party.

  www.crfonline.org/orc/glossary/p.html

- The provision in a lease naming a guarantor who is held personally responsible for the payment of all the amounts for rent and additional rent and other terms as set out in the lease.

  www.gtacommercialrealestate.com/resources.asp

How can you avoid giving a personal guaranty when signing a lease? For almost all new businesses, landlords will want you to sign personally. We recommend signing as a limited liability entity such as a corporation, limited liability, or limited partnership. Try to avoid signing a personal guarantee at all costs.

You should not grant the landlord a security deposit with an interest in the dispensary furniture and grow equipment or trade fixtures. A security deposit of first and last month's rent payment should suffice.

BUYOUT CLAUSE

You should negotiate, upfront, a buyout clause in the lease negotiations. Doing so will allow you to get out of the lease should the business fail. If you should desire to terminate the lease, the "buyout" clause would be in place. The buyout should provide that you can pay a specific amount of rent, usually from three to six months', to terminate the lease. This is a good back out plan if things fail.

FREE RENT

It's important in the first year to negotiate a very low rent to allow you to turn a profit quickly or utilize your dollars elsewhere, such as in advertising and marketing. You might be able to negotiate six months free rent in the beginning or half rent. There are so many ways to be creative.

Free rent can be very helpful in the beginning stages of setting up your business. The overall expense of setting up a dispensary and or grow facility is not cheap. Although you may hit the ground running due to the success of other marijuana businesses, knowing that your rent is prorated or not having to pay for the first few months will enable you to absorb the startup costs and get on your feet and started without the burden of a rent expense.

Reasons why free rent is so important:

- Construction time, including permits, takes 3-4 months, best case scenario. With the process of getting approvals on city and state levels, it will take longer. Free rent during this building process (no revenue at this point) will be very helpful.

- Legal fees.

- Training your staff and incurring payroll expenses as the business is being built.

- Leaving your other employment while building your new business. You'll need money to pay your bills.

- Running your grow operation until it produces revenue; it will be a four-month minimum until you harvest. You will be paying laborers to garden.

- Upfront expenses, such as building out your grow operation and/or dispensary.

DETAILS OF YOUR COMMERCIAL LEASE NEGOTIATIONS

Check off the issues below as they are addressed in your lease:

○ Acceptable signage is detailed.

○ What happens if you need to relocate?

○ What if someone wants to buy your business? Can they take over the lease?

○ What happens if you outgrow your space?

○ What happens if you want to downsize?

○ What happens if you go out of business?

○ What happens if the Federal government shuts you down?

FINAL STEPS—LEGAL ADVICE

As a final precaution, take the lease to an attorney who specializes in lease agreements. You can never be too careful about signing a commercial lease. Your lawyer will raise any red flags, answer your questions, and explain exactly what you are signing. Due to the fact that the marijuana business is new, the feds have the right to shut down your dispensary business under the U.S. Controlled Substance Act and can shut your business down for any reason. Also, the state can shut you down as well.

It is extremely important that your lawyer puts into your lease a "get out of your lease" clause that will protect you if any unforeseen things do come up. The marijuana business is new and changing daily. Yes, regulations will settle down eventually, but until they do you must protect yourself from these uncertainties.

NEWS FLASH

The CSA is the Federal U.S. drug policy under which the manufacture, importation, possession, use and/or distribution of certain substances is regulated. This act is in place for public health and consumer protections. If the Feds feel you are in any way a harm to the public, they can come in and close your business operations. No questions asked! Done.

Working with Architects and Contractors

IF YOU CANNOT BE ON THE PROJECT EACH DAY to check on things, then you should not try to be your own contractor.

> *"A doctor can bury his mistakes,*
> *but an architect can only advise his clients to plant vines."*
> — Frank Lloyd Wright —

At this point, you have a layout design and a floor plan, and you have a good idea what type of equipment you will need to purchase for your dispensary and/or grow facility. The next step in the build-out phase is to find the right people to help you build it. If you have leased your space, keep in mind that your landlord or other tenants may be able to direct you to contractors that they used when they built their places of business. In the case of a grow operation, because this is a new business for you and your landlord, this may not apply. He or she still may be able to recommend a viable candidate that they have used in the past.

ARCHITECT

An architect can help you design and space-plan your location. Having a solid design plan will save you a ton of time and money with your architect. We suggest visiting as many dispensaries or grow operations that you can to get ideas before you meet with your architect for the first time. Having a clear vision and understanding of what your business may look like will help you enunciate the process and get things moving on the fast track. Keep in mind, an architect charges by the hour and it will not be cheap. The architect is not likely to have experience in designing dispensaries—it's not something they do on a daily basis. They will have to spend time researching how to space-plan this type of business. From the floor plan you provide, they should be able to quickly draw up a blueprint. Supply your wish list before your meeting, as this will also reduce the guess work and, therefore, the time spent by the designer and/or architect.

Note: Your architect works with contractors on a daily basis; he knows the good ones and the bad. Ask him to give you a couple of names. I am sure you will not be disappointed.

Here are a couple of sources for architects:
- www.architectfinder.aia.org
- www.servicemagic.com

It is critical for you to spend a lot of time with the architect to make sure he or she puts everything in the right place. The architect is responsible for:

- Transferring your floor plan into a blueprint; work with him/her to ensure that everything is in the right place.

- Creating and providing you with hard copy blueprints for your new space, including:
  - Two "certified plans" for submitting to the city for building permits.
  - 15 contractor copies that you can use for getting bids on your project.

Before you take the finished plans from the architect, it's important to review it carefully and make sure every detail is included. **Note: Do not misplace or mix up the "certified plans" with any other copies.**

BUILDERS/CONSTRUCTION CONTRACTORS

Once you have the architect's plans, you should move quickly to get some prices on the cost for construction. Why?

- At this stage, you will probably have already signed the lease, and the clock will be ticking on any "free" rent periods that may have been negotiated for the build-out. TIP: Negotiate with the landlord to not pay rent until you get your final Certificate of Occupancy (CO) from the city.

- The process might take a couple of weeks to get final bids from, say, three prospective contractors.

- Your contractor will be the one to submit the plans to the city. In our past experience, it can take anywhere from two to six weeks to submit them and get them approved. The city can also reject the plans, which will have to go back to the architect to be redrawn and then resubmitted.

- The marijuana industry is new and many of the inspectors will in many cases be over stringent in the approval process on inspections. Make sure every detail is addressed and do expect delays.

Friends, family, and associates can usually recommend a good contractor. You can even ask the owner of other dispensaries or grow operations what contractor they used. If you cannot find someone you feel comfortable with, you can try these Web sites:

www.1800contractor.com

www.needacontractor.com

www.agc.org

www.angieslist.com

QUICK STEPS TO GET STARTED:

1. **Identify at least three contractors.** Collect as much information as you can about each contractor before you ask for a bid:

   a. **Type of Contractor**—Find out what their specialties are.

   b. **Quality of Work**—Visit job sites and/or recently completed projects.

   c. **Client Satisfaction**—Get list of referrals and call them.

   d. **Licensed/Insured**—Get the physical proof of their builder's license and insurance policy. Never hire a contractor who is not licensed and insured.

   e. **Stability**—Ask how long he/she has been in business. Look for those who have been in business for more than five years.

   f. **Project Management**—Find out if your contractor will be your main contact and always on site to oversee the work being performed.

   g. **Payment Terms**—Ensure that you agree with how the contractor will bill and receive payment for services. Never, never, never pay in advance or in full.

2. Get bids from the three contractors that you identified.

3. Give each contractor four to five sets of plans. General contractors will most likely give a copy to a plumber, electrician, and an air conditioning company.

4. Assess the bids and choose your contractors. Here are some thoughts around coming to a decision:

   a. **Price**—We all understand that price is a BIG factor, but we must look at each contractor's bid and compare.

   b. **Thoroughness**—You must make sure that each bid includes everything on the plan. You must remember that a contractor is only as good as the plans he works from. If the plan is not complete or is missing something, a contractor will do the rework to correct it, but he will also charge you for the change.

   c. **Timeline**—Look at the overall timeline and when the contractor says that work will be completed.

   d. **Quality**—Do your homework and visit former jobs that the builder/contractor has completed. Check that the customer was satisfied with the process of working with the contractor and with the end product. Inspect the work yourself to ensure that it meets your standards and expectations.

Building your new marijuana business should be something you always remember, but not because you picked the wrong contractor or it took twice as long to build and cost twice as much money as you originally were told. Take your time when choosing the contractor. Do your due diligence by getting references. Make sure you visit the job site as much as possible so if changes need to be made you can catch mistakes on day one, not a week later after walls have been put up and the flooring you chose came in the wrong color. If you're not watching and keeping an eye on things, rest assured corners will be cut and problems will arise. Get involved, get your hands dirty, do research on some of the things that the contractor is doing. Just because you may or may not have used a hammer and staple gun doesn't mean you can't use a paint brush to help get things done.

EXPECT DELAYS

Building your facility and grow may be an arduous undertaking and most likely have delays because of plan review within your municipality. The inspector may not understand the dynamics of an indoor grow and delay it in review. There are so many factors in this business; expect delays. This will weigh heavily on the timelines when considering how long it will take to get your new business open. Every day that you delayed will cost you money.

How do you protect yourself from this happening? Unfortunately, issues come up with construction or municipality delays. Just think, your application goes into the city and all the departments have to review it for approvals. It's not only pulling a permit, it's reviewing you as the owner personally with a complete background check. All of this takes time and money. You can't protect yourself from all delays but you may be able to speed up the process with good planning.

PLANNING POINTS

Think through your project and consider the following:

- If you're moving into your retail location will you have to move walls, electric, plumbing, install security glass? You will never know what you discover once you start to take down walls or sheetrock. Issues like wiring, plumbing and support structures are often more complex than you realize.

- If you're moving into your grow facility do you need to add security measures to windows, doors, walls, etc.?

- Does your new grow facility need extra air conditioning on the roof, or does the roof need to be reinforced?

- Who is involved? What contractors do I need to bring in? Will you need carpenters, engineers, architects, interior designer for your dispensary, cabinet makers for your display cabinets, tile guy, plumber, electrician, sign person, alarm specialist, fire inspector? All of these people will walk through your new business' doors before you open at some point in time.

- Scheduling the work. Your contractor should be able to schedule the arrival of all the workers (and the supplies) for maximum efficiency.

- Inspection. Do you need to have the work inspected? When does the inspector make site visits? Who calls the inspector? If things need to be corrected when do you call them to come back?

- Always consider the longer, more expensive option when planning your finances.

- Any delays in opening mean lost revenue for you; the clock starts ticking when you sign that lease.

All of these items may seem overwhelming, but like opening a new gadget without instructions it's impossible to do on your own. Let us continue on the journey of opening and successfully running a new marijuana business. Read on . . .

Defining Designs and Layouts
For Your Dispensary

WHEN DESIGNING YOUR DISPENSARY, there are key components that many of us seem to forget. Your customer base will be of all ages, shapes and sizes. There is no one-size-fits-all customer. The design focus needs to be geared toward making the dispensary space pleasing and appealing to the eye, yet focused on keeping comfort in mind for individuals with different abilities.

If you are a medical marijuana dispensary, your design must have the needs of the disabled customer in the forefront of your design planning. This aspect of designing for your customer makes your dispensary applicable to all, regardless of their age or ability. It is useful to meet the needs of many, from a multigenerational family to the youth of today, and be able to meet the needs no matter their status in life.

Universal design is very important. It takes the traditional design and incorporates elements that offer comfort, convenience and ease of use. Universal design should be transparent to your customer and subtle to the eye.

Some examples of universal design include:

- Wider hallways to accommodate wheelchairs, walkers, and strollers.

- All counters must be handicap accessible.

- Porch or entrance without steps that will increase access and convenience without compromising aesthetics of the dispensary entrance.

- Handles or grab bars in the bathrooms (most bathrooms today will have to be handicap accessible).

The design aspect of the dispensary is one of the first steps in planning your space. The designs you incorporate will be in place for many years once you break ground, start construction, order equipment and display cases, and open for business. If you then realize that mistakes were made in the design process, the expense to change them will be extremely costly and you will have an interruption of your business to make any alterations necessary. Take the time, plan accordingly, and remember no two customers are alike!

DIFFERENT SMOKES FOR DIFFERENT FOLKS

With many people interested in the medicinal and recreational uses of marijuana, your potential for a varied customer base is huge. By meeting the needs of many and being accepting of all people, you will encourage individuals and families of all types to become patrons of your dispensary.

Think for a moment of individuals in your family, your friends and their families, and those in your community. Within the network of people that your dispensary will touch, you will know of someone (directly or indirectly) who either has some form of disability (from birth, from an accident, veteran of war, through an illness or the aging process, etc.) or is caring for someone who is disabled. Your design and layout of your dispensary will have to keep these customers in mind.

CHECKLIST of things to think about in your dispensary design stages:

- ○ Is your front entrance wide enough for a wheelchair, walkers and baby strollers?
- ○ Are the aisles wide enough for more than one customer at a time?
- ○ Are the display cases installed at the right height for wheelchair patrons?
- ○ Is the area around your entrance lit up enough?
- ○ Is the checkout area big enough for multiple customer checkout?
- ○ Is there an adequate waiting area for more than a few customers?
- ○ Are your bathrooms handicapped accessible?
- ○ Do the doors have lever handles versus knobs for easier entry?
- ○ Is the entrance wheelchair accessible?
- ○ Is there lots of lighting inside and out?
- ○ Is the flooring stable, firm and slip resistant?
- ○ Are there handles and handrails in the bathrooms?

Decorate your retail space for aesthetic appeal, but also for the functionality of your customer. Complicated or hard-to-reach shelving systems, for example, may cause customers to shy away from purchasing products displayed on them. If products are not clearly labeled and easy to find, customers might give up and look elsewhere. Providing areas for your customers to make themselves comfortable is ideal in many retail situations; if a customer feels comfortable, he or she will be more likely to stay inside the shop. Designing a comfortable lounge area or reception waiting area with televisions or magazines will give your customers a relaxed environment for lounging. The longer a customer stays, the more likely they are to make a purchase

For a retail marijuana store design, aesthetics are developed to form a backdrop to the wares on display. Yes, design is important—but selling marijuana is the emphasis of this design/ layout process. The focus is on the merchandise (marijuana) followed by the comfort of the customer and by the actual functional aspects of the business. Functional aspects that are integrated into a retail store design such as the cash counter, the storage area, the safe area, and the computers must be discreet and unobtrusive. The challenge is to integrate all of these functions within the actual retail space without it being too cluttered, while also keeping safety in mind.

SECTION V

CONSTRUCTION OF YOUR DISPENSARY AND GROW FACILITY

Lighting the Way

GROWING YOUR MARIJUANA RETAIL BUSINESS will take many different tactics to become successful. The location you choose to open your store. The display cases you purchase to show off your products. Trained and confident sales people that you and your customers can trust. And, of course, the products you choose to sell. It may seem easy selling a product that everyone wants, but having the correct lighting to display your product is extremely important.

There is so much that can happen to either drive business to you and keep patients loyal, or turn customers away from you and send them to your competition. The weather, a broken water main in the street that diverts traffic from your store, an unhappy employee that is turning off your customers in the dispensary, or a disgruntled employee sabotaging your garden could all negatively affect your customer flow. Some of these are things are impossible to control and may be an act of God, but there is certainly one thing you can do to make sure that your customers see the very best aspects of the products you sell: the lighting you use in your store.

Maintaining and growing a retail business means always showing off the best characteristics of your products. Whether you sell shampoo, diamonds, or doughnuts, you want your customers to look at the very best qualities of your products. The way you display them and the lighting you choose will set your store apart from the competitor down the street.

There are many different strains of marijuana. Each strain has a different look and color, as well as smell. The fact that your customers have the ability to see the different qualities of your marijuana is essential to driving sales.

Each strain of marijuana usually has completely different characteristics. Color, smell, THC concentration, and crystallization are important. Customers will look closely at each strain before they purchase, and good lighting will help facilitate the sale.

Most small retail stores forget the significance that lighting plays when attracting customers and stimulating them to buy. Have you thought about the importance of lighting when building your store? Most business owners get wrapped up in the fixtures and walls, putting up "Grateful Dead" posters or trendy pictures to give an upbeat feel. They forget about the actual product itself and focus on décor. The lighting fixtures you choose can have a big impact on customer decisions when choosing their strain. A client may not appreciate the "quality of the medicine" if they can't see the detail of the product because lighting is poor.

WHY LIGHTING IS SO IMPORTANT

Common sense tells us that light is an integral part of a retail environment, but most of us take lighting for granted. Most business owners think that if they can flick a switch and the lights turn on, they are ready for business, and that just isn't the case.

As a retailer, you will have a business to run. You will be consumed with the everyday duties of managing the store, employees, marketing, ordering inventory, growing, harvesting and, of course, dealing with customers. Until now, the thought of becoming a lighting specialist probably has never crossed your mind when thinking of opening your medical and/or recreational marijuana store.

The great thing about lighting is that you do not have to have a Ph.D. in lighting to be able to get the results you want; just a little knowledge will go a long way. Nontechnical people make lighting decisions every day. The trick is to know enough to make the right decisions. These decisions will improve employee productivity, retail sales, safety and security, identification, and your bottom line.

THE DANGERS OF INADEQUATE LIGHTING

- Many marijuana strains are different colors, some more vibrant than others. The ability to actually see this under specific lighting can enhance a customer's decision-making experience. Without good lighting, your facility stands a chance of losing the sale to a competitor who has invested in a good lighting system.

- Customers may not be able to read the fine print regarding a product, such as potency, medical remedy awareness, etc.

- Customers may not be able to see the price of an item.

- Employees may mismark an item or SKU number.

- Employees may not realize stock is out and order new product or misplace and put in the wrong spot.

- Employees will take longer finding items that may be in a stock room without adequate light, thereby leaving customers at the register.

- Employees may undercharge or overcharge your customers due to inadequate lighting at the point of checkout.

- Safety concerns are greater in your store if you have inadequate lighting.

- Employees and customers can easily mistake one marijuana strain from another if adequate lighting is not available.

- Employees may not adequately put the sale through for the correct amount or to the right customer.

SETTING UP YOUR STORE LIGHTING

When setting up your medical and/or recreational marijuana dispensary, everything matters—from your choice of flooring to your display stands. When first designing your location, you should make the lighting in your space a priority. The lighting you use in your store will have a major effect on how the products for sale appeal to customers. Obviously, you want lighting that makes your products look attractive to shoppers. Most electric supply stores will be able to assist you or recommend someone to help with your project. However, you should hire a lighting professional if your electrician or architect cannot assist you with the lighting design. Impressions matter greatly, and choosing the right fixtures can make all the difference.

SPOTLIGHTS

If you plan to feature certain items or will have a display case that you want to use in a specific area of the dispensary, a spotlight is an ideal way to draw attention to these items or areas. The spotlight shines from the ceiling or wall toward its target. You can also install task or accent lighting, which puts a smaller spotlight on certain items on your selling floor, like items on a shelf or inside a cabinet. If you are building a custom cabinet with spotlights, make sure the shelving is glass and at least 3/8" thick. Using wood or laminated shelving will reduce lighting throughout your case.

NOTE

Glass, although tough to keep clean, is the best product showcase for any retail sales!

LED LIGHTING

LED lighting fixtures offer a more natural-looking light (traditional light bulbs and fluorescent lighting lack luster and tend to give a yellowish or gray color). LED lighting will bring out the best appearance of virtually any retail products. LEDs have been praised by many interior designers for providing the most authentic-looking light, and you will find that neutral white LEDs provide the closest appearance to what an item would look like under bright, natural sunlight. When you want your customers to see the most intricate details of your products, the best light to use is LED light. LED simply cannot be beaten. They now have "strip LED lighting" for showcases that are highly recommended. They also do not create much heat, which is important when displaying any edible products.

ENERGY EFFICIENT RECESSED LIGHTS

No matter what size your store will be, you must always consider your electricity bill. If your dispensary is located in a strip mall, you may be required to be open the same hours as other tenants. That could be seven days a week and as much as fourteen hours a day. Your electricity bill could be outlandish if you don't choose the right lighting. Since you will probably have to install a large number of lights at your location, look into energy efficient fixtures; recessed are the most popular. Recessed fixtures sit within the ceilings of the store, while standard fixtures hang and are sometimes adjustable. Energy efficient light fixtures contain lamps that use less energy compared to standard lighting options.

NATURAL LIGHT

A retail store designer or a lighting expert will always suggest using natural light as a means of showing off your retail products, but in most cases there will be too many obstacles to achieve that goal. If you are an interior store or inside a mall this will be almost impossible to accomplish. Natural lighting is the light that shines through the windows of your store from the sun or other lighting sources outside. This usually doesn't require anything done on your part; you must simply make it a point to open all window coverings in the store each day to take advantage of the natural outside light. Natural light is a great supplement to your artificial lighting.

The bottom line is that lighting makes a big difference in any retail shop. Whether you are selling products or services or budget goods, the right lighting can make all the difference in the world.

Investing in the correct lighting while designing your retail store is the most cost effective way to approach successful retailing.

BASIC MAINTENANCE GOES A LONG WAY

- Improving your lighting system can be as easy as replacing the lamp or bulb. When leasing your store, you may inherit old, ineffective lighting, which would need to be replaced. The good news is that the lighting industry has come a long way in the past few years. The lamp efficiency and brightness has increased dramatically. By replacing one lamp type with a more efficient version you can enhance light and also reduce your overall energy costs.

- Lamps and luminaries, like any other surface, collect dust and dirt over time. When these lamp surfaces become dirty, they lose the luster and intensity of the light that they give off. They work harder to give off the light they would normally give off when clean. They become overheated and draw more energy, despite the poorer quality of light they are giving off.

- Bulbs lose their lumens with age; they are not working as efficiently during the latter stages of their lives. We recommend group replacement. This involves replacing all the lamps in a retail store at the same time. This will guarantee the light levels in your dispensary are above par at all times.

- The lighting in your retail store will slowly get worse over time. It may not be noticeable, but once you clean and/or replace your bulbs you will immediately notice a big difference.

- Keeping a scheduled maintenance of cleaning or replacing the lights will keep your lighting at peak performance.

CLEANING YOUR LIGHTING FIXTURES AND BULBS

- Make sure your lights are off.

- If using a ladder, set to the side of the fixtures (do not set directly underneath a florescent bulb or light fixture). Fluorescent bulbs can easily come crashing down when slightly loosened. If you are standing to the side, you will be out of danger.

- Use a dusting cloth or large feather duster. If bulbs cannot be cleaned by dusting, replace them. It is not recommended to use water on any bulbs or fluorescents. Electricity and water don't mix well. You may cause the bulb to blow up or— even worse—get electrocuted.

- There are many lighting resources available to retail store owners. Most people get the bulk of the information from local lighting stores. These stores have sales people that are well versed in setting up stores and/or guiding you to make the right decisions when choosing your store's retail lighting

Online references for Lighting Section: E-zine articles (Kim Zheng); Ehow.com (Louise Balle); and www.nlb.org (John Bachner)

The Importance of Signage

THE SIGNAGE AT YOUR STOREFRONT IS YOUR BILLBOARD, the single most effective way of communicating what your business is and what you have to offer. You want your sign to work for you and to attract a variety of potential customers: people passing by, people new to the neighborhood, people curious about your dispensary.

If your business site is in an area not easily accessible, then your sign is the only thing that can communicate to people who happen to be driving by. The dispensary located off a freeway, for instance, can use a high-rise sign to attract travelers on nearby roads and expressways.

SIGNAGE—A WAY OF LIFE

For as long as anyone can remember, signs have been used as a marketing tool for all sorts of occasions, events, and business purposes. From the moment you leave your house each day, you see sign after sign. You notice some of them, but the rest will simply blend in with the scenery. Your goal should be to create a sign with a lasting impact on a customer, one of the few that don't get overlooked.

So what type of sign do you choose? What material should it be made of? These can range from PVC to neon to steel or aluminum. Signage designs can suit a variety of budget, landlord, and city requirements.

Business signage does not necessarily have to be metal or large neon. You can choose from all kinds of modern technologies, including plastics that do not rust (and which allow for interchanging graphics) and weatherproof digital signs. If you go digital, you can add these signs to your store windows or personal car. Above all, be sure your sign is easy to read and placed in a high-traffic area where it can be seen.

When you're choosing colors for your sign, be sure to think about the clientele you hope to bring into your dispensary.

- Impulse shoppers are attracted to red, orange, black, and blue.
- People who plan ahead when purchasing lean toward pink, light blue, and navy.
- People in high-income areas, where status matters, look for classic, subtle colors.
- People in middle-class areas, hot climates, and coastal regions welcome bright colors.
- People in colder climates prefer neutral, more traditional colors.

Each city will impose different requirements and restrictions on signage, including height, placement, colors, and/or material. Your area may not allow signs in windows and/or obstructions on the front lawn. To find out what is acceptable, contact your local building department and request the current guidelines.

Your landlord might also have requirements for everyone in the plaza. Read your lease carefully for any restrictions, such as size and type, and whether window signs and neon are allowed.

The cost of your sign will vary depending on what it's made of and whether it's illuminated. The least expensive signs are aluminum and steel, which typically range from two to four thousand dollars. An illuminated block-letter sign will cost in the neighborhood of three to seven thousand, depending on the size and number of letters. Graphics for your store windows will also vary in price—based on size, layout, and number of colors—but will typically price between five hundred and one thousand. Weatherproof sign graphics for your car cost between one thousand dollars for half a vehicle and two thousand dollars for a full-size car or van.

Air Conditioning: Life or Death for Your Plants

THERE ARE MANY KEY INGREDIENTS in developing a beautiful, healthy marijuana crop. Your gardener, of course, is essential to maintaining and controlling your harvest. One of the most crucial parts of a successful crop is the proper air control and temperature. Who would think that the air in your garden and the temperature would play such a key role in harvesting a banner crop? This is one more thing to think about when designing and building your grow facility. Without the correct air systems in place, it will be almost impossible to cultivate big dollar marijuana crops.

Cannabis loves warm temperatures, but too much heat can dry out the plant and stop production. Plants will naturally stop production of Kola buds (the fruit of marijuana) when temperatures climb above 92 degrees Fahrenheit.

The ideal temperature range for plant growth without CO_2 supplementation is 70-75 degrees. Temperature is probably the factor that causes the most problems in an indoor garden. When the temperature in a garden climbs higher than 85 degrees, plant growth damage can happen quickly. When it comes to temperature, you have the following factors working against you when you begin to design your garden area:

KEY REASONS FOR A FAILING HARVEST

- Improper nutrient feeding
- Failed regular watering
- Power outage for more than 24 hours
- Poor enthronement
- Unskilled gardener
- Poor plant genetics
- Insect infestation

Read more: http://www.ehow.com/facts_7209643_much-vegetable-plants-need-garden

NOTE

Proper spacing reduces competition among plants for water and nutrients. When spaced appropriately, each plant will have access to the resources it needs without taking them away from others. The result is a huge banner crop. The larger your plants and buds the more money you make! Spacing is essential!

OUT WITH THE OLD AIR AND IN WITH THE NEW

The general idea for controlling heat is to exhaust the hottest air out of the area and, at the same time, introduce cool, fresh air in to replace the exhausted air. The source of the cool air is critical. Plant growth slows in hot, humid conditions, and your ability to control the temperature in the garden area (and thereby directly controlling the success of your crop) is only as good as your source of cool, fresh air.

The most important thing is to know the temperature in the hot spot of your garden area. This is usually directly under the center of your grow light, at the tops of your plants. The plant growth in this area is the most vulnerable to damage from high temperatures. In order to keep an eye on this temperature, every indoor gardener should have an indoor/outdoor thermometer (the kind with a cord and remote probe).

Here are four strategies you can use to help reduce the temperature in the plant growth zone of your indoor garden area:

- Open the grow area to allow air circulation with a larger volume of air.

- Keep the grow light exhaust and the garden area exhaust as two separate systems.

- Increase the size and number of exhaust fans for the area.

- Add air conditioning.

An air conditioning specialist who has worked on other grow facilities or indoor gardens should be used for your new indoor grow facility. The key is to have a professional consult with you on what system is best for your space with the correct tonnage to handle your facility. You should also consider having a system installed that is larger than the one recommended—just in case you need the space for expansion. This is cheaper over the long haul.

Large ceiling fans or wall mounted oscillating fans on timers also control temperatures and assist in maintaining the movement of air circulation. This helps rid the garden area of still air, resulting in a steady airflow pattern. This reduces hot air pockets or cool air in smaller-spaced grow facilities.

Like any other plants, cannabis put out toxins through the stomata of the leaves. If you are growing cannabis in a small room, opening the door or window is quite enough to allow proper exchange of air. Good air flow will help promote healthy cannabis growth. You can install circulating fans, ventilating fans, exhaust fans, and blowers in your indoor pot garden to provide the room with proper ventilation. Stagnant air stunts the growth of marijuana from pot. Quality air movement at the right temperatures is essential for a quality harvest

ADVANCED CLIMATE CONTROL

Air conditioning is the final solution when it comes to controlling indoor garden temperatures. With AC, you are always guaranteed a quality source of fresh, adjustable, cold air. Air conditioning set at a specific temperature eliminates the need for constant worry about maintaining air quality and movement.

The strategy for using air conditioning is to run the lights on a separate exhaust system from the garden area. Whenever the temperature gets too warm, the garden exhaust fan kicks on at one end of the area while the air conditioner operating at the other end acts as the fresh air intake.

AN IMPORTANT SIDEBAR ON CO2 AND TEMPERATURE

It is generally accepted that gardens can be run at higher temperatures when using CO_2 supplementation to maximize plant growth. Elevating carbon dioxide levels can increase marijuana growth speed a great deal, perhaps even double it. It seems that the plant evolved in primordial times when natural CO_2 levels were many times what they are today. The plant uses CO_2 for photosynthesis to create the sugars it uses to build plant tissues. Elevating the CO_2 level will increase the plant's ability to manufacture these sugars and plant growth rate is enhanced considerably.

While this is true, it is important to understand that this is only the case when all other growth influencing factors are kept in their ideal ranges. The ideal temperature range for the indoor garden is seventy to seventy-five degrees. With the addition of CO_2, you can run your garden up to ten degrees warmer without seeing any negative effects.

TEMPERATURE AND YOUR NUTRIENT RESERVOIR

The other place where temperature is a concern is in your nutrient reservoir. This storage tank is loaded with the necessary nutrients to assist in the ability to harvest your crop faster and healthier. Your farmer or farmers will register the temperature of your nutrient reservoir. The wrong temperature can have a negative effect on your nutrients. The uptake of nutrients (in the root zone) only occurs in the presence of oxygen. Water loses its ability to hold dissolved oxygen as it warms up or is too cold.

If the nutrient solution gets too warm, your plants will not be able to take up any nutrients (and, therefore, they will not grow). Worse yet, the nutrient solution will begin to favor a number of pathogenic microorganisms at a warmer temperature—nasty things like fusarium and pythium. These two plant diseases are two of the most destructive plant diseases of modern times. The

NOTE

Tepid water is best. Water that is too hot will cook your cannabis and water that is too cold will shock them.

ideal temperature for your nutrient solution is sixty-five to seventy degrees Fahrenheit. If your garden is in a commercial building that has a slab floor, keeping the nutrient reservoir on the concrete floor will usually help keep it at an ideal temperature.

TYPES OF AIR CONDITIONING TO BEST SUIT YOUR FACILITY

Portable Air Conditioning

Portable air conditioners have few advantages and many disadvantages. This type of air conditioner is the least adequate choice for indoor growing environments because it is extremely inefficient. The need to exhaust the heat through a run of ducting means less heat is ultimately transferred out of the grow room. The longer the exhaust duct runs, the less efficient a portable air conditioner is. These units appear to be relatively expensive for their BTU ratings, but these ratings tend to be inaccurate because they are measured without the exhaust duct run being considered. These units also take air directly from the grow room, thereby affecting CO_2 enrichment and causing odor control issues. The only real advantage is that these units are generally on wheels and are portable, making moving or changing locations easier.

If you are expanding quickly this may be a quick, temporary solution, but over the long haul this would be the least adequate for your overall production.

Wall Mount

Wall-mount or window-mount units are the old standard. These units are self-contained, exhausting heat directly outside and taking in fresh air from outside, cooling it and blowing it into the room. These units are more efficient than the portable air conditioners, but they require either a window or that a large hole be cut in the wall. These units tend to be noisy, and like the portable air conditioners, they either draw air directly from the room or from the outside, which is a slower cooling process that also causes odor control issues and affects CO_2 enrichment.

This type of unit is a quick fix and is not recommended for large production facilities. Airflow is difficult to manage, and taking hot air from the outside takes longer to cool. The amount of air these units provide is likely adequate only for a small space.

At the start-up stage of your grow facility, the cost of building out your operation will be very expensive. Through-the-wall or window-mounted air conditioning will cost much less than going for the outdoor or rooftop system.

One additional thing to consider: wall-mount or window-mount air conditioning may be a cheaper way to get your much-needed air conditioning, but these units open the door for easy break-ins. No matter how they are installed they can be pushed into the facility, and criminals can quickly gain access to your grow operation.

Mini Split System

Possibly the best A/C unit for marijuana growers is a mini split system. A mini split system is made up of two components: a compressor, which sits outside, and an evaporator, which is mounted within the room. Heat is removed from the room through refrigerant that is pumped between the compressor and evaporator. These units are extremely efficient due to their duct-free design, and they do not interfere with a grow room's CO_2 levels. Also, because the air from the room is not removed, these A/C units do not create additional odor problems.

There are many factors involved in the success of your grow facility. Putting the correct systems in place from the get-go will only make your life and your gardener's life easier. Take a look at new trends in air conditioning—particularly high efficiency and low noise. Adding a dehumidifier as part of the AC unit assembly at the factory can keep PM (powdery mildew) out of your garden. Powdery mildew occurs when humidity levels are too high and when there is poor air circulation.

Air Quality

YOU HAVE MADE THE MOMENTOUS DECISION to open a legal medical/personal use marijuana business. Part of the design and management of your store/grow facility involves air quality. This aspect needs to be a part of the financing section in your business plan. Marijuana has a very potent aroma and it is your responsibility to make sure your store/grow facility is in compliance with the requirements of your local municipality.

If your municipality requires an air quality inspection certificate, you will need to hire a Certified Industrial Hygienist (CIH) or an Industrial Hygiene Technician to certify that your store/grow facility is in compliance. Industrial hygiene is the science of anticipating, recognizing, evaluating, and controlling workplace conditions that may cause workers injury or illness. Industrial hygienists use environmental monitoring and analytical methods to detect the extent of worker exposure, and they employ engineering, work practice controls, and other methods to control potential health hazards.

CIHs are experts in detecting Indoor Air Quality (IAQ) problems in commercial buildings, public buildings, government offices, industrial facilities, warehouses, small offices, hotels /motels, casinos, etc. Indoor Air Quality surveys include testing and sampling for Sick Building Syndrome (SBS) and Building Related Illness. Their IAQ site inspections include the HVAC systems as well as occupied spaces. Their reports include specific recommendations of corrective measures where IAQ problems are identified. These indoor air quality specialists can also provide expert witnesses, litigation support, and insurance claims assistance.

The following shows an example of the type of inspection an Industrial Hygienist may conduct for compliance with a local municipality. The evaluation focuses on health and safety of employees, visitors, and the general public. The review includes the written waste disposal program, where they want to determine that any medical marijuana or medical marijuana-infused product that is not sold is disposed of in a manner that protects any portion thereof from being ingested by any person or animal.

- Review of chemicals and Material Safety Data Sheets (MSDS).

- Review of personal protective equipment used.

- Review of posted fire evacuation plan.

- Perform walk-around of perimeter and adjacent properties for marijuana odor.

- Ventilation smoke tube verification of negative pressure within the building with respect to outdoors and adjacent properties.

- Evaluation of HVAC system to determine type of system and controls to effectively control marijuana odors to the interior of the facility. This did not include a mechanical engineer's evaluation of the HVAC system for ASHRAE or any other engineering standards or building codes.

• Review of written marijuana item disposal policy.

ALTERNATIVE ENERGY SOURCES

When creating the business plan for your store/growing facility, you must have a realistic idea of what your electricity costs will be. The lights, heating, cooling systems and ventilation in a growing facility hourly devour electricity by the kilowatts; my friend, by any stretch of the imagination that is not going to be cheap. This is a critical issue that cannot be glossed over or taken lightly.

You need to invest some of your time in investigating alternative sources of power. Talk with your contractor and/or architect about the possibility and costs related to utilizing alternative energy resources. Ask your tax advisor about the long-term benefits of installing these systems for your business.

NOTE

Many states now require offsite backup and onsite memory of 40 days. A backup battery of over one hour is usually required. Your regulatory agency or police department will want to review your history in case there is a robbery.

Solar Energy

Solar energy, radiant light and heat from the sun, is harnessed using a range of ever-evolving technologies, such as solar heating, solar photovoltaics, solar thermal electricity, solar architecture and artificial photosynthesis. Solar technologies are broadly characterized as either passive solar or active solar, depending on the way they capture, convert and distribute solar energy. Active solar techniques include the use of photovoltaic panels and solar thermal collectors to harness the energy. Passive solar techniques include orienting a building to the sun, selecting materials with favorable thermal mass or light dispersing properties, and designing spaces that naturally circulate air.

In 2011, the International Energy Agency said that "the development of affordable, inexhaustible, and clean solar energy technologies will have huge longer-term benefits. These advantages are global. Hence, the additional costs of the incentives for early deployment should be considered learning investments; they must be wisely spent and need to be widely shared."

Agriculture and horticulture seek to optimize the capture of solar energy in order to optimize the productivity of plants. Techniques such as timed planting cycles, tailored row orientation, staggered heights between rows and the mixing of plant varieties can improve crop yields. While sunlight is generally considered a plentiful resource, the exceptions highlight the importance of solar energy to agriculture. During the short growing seasons of the Little Ice Age, French and English farmers employed fruit walls to maximize the collection of solar energy. These walls acted as thermal masses and accelerated ripening by keeping plants warm. Early fruit walls were built perpendicular to the ground and facing south, but over time, sloping walls were developed to make better use of sunlight. In 1699, Nicolas Fatio de Duillier even suggested using a tracking mechanism which could pivot to follow the sun. Applications of solar energy in agriculture, aside from growing crops, include pumping water and drying crops.

In the United States, heating, ventilation and air conditioning (HVAC) systems account for 30% (4.65 EJ) of the energy used in commercial buildings and nearly 50% (10.1 EJ) of the energy used in residential buildings. Solar heating, cooling and ventilation technologies can be used to offset a portion of this energy.

Thermal mass is any material that can be used to store heat—heat from the sun in the case of solar energy. Common thermal mass materials include stone, cement, and water. Historically, these materials have been used in arid climates or warm regions to keep buildings cool by absorbing solar energy during the day and radiating stored heat to the cooler atmosphere at night. However, they can be used in cold areas to maintain warmth as well. The size and placement of thermal mass materials depend on several factors, such as climate, daylight, and shading conditions. When properly incorporated, thermal mass maintains space temperatures in a comfortable range and reduces the need for auxiliary heating and cooling equipment.

A solar chimney (or thermal chimney, in this context) is a passive solar ventilation system composed of a vertical shaft connecting the interior and exterior of a building. As the chimney warms, the air inside is heated causing an updraft that pulls air through the building. Performance can be improved by using glazing and thermal mass materials in a way that mimics greenhouses.

In 2011, the International Energy Agency said that solar energy technologies, such as photovoltaic panels, solar water heaters, and power stations built with mirrors could provide a third of the world's energy by 2060 if politicians commit to limiting climate change

Wind Power

Wind energy is a free, renewable resource, so no matter how much is used today, there will still be the same supply in the future. Wind energy is also a source of clean, non-polluting electricity. Unlike conventional power plants, wind plants emit no air pollutants or greenhouse gases. According to the U.S. Department of Energy, in 1990 California's wind power plants offset the emission of more than two and a half billion pounds of carbon dioxide and fifteen million pounds of other pollutants that would have otherwise been produced. It would take a forest of ninety million to one hundred seventy-five million trees to provide the same air quality.

Even though the cost of wind power has decreased dramatically in the past ten years, the technology requires a higher initial investment than fossil-fueled generators. Roughly eighty percent of the cost is the machinery, with the balance being site preparation and installation. If wind generating systems are compared with fossil-fueled systems on a "life-cycle" cost basis (counting fuel and operating expenses for the life of the generator), however, wind costs are much more competitive with other generating technologies because there is no fuel to purchase and minimal operating expenses.

The major challenge to using wind as a source of power is that it is intermittent and does not always blow when electricity is needed. Wind cannot be stored (although wind-generated electricity can be stored, if batteries are used), and not all winds can be harnessed to meet the timing of electricity demands. Further, good wind sites are often located in remote locations far from areas of electric power demand (such as cities). Finally, wind resource development may compete with other uses for the land, and those alternative uses may be more highly valued than electricity generation. However, wind turbines can be located on land that is also used for grazing or even farming.

If you can take advantage of any of these renewable resources, you are eligible to receive tax benefits on your state and federal returns. While the initial expense may seem intimidating, the rewards down the road will more than make up for it. The fewer kilowatts you pay for each month, the faster your profit margins will increase.

SECTION VI

SECURITY

Alarms, Video Surveillance, and Employee Emergency Procedures

MOST SMALL BUSINESS OWNERS ARE VERY CAREFUL with their business plans and money management. Much of that focus goes into developing a quality product or service for their customers. The expenses of opening a marijuana business are overwhelming, and sometimes one of the most important things gets overlooked. Expenses, like display cases, lighting, computers, software, signage, staff and the storefront are vital items to factor in and are usually the focus when allotting dollars to getting set up and opening. But don't forget your security system! Security and video surveillance cannot not be overlooked, and most states require a system to be in place before you are allowed to open.

Every operation must have a good security system in place. After the burden of spending almost every dime they have saved to open their business, many small business owners do not include this on their immediate "to do list." They might believe they aren't targets because they are only a small operation. This type of thinking is dangerous—and incorrect.

Proper security measures for your business means everything to your success. Just locking your doors at night as you go home is clearly not enough. A business can only benefit from an alarm system and security camera system, which will offer break-in prevention, panic buttons in case of robbery, and evidence in case of a crime or employee theft. It may also be a way to address complaints, questions, or other issues that may surface in the course of doing daily business.

PREVENTION
When a security system is in place and people know that they are being monitored by cameras inside and outside of your business location, issues like theft are less likely to occur. On the other hand, if a would-be thief knows that he or she is not being filmed, there may be little to deter him or her from trying to steal from you. Thus, having a security camera system in place can help prevent things like theft on your business property. It might also help your customers feel safer in general, knowing your dispensary is constantly being monitored by surveillance.

TYPES OF SYSTEMS
There are so many options available that you will have a hard time finding what you need. Before you decide what security system you are going to get, you will want to make sure that you do some research and check your state guidelines. They will indicate what is needed and required to be compliant.

It is recommended that your dispensary and grow business have a security system that has multiple cameras covering every aspect of your property. It can be a system with CCTV or a wireless system. Either one will work. Just do your research and find out what each system can do so you can make the best choice for what you need in your situation.

Having multiple cameras in your system will help stop criminals from within your operation, and will also help law enforcement catch anyone that breaks the law at your business.

POINT YOUR SECURITY CAMERAS AT THE RIGHT SPOTS

The State of Colorado has made it clear that every camera system must contain "NO BLINDSPOTS." Every inch of the facility must be shown by placing cameras directly over areas such as the trimmers, your safe, and all cashier locations, just to name a few. Remember to check your state requirements on camera placement.

RECOMMENDED CAMERA LOCATIONS

Dispensary Hot Spots

- Outside of front entrance
- Inside camera facing front entrance
- Front desk or check-in area
- Multiple locations in retail area
- If you have multiple cash drawers, cameras on each
- Safe area

Grow Facility Hot Spots

- Outside perimeter
- Outside garbage area
- Windows and all doors
- Roof top covering entire roof and parapet walls
- Interior front entrance
- Bud room
- Trim Room
- Drying Area
- All offices
- Storage room
- Growing area
- Maintenance area

SILENT ALARMS

Silent alarms are used by banks and retail store owners who want to protect their employees and help catch would-be criminals in the act. There are a wide variety of manual and automatic triggers for silent alarms, but they all have one purpose: to let police know that a robbery is in progress without alerting a criminal that the alarm has been sounded.

PANIC BUTTON

When and if your employees are faced with a dangerous robbery and/or a thief brandishing a gun, your employees will want to make sure that the thief isn't aware that they hit a secret trigger to the local police station. This could make a bad situation worse. Ideally, the robber wouldn't know the silent alarm or trigger has been tripped, then when he or she leaves, the police are waiting for them outside.

Recommended locations for the silent alarm "Panic Button"

- Behind the counter next to the check-in area

- Behind the counter next to the budtender/check-out area

- Next to the phone or close to an area where your manager is stationed

The details of these panic buttons or silent alarms should be kept secret in order to protect those who might have to use them. Where they are and what they look like should only be discussed with your employees who would be the ones to use them.

BUSINESS PHONE (E-911)

One area that you should also explore as a business is **E911**. Having this feature as part of your telephone plan means that as long as someone dials 911, the police and emergency services will be dispatched to your location immediately. There's no need for anyone to speak with the 911 operator; having **E911** means your address is already in their database and is readily accessible. This should be on speed dial and is a great for any type of emergency in your place of business.

HAVE EMERGENCY PLANS IN PLACE

Make sure that you already have documents outlining steps to follow in case of an emergency. It's best to always be prepared for eventualities such as fire, theft, floods and the like. And even if it does sound cheesy, having drills performed regularly will pay off, not to mention that it is sometimes required by fire prevention or insurance agencies. The better safe than sorry approach is a good one to follow in this type of business.

Evacuation plans should always be displayed in an area where employees will see them often and can familiarize themselves with them. Important telephone numbers should be included in the same document, including numbers for the police and emergency services.

Robbery rules and procedures are extremely important in your business. Let's face facts: currently the marijuana business is all cash. Your employees are handling two things that any common criminal wants: marijuana and cash. Dispensaries and grow facilities are targets for thieves and at all times your employees have to know exactly what needs to be done when and if there is a robbery.

By following this simple advice, you can keep yourself and your employees safe should your workplace ever be the target of a robbery. While countless business establishments are robbed each year, the fact of the matter is that very few employees are injured during these robberies. The most important thing to remember is to keep your cool and give the robber whatever he wants without resisting. If you can remember that rule, you know the single most important step to staying safe during an armed robbery.

Let your employees know that their life is more important than cash or marijuana. Explain to them that they should not in any way try to negotiate, fight, talk back or agitate the thieves. They should give the thieves what they want and let them go. Most of the time this will take seconds and the bad guys will be on their way. They should not try to be a hero by chasing or following the thieves. Money and merchandise can be replaced, but a life cannot. As soon as they feel it is safe, they should close the store and call 911, not allowing anyone to enter the store until police arrive and can assure their safety.

SECURITY TIPS

- **Security Mirrors:** Attach these above areas leading into hallways, around corners, and those that aren't completely visible from your location. Security mirrors come in a variety of shapes and sizes and come with vandal-proof designs.

- **Signage:** Signs on the building inside and out letting people know that your business is alarmed and that cameras are rolling at all times.

- **Motion-Detecting Sensors:** If incorporated with your security system, motion detecting sensors will trigger cameras to zoom to the area where movement has been detected. You can also have your security floodlights activated when your sensors detect movement. It all depends on your configuration.

- **Monitor and DVR:** Depending on your security system, you can use a single monitor and have its screen divided according to the number of areas under surveillance, consequently allowing simultaneous surveillance.

- **Security Cages/Wire Window Partition:** Outside of office hours, the windows and doors should be boarded up with metal wire barriers. This is an ideal way to reduce the risk of late-night burglary.

- **Break-in Alarm:** You will want to have an alarm system that goes off if someone tries to get in, as most burglars will be scared away when they hear the noise.

Of course, another option is to hire a company and have them set up everything for you instead of you doing it yourself. Many business owners choose to go this route and leave it to the professionals. Depending on your budget, this may be worth checking out. You can have them come out and survey your business and make suggestions. They can take care of everything, including the design, installation, and monitoring. Many times this can be done for an affordable monthly fee.

Hired Gun: Do You Need One for Your Business?

WHEN BUSINESSES, BOTH LARGE AND SMALL, MUST DEAL IN CASH PURCHASES, they have to be aware that thefts and other crimes can occur on business premises. Some businesses with a higher percentage of cash transactions, such as the medical and/or recreational marijuana business, convenience stores, liquor stores, and banks may be targeted more than others by criminals, petty thieves, and gangs.

With the growing medical/recreational marijuana business and the unwillingness of banks to recognize marijuana as a legal business or open business accounts for those businesses, the danger lurks for every dispensary owner.

Thieves read the local papers and watch the local news. Marijuana dispensaries have received a lot of media attention, what with Colorado hitting unforeseen sales numbers and running out of merchandise to sell because of approved recreational use. The cash that dispensaries have on hand is enormous. Cash is king and who doesn't love it, but there is a danger of having it laying around or in a safe on premises. Thieves understand this and figure that if they rob your place of business they can quickly make a very big score. Many of these businesses choose to hire security guards and/or retired law enforcement for the protection of the employees, customers, and business.

Does your marijuana dispensary business really need security guards or a hired gun? To take a logical position on this question, you should first define the security needs of the enterprise, and then examine what type of service would provide the benefits you seek.

SENSE OF SECURITY

Security guards are uniformed personnel that are employed to protect property and people from all kinds of dangers. Uniforms give the guards high visibility. The presence of a security guard can provide piece of mind and a sense of security to the business owner, employees, and customers. Employees working in dispensaries are more productive knowing that security is close by, and when it comes to handling the two things that may make them wary of taking a job in your place of business in the first place—marijuana and cash—they feel better about their personal safety when there are security guards present.

Security guards help deter theft of property or other illegal actions. Furthermore, they are readily identifiable and available to the public in case their assistance is needed. If they have a license and can carry a gun, that makes them that much more intimidating.

PREVENTION

Almost since birth we are programmed to know that a man or woman in a uniform is there to protect us. When you see a policeman, fireman, soldier and, yes, even a security guard, there is a sense of well-being. The fear of being attacked or being in danger is mitigated once you know they are close by. Simply put, having security guards present in your place of business is a great deterrent to crime. Thieves will think twice about targeting a business that has uniformed protection. Professional guards are trained to look for suspicious activity on the spot. They can assess a situation and react to a security problem. Having a security guard sends a message to potential criminals that you are serious about protecting your business, employees and customers.

Job Description: Most of us have seen security guards in different businesses. They usually stand close to the front door of the business or near the checkout area. In the case of the dispensary, they should stand at the entrance/exit of your dispensary to discourage or to deny admittance of undesired callers, to guide legitimate visitors to their destination, and to make sure that no one leaves with anything they didn't pay for.

They may also patrol the premises on foot, taking care of problems before they become big issues and maintaining order, and can be summoned by loudspeakers or other means if something requires their immediate action.

We recommend that they take a look at your trash, inside and out, and also monitor employees coming and going at shift changes. Not only should they be used as a warning sign to deter criminals, but also as a way to help keep employee theft under control.

All Hands on Deck: Security guards can also be customer service ambassadors. A guard may be able to pick up the slack when your dispensary gets busy, when someone needs a potty break, or when a delivery of merchandise arrives. This may mean they have a substantial amount of interaction with your dispensary customers, vendors, postman or delivery man, and employees. Guards may be able to help to check in medical and recreational clients at the reception area. The extra set of hands can come in very handy at times when things just seem to get out of control.

Guards can also be used as escorts for customers and employees going to their cars after dark, or to assist when picking up merchandise (marijuana) from your grow facility if that is not in the same location as your dispensary. Hiring personable and capable guards lets you communicate that your business is secure and customer oriented.

Monitoring: Your security guard shouldn't just stand at attention at your front door. They can watch customers for shoplifting and keep an eye on your security monitors for your dispensary. They can also watch the cameras at the grow facility to make sure your growers, trimmers and maintenance team are working and doing their jobs as well as monitor for employee theft.

They also may be on active patrol of your dispensary property and/or grow facility, making sure that the premises are not being compromised in any way. These monitoring duties take a lot of security responsibility off the shoulders of the business owner and managers, allowing them to focus on their jobs.

Handling Crime: Security guards can have varying levels of training when it comes to actively responding to a crime. Some may simply take down details and contact the police. Some may be able to detain suspects. It is up to the business owner whether to have an armed guard or unarmed guard, and what procedures should be in place for handling a suspect should a crime occur. Hiring a trained and licensed guard from a reputable company can ensure that when a problem does arise, the situation will be handled with the utmost professionalism.

It is uncommon that security guards be authorized to perform arrests if needed, but they certainly can summon police or authorized personnel, can ask for personal identification of suspects and, given their training, they are in the best position to submit witness testimony if required.

It is widely recognized that the number of security guards that will be employed in the marijuana business in the coming years will grow substantially, given the uncertain climate and the perceived dangers of running and operating a cash business. Until the banking regulations change and dispensaries are able to open and operate as a regular business, they will be continue to be a target for thieves and robberies.

How to Stop Employee Theft in Your Retail Store

EMPLOYEE THEFT CAN COST A RETAIL BUSINESS thousands of dollars a week. It is one of those business ownership or management experiences that is all too often ignored until it happens to you. Preventing the inevitable from happening may be impossible, but putting the necessary procedures in place to prevent it is one of the first things you should do as an owner of a marijuana dispensary and grow operation. Procrastinating will only cost you money. Money that, most times, you will never see again.

It's Thursday afternoon and your grow facility has been harvesting at a wonderful pace. Everything seems to be in order. You have been trying to reconcile your inventory with your written records. To take a break from looking at numbers, you begin to straighten up the back room. What you find is a pile of one of your high strains of marijuana sitting on a table, definitely out of place and in an area not normally used for packaging or trimming. It's only a few steps to a door that exits to the parking lot. So that's what's been happening to your inventory, but who's the culprit?

Retail store managers and owners need to take the risk of theft seriously rather than thinking that it won't ever happen to them. This means considering that everyone working in your retail business is a potential thief. Tough as this is, it is the only way to operate—especially in a business that currently operates as cash only and sells a product that is easily able to be concealed in clothes quickly. In the blink of an eye, hundreds, if not thousands, of dollars' worth of marijuana and/or hard earned cash can be picked up and stolen from right under your nose.

The tragedy is that retailers usually have at their disposal tools which, if used properly, can reduce the opportunity for theft and protect the cash within the business. To help you protect your business, we have compiled some tips and procedures you can use in your marijuana dispensary and grow operation that can help control this kind of loss.

HIRE AND TRAIN WELL

Your first line of defense against employee theft is to hire honest employees. That means taking the time to check references thoroughly, including verifying dates of prior employment, and screening for past shoplifting arrests or other criminal activity. I know a crystal ball would be so much easier to tell us that the person we are considering is going to be the employee of the year, or at least not a thief, but that is unrealistic. Without spending the time to do as thorough of a background check as you can with the material you are given (usually just a resume), then you just don't know what you may end up with. Calling a few references only takes a few minutes of your time. This time is time well spent.

Thirty minutes today may mean you save yourself and your business thousands of dollars tomorrow.

Train new recruits thoroughly, both in the actual job procedures and in the level of integrity you expect from them. Let them know they are accountable for their actions. Set realistic rules and let them know you will enforce them daily. Selective enforcement encourages dishonesty.

At every opportunity, make it clear that you have a zero tolerance approach to theft. This will separate you from your employees; so be it. It is essential that you put your desire to cut theft ahead of friendship with an employee. Your business is at risk, after all. If they think you are their friend, the fear of stealing becomes less. People usually will not punish their friends, and your employees may think they can get away with stealing from you without the danger of legal penalty and/or loss of their job.

Everything in your business with value must be treated with respect, every day. And you, as the owner or manager, need to demonstrate leadership in the mission to keep theft at a minimum.

BE AN EMPLOYER OF CHOICE

Employees who feel they are underpaid or treated unfairly feel justified in being dishonest or in failing to report other employees' dishonest acts. If an employee feels that they are not being treated as well as others and/or that their pay is not equivalent to other employees who work with them on the same level, in their mind they may feel they can make up this deficit in a couple of ways. How? For starters, by not being a good employee: exhibiting poor treatment of customers or being lazy with job tasks.

Another way is by stealing. Both are damaging to your business and will have a major overall effect on the daily operation and success of your retail marijuana business.

Give your employees the tools to be honest. Make sure they know how to respond when friends (customers) ask them to steal or ask for discounts on marijuana your dispensary is selling. Let them know they are trusted and you are counting on them to be fair and honest, just as you are with them.

ESTABLISH ZERO TOLERANCE

Every preventive action you take reinforces the impression that stealing from your business is a bad idea and that if they are caught they will be punished by you and the law.

Consequently you must always be highly visible on the sales floor, as well as the grow facility if you have one. Being nonexistent promotes employee theft. The old adage out of sight out of mind comes in to play. If you're not watching the till, your employees will—and will surely have their hands in it.

Obviously, you can't be in all places at every waking minute of the day. The solution to this problem is to pop in every day at different times. Have no set schedule to visit the grow facility or to check inventory. Try to walk in and inspect the entire operation at both the dispensary and grow facility every time you visit, if possible. This will keep your growers, trimmers, inventory people and budtenders at attention. They will also understand that you truly have a finger on the pulse of your

TIP

A clever way to counter the problem of friends asking employees for discounts is to give your employees a discount that they can use to buy product at a reduced rate. This rate can be applied to family and friends. The discount has to be enough that it prevents them from stealing. Also, they have to understand that every one of their friends isn't subject to the discount. This added employee benefit should eliminate the urge to steal your hard-earned marijuana and keep your employees happy. The price point on the discounted inventory will cost you far less over time than just one person helping themselves to product and or cash from your register.

business and know everything that is going on. This procedure will help deter any would-be employee theft by the worry that if they do try and steal they may be caught.

The more you make it clear that you intend to protect your business, the less likely you'll experience employee theft, and you will see your bottom line improve. Zero tolerance for employee theft is good for your business and good for the retail industry overall. Explaining to your employees when you hire them if they get caught stealing just once, they will be fired. This leaves no room for interpretation when and if it does happen. FIRED! They should also know that you will call the police and press charges if they steal from you and your business—no ifs, ands, or buts.

Have your employee sign an employee agreement when taking the job to ensure they understand your rules for their employment. This agreement can be a simple one page document that explains their job role and the ramifications if they do steal from your place of business. Make them read this document and sign it. The agreement should set the expectations from day one of their employment going forward.

> **TIP**
>
> **Check garbage daily. A bud or two in the trash is an easy score for an employee trying to sustain a marijuana habit or make a few bucks after work. Also let employees know that you may check lunch boxes, backpacks, or handbags periodically. Your staff knowing that you have rules in place that will warrant periodic checking will hopefully curtail theft.**

TIPS FOR ELIMINATING EMPLOYEE THEFT

- Establish one door as the official employee entrance and exit.
- Establish rules for who checks inventory and have these checks documented: signed, time stamped, and dated.
- Monitor trash disposal.
- Keep all debris, including garbage pails, away from the building.
- Require at least two employees to be present at opening and closing.
- Handbags, backpacks, jackets, and lunch bags should be checked periodically.
- Replace the locks and/or keys whenever an employee leaves your employment.
- Replace and/or change computer and alarm codes whenever an employee leaves your employment.
- Check places that normally do not get inspected for unusual bags or supplies whenever possible. You may never know what you may find.
- Light bulbs that are burned out or fixtures that are broken need to be replaced immediately. Dark, unused areas foster employee theft.
- Look for unlocked or disabled doors.
- Check alarm system daily.
- Hang signs in your place of business, including employee areas and restrooms, stating that shoplifters will be prosecuted.
- A camera system is mandatory in a retail business, especially in the marijuana business. Again, you can't be everywhere.

- Keep all employee coats, bags, lunch boxes, etc. in a designated area. Nothing personal should be in or around counters or inventory areas.

- Invite a law enforcement officer to walk through your place of visit for a tour.

- Place cameras on all doors in and on the outside of the building, cash registers, front desk, trim areas, storage areas, drying areas, and grow room. Make sure cameras are visible for all to see. The bigger the camera the better. If they see it, they will know it's there. Small capsule or hidden cameras are great from a decorating standpoint, but you want your employees and customers to know they are being watched.

- Initiate procedures for balancing the cash register or drawer after each employee's shift.

- Having employees wear a tee-shirt, golf shirt or overcoat with no pockets that covers front and back pants pockets won't ensure they can take anything, but it will make it more difficult for them to pocket something. This also keeps all of your staff looking professional.

- Check daily receipts against a list of items sold.

- Randomly monitor the inventory of particular items and compare with recorded sales over a period of time.

- If you suspect an employee of stealing, randomly audit sales by contacting customers to verify sale details. You can do this as a routine survey of customer service.

- Take steps to monitor employee/vendor friendships.

- Require a designated manager or trusted person when goods are received.

- Watch all invoices and spot check to make sure all inventory was actually received.

Don't be so obsessed with catching a potential thief that you treat your employees with suspicion and disrespect. They deserve to be trusted and treated with respect and confidence unless evidence indicates otherwise. The simple controls outlined above will not catch all pilferage, but they will usually disclose discrepancies if you use them consistently.

Is Your Safe . . . Safe?

A MONEY SAFE IS IMPORTANT TO HAVE. Most business owners find peace of mind in keeping their cash in a place they know is secure. It is possible to do this, but there are several factors to consider with money safes. Some shopping around might be necessary as choosing a good model involves looking at factors such as the safe's effectiveness at deterring burglars, its fire rating, the storage space it affords, lock configuration it has, and price.

The main objective for getting a money safe is theft prevention. Each one has a cash rating that indicates just how well the unit will hold up to an attempted break in. This rating is calculated using an assessment of a combination of features, such as how strong the door and walls of the safe are, what kind of locking system the safe has, and how possible it is to remove the unit from where it is being stored. A high cash rating means that all of these features account for a more secure system of storing money or other valuable items.

A money safe should also have a good fire rating. By analyzing this rating, it is known just how long the money vault will maintain its integrity when exposed to fire. The longer it can be exposed without the contents inside bursting into flames, the higher the fire rating. A safe rated to withstand exposure to fire for an hour is generally considered to be good.

CHOOSING A SAFE TO FIT YOUR MARIJUANA BUSINESS NEEDS

- Choose a safe that is large enough to store your cash and marijuana. Consider the possibility of future business growth when you compare safes to make sure the safe you choose will meet your needs further down the line.

- Ask yourself which type of lock you prefer. You can buy a safe with various locking mechanisms, depending on your preference. Note that you can expect to pay more for the more secure safes.

- Consider whether a fireproof and/or waterproof feature is desired. We suggest you contact your insurance company to see what fire rating meets their policy in case of fire, theft, and/or water damage.

- When you choose a safe, look for a safe that has been tested by Underwriters Laboratories, Inc. (UL) and has earned their certification for a residential security container. Basically, this means the higher the rating by UL, the more difficult it is to break into the safe.

- Before you buy your safe, read the state regulations, as they may require certain features. Make sure when you design your area for the safe that there is room for another one. As your volume grows, you will need to store more products away when you close. One safe won't be enough.

- Most safes are rated on the thickness of the steel and the type of locking mechanism. Keep in mind that the more you pay doesn't necessarily mean the average safe cracker can't open your safe. Yes, some locks are better than others in terms of slowing down a break-in; i.e., a combination of digital and mechanical. Keep in mind, most locksmiths today can open a safe. It may take them awhile, but it can be done.

SECURING YOUR SAFE

How often have you seen a movie where the thieves break in to a bank and successfully break in to a safe—or better yet, steal the safe by blowing up the bank and escaping with both the safe and money in one shot? Well, that's Hollywood. Owning a medical marijuana business may seem like a Hollywood movie, but securing your safe and making sure it's a good one will slow down any thief, hopefully preventing them from pulling off a Hollywood caper.

- You should attach the safe directly to the floor joists. You must first remove the flooring and sub floor to have access to the floor joists.

- If your space is on a slab, set the safe in six inches of concrete. We suggest you do this yourself and not have the assistance of any outside help. This will eliminate anyone from knowing how secure the safe is and how difficult it would be if they should decide to rob your marijuana business. Placing a rug and or flooring over the concrete will make it look like the safe is part of the room and is simply a piece of furniture.

- If you are constructing a new building, you can encase the safe directly in the concrete foundation.

Many of these suggestions may seem like overkill, but the more difficult you make things for any thief, the more secure your business and your marijuana harvest and hard-earned cash will be.

Protecting Your Business Property from Theft

FOR MANY BUSINESSES MAKING THEIR WAY IN A TOUGH ECONOMY, burglary can mean the difference between staying afloat and going under. The marijuana business is no different. The grow operation is a crucial part of your business. The majority of your profit will come from the marijuana you grow and harvest. Any type of disturbance, in this scenario a burglary, can interrupt months, if not years, of cultivating and harvesting to create the ultimate product for your customers and wholesale operation. A few relatively simple and manageable precautions designed to make a burglary much more difficult can go a long way toward protecting your investment.

LIGHTING IS UNINVITING

It might seem like a cat burglar cliché, but you can't deny that intruders like to work in the cover of darkness. Good interior and exterior lighting is one of the most effective deterrents against crime. These lights must provide optimum visibility. Pay special attention to areas that are not in plain view—this is where intruders often try to enter. It's also important to make sure that the lighting fixtures stay in good working order. The chance of breakage can be reduced by paying attention to where the fixtures are placed, using lights in cages, and choosing durable products with vandal-proof covers over the lights and power sources. Damaged or burned-out bulbs should be replaced immediately.

Keep valuable merchandise illuminated, but away from display windows, where they could be a target of a quick "smash and grab." A "smash and grab" is just what it sounds like: in a matter of seconds, thieves break a window, grab whatever's nearby, and flee the scene.

The more light you use around your grow operation, the less likely intruders will try to enter. We recommend heavy lighting around any doors, garbage areas, and/or areas that may be difficult to be seen from the street. These lights should be on timers so that forgetting to turn them on is something that never happens.

MAINTAIN THE EXTERIOR

Overgrown shrubbery, vehicles, and trash dumpsters near the building provide excellent cover for burglars. Keeping trees and shrubs trimmed away from windows and doors can help minimize hiding places around buildings. The grow operation can quickly accumulate trash—sometimes a lot of it. Make sure any trash is not placed next to the building. Piling up garbage and or trash pails against the building allows burglars a place to hide and break-in from these unsuspecting hiding spots.

LOCKS AND PADLOCKS

Locks on all outside entrances and inside security doors should be double-cylinder deadbolts with removable collars. The deadbolt should have at least a one-inch throw containing a hardened steel insert and protected by a latch guard. Padlocks should be made of hardened steel mounted on bolted hasps and always locked to prevent exchange. All serial numbers should be hidden so no new keys can be made.

MAKE IT HARDER TO GAIN ENTRY THROUGH WINDOWS AND DOORS

Exterior windows can be covered with burglar-resistant glazing, which provides the appearance of glass and increases security. Most windows in the growing areas of your operation should be covered with ¾ plywood then ¼ metal on the interior and exterior. Any windows in the rear of the building should also be covered with heavy metal grates, since these will most likely be targeted because of their vulnerability. Even though natural light is a desired source for plant growth, the security of the business overrides that tenet.

Bars on the exterior or roll down gates on the windows are other ways to protect your grow facility. The more precaution in these areas the better.

Consider installing exterior doors constructed from solid-core wood or metal that fit tightly into the doorframe. A heavy-duty deadbolt lock with a heavy-duty strike plate can be installed using three-inch screws that penetrate the wall stud. This, as well as doorjamb reinforcement, will provide extra strength if a criminal tries to kick open the door. Cross bars on the interior of doors are also recommended.

Side and rear doors should be made of solid wood or steel construction and installed in reinforced steel frames. Avoid using doors with hinge pins on the outside where they can be easily removed. Equip outward swinging doors with hinges that have non-removable pins. Secure overhead garage-type doors with padlocks on roller channels. All doors should have roll-down gates no matter what type of material they are made out of. Yes, this is all a precaution and will not be inexpensive, but it is certainly worth the investment.

ROOFTOP INTRUDERS

Who would think a thief would go out of their way to rob a grow facility by entering through the roof, skylight or air-conditioning vent? Stealthy burglars are out there—and plenty of them. There are also desperate people that will try anything for a quick fix or score for drugs.

You must remember the damage done by an intruder in your grow facility does not necessarily have to be by taking product or trying to steal your safe filled with money. This intruder may shut down your heating or air conditioning system, thereby destroying your harvest, or steal your newly germinated seedlings that your have been crossbreeding for months, maybe years. The damage will be done, but could have been avoided.

We recommend putting metal cages on all rooftop air conditioners. Any skylights should be boarded over with plywood and steel sheeting on the inside. If there is a bulkhead roof top door, a steel cross bar must be used on the inside to prevent the door from being kicked in. If the door is not being used and is not required by the fire department as a means of egress, then simply board the door up and be done with it. To a normal person, the roof would seem like the last place a thief would strike, but in most cases it is the easiest way to break into a commercial building.

ALARM SYSTEMS

The best and most effective way you can help protect your property against burglary is with an alarm system. There are a variety of different alarms available, ranging from very basic local alarms to central station systems. Detection equipment alarms can involve protection of the perimeter, area, or object.

Perimeter protection covers the outside surface of the building. Area protection covers an entire space or area, such as the inside of a building. Object protection covers a particular object, like a safe.

Alarm and video monitoring alarm systems offer a network of surveillance equipment that automatically notify a central monitoring service when the system detects unauthorized intruders. Trained staff at the service will then contact both the owners and the authorities. Video technology gets smaller, better, and cheaper every year. For a modest investment, you can cover the perimeter of your business with video surveillance, and also digitally record substantial amounts of footage. What you capture could play an important role in catching a thief and retrieving your property.

BIGGER THE BETTER

The medical marijuana industry is one that requires a big safe, the bigger the better. This safe will be needed to house your harvest of marijuana and the cash that you accumulate from your daily retail merchandise sales. You will most likely have large sums of cash and merchandise on hand at all times. It is important that you safeguard your harvest and money in a safe for protection from employees, burglars and fires.

Safes are classified as either fire resistive or burglary resistive and are rated for performance by Underwriters Laboratories, Inc. Select a safe based on the valuables to be protected. A higher level of protection should be chosen for high value merchandise or large amounts of money. By anchoring a safe in a well-lit area, there's a better chance burglars would be noticed if they try to open or remove the safe. The bigger the safe and anchoring system you decide to use to bolt, cement or build your safe into a room will make taking or trying to steal the safe almost impossible. *Almost* impossible because anything can be taken, but the longer the thief has to plan or stage a robbery, the better off you are.

STOP IT FROM HAPPENING BEFORE IT HAPPENS

You're a business owner, not a vigilante. Chances are you don't have time to guard your property twenty-four hours a day. However, it doesn't take a superhero to take a few simple steps to make a burglary less likely. Check those lights. Close up windows and get roll-down gates for your doors. Consider an alarm system. Reconsider your safe. Most burglaries can be prevented with a little foresight and planning.

SURPRISE! You Hired a Thief!

SOME OF THE MOST LIKABLE PEOPLE YOU'LL EVER MEET may have few morals and little or no integrity. Employee theft usually comes as a "complete surprise" to coworkers and business owners. "He (or she) always seemed so nice and energetic; I never dreamed I'd hired a thief," lamented a business owner. Obviously, no employer wants to believe they hired and trusted someone who would even consider stealing from them, but facts from law enforcement tell a different story. Furthermore, most employers believe that their employees have the same opinions of what theft actually is as they themselves do. The sad truth is that they do not.

In the marijuana business, it is difficult to pick and choose who you can hire. Most states require employees to be twenty-one years old and be a resident of the state. They must show a lease and utility bill in their name. These states require an advance background check on employees. If they have a drug related felony in the past, most probably they won't be able to work in the industry. They can have misdemeanors, but they must show evidence of the case and whether it is settled or not. If they owe back taxes or child support, this may deny them a license to work as well. Each state is different, so check with the agency that is regulating the industry in your state. Some municipalities require background checks as well, so go into your municipality and ask for all of their requirements too.

Most of the time, the people who want to work in the marijuana business are intrigued by marijuana and are comfortable working and selling in an industry they are familiar with. They steal product from you. The temptation to steal is always there, and they most likely smoke and use recreational drugs themselves. The reality here is that the industry attracts marijuana users. The fact of the matter is your employees will be around quality merchandise up to eight hours in a given day. Like a bartender in a bar, there may be urges to use if they should choose to do so. Remember, you are responsible for your business and your employees. If they steal marijuana and sell it out the back door, it will not only be a theft problem—then your entire business will be at risk. What this means is that you are responsible for all product being produced; if marijuana is found by a citizen outside your building, it is a criminal offense. So if an employee puts product by a dumpster to grab later after work and a citizen finds it, the owner of the business is in big trouble. Systems and procedures need to be in place to help curb potential theft opportunities. Monitoring your garbage and waste that goes out is important. A thief will bury product in the garbage and grab it after work. A manager must have a check system in place.

Another way to potentially curb theft is to offer employee pricing for all of your product and merchandise. Perhaps offer employees a 10-20% above cost. For example, an employee could buy an eighth, or 3.5 grams, for $20.00, which normally sells for an average of $40 in Colorado. Why jeopardize a good job when buying it can be so cheap?

BELOW IS A CLEAR DEFINITION OF A THIEF

A thief is someone who takes property by stealth belonging to another without the consent of the other. Part one of the theft psyche is the conscious choice to take something belonging to someone else.

Further, a thief takes without consent. While this seems very clear-cut, many people do NOT consider unauthorized "borrowing" to be stealing. An example is comes from a current grow/dispensary owner, where an employee "borrowed" (without permission) money from the till then replaced it a few weeks later—many fellow employees did not feel she had done anything wrong. Many responses to this woman's complaint against her employer were that the employer needed to have compassion. The woman had been "borrowing" from cash deposits for years whenever she found herself short of money and then paying the money back on payday. She was not caught until she fell behind and was not able to replace everything she had borrowed one month. Talk with your employees TODAY. Be sure your employees know that borrowing without permission FOR ANY REASON is stealing!

Your dispensary or grow facility should not allow:

- Borrowing of any products or supplies of inventory from storage or retail displays without asking, then paying for it later. If an employee of the dispensary should do so they should be written up and monies taken from pay. If it happens again they should be terminated and it is the choice of the owner or manager to have them prosecuted by the local police.

- Borrowing of any money or any other items used for business purposes should only come with permission from the owner of the said properties (tools, products, merchandise).

- Products, tools, stationery, laptops, customer information and any other items in the dispensary that are supplied by the owner are to conduct work in the dispensary or grow facility. If any of these items should be taken out of the business by an employee without asking, that could be grounds for immediate termination.

Above are standard rules of thumb, but for this industry, immediate termination is suggested; a zero tolerance policy. Make sure when you hire an individual that this is clearly understood from the beginning.

While this addresses the theft of merchandise and supplies, an owner must also be vigilant about time theft. Those long lunches or short days or personal business on company time also take a big bite out of company profits. Some authorities on the subject estimate that the cost of time theft is comparable to that of merchandise theft. While all employees have the occasional emergency to deal with, as an employer you must be diligent to protect your business from this theft.

Cash Procedures to Live By

MARIJUANA CASH HANDLING PROCEDURES are very important to minimize theft, both from robbery and internal skimming. The type of systems you put in place and the tools you install for safety and lockdown will ensure the money your business earns will stay safe and secure.

The most common cause of theft is employee theft, although a business can also lose money to thieves and others not associated with your business. In this industry, it will happen not only at the dispensary but the garden area as well, so steps need to be taken to prevent this. Having cash procedures in your dispensary business is one of the most crucial steps to eliminate daily setbacks. Some of you might be lucky enough to have credit card processing in place or a checking account, which would eliminate 30-40% of the cash being handled, so hopefully you are able to set that up within your dispensary. If not, some of the ideas below will help you keep control of your enterprise, while keeping theft to a minimum.

PHYSICAL CONTROL

All businesses should have procedures in place to ensure physical control over cash. For example, businesses should not allow employees to have more than a certain amount of cash in their registers during their shift. This cuts down on losses in the event of a robbery and reduces employee temptation to steal. Excess cash should be stored in a secure location, such as a locked safe, and managers and or owners should check receipts every couple of hours based on your dispensary's active sales. Everything has to match sales and receipts. This is the primary responsibility of the manager on duty. You should do no less than three pulls a day. This system allows a quick way to check receipts, so if there is a problem you can quickly trace by whom and where the mistake was made.

Most Common Employee Mistakes

- Putting an order in twice.
- Giving the wrong amount of change.
- Collecting the wrong amount of money.
- Not adding the order up correctly.

DESIGNATE WHO HANDLES THE CASH

As in most cash businesses, it's important to hire trustworthy employees to handle cash and work with customers. Employers should do their own criminal background checks on all new employees prior to hire. The State of Colorado does a background check on each registered employee before they can work in the industry. If someone has a felony, they can be denied employment by the state. As an owner, you can only employ someone who has a current state badge, so there has been some background work done already. All states have different regulations concerning employment, so do your homework before you hire. Depending on the amount of cash an employee may be expected to handle, employers should run credit checks on potential employees themselves. Employers need to document who is authorized to handle cash and what responsibilities each person who handles cash is allowed to perform.

Your dispensary's budtenders must understand exactly what their responsibilities are when dealing with customers. If their job is just to assist with sales and recommendations to customers on retail products, then that is all they should do. Designate one person to handle the register and cash. If you have a larger dispensary, you may have several budtenders. Seniority and trust will guide you on who should handle the cash registers if you have more than one.

No one employee should be responsible for all aspects of cash handling, as this puts too much responsibility, and perhaps temptation, in one person's hands, increasing the risk of loss. Instead, any business that handles cash should hire several people to engage in cash-handing duties. One person should receive cash while another records it and still another deposits it into the safe. This allows employees to check one another for honesty (i.e., if the recorder notes something wrong when recording cash, he or she can consult with your budtenders or with a supervisor.)

DOCUMENT ALL TRANSACTIONS

All cash going in or out of the business must be documented, as well as the duties of each person handling cash. Employers should audit records regularly and should periodically conduct independent audits of each cash handler's records. Employers should conduct at least some audits without announcing them in advance so that employees do not have the opportunity to hide any inappropriate behaviors regarding cash handling.

KEEP IT SAFE

Cash should be placed in a secure location from the time it is removed from the cash/drawers. For starters, one option is to seal each drawer's cash in an envelope and sign it. That way, it's tough for anyone to break the seal and forge a signature. Deposit that into a safe, which should be located in a locked room. Keep a record of times and dates of deposits. Decide how you want to secure the room as well. Using some combination of buzzer door entry and closed-circuit TVs can remove the opportunity and temptation for theft. Most of this security is required as part of the state's regulations.

STATE REQUIREMENTS

Any state regulatory agency is a public authority or government agency responsible for exercising autonomous authority over areas of human activity in a regulatory or supervisory capacity. Their job is to make rules for any industry and supervise that the rules they put in place are followed. These rules, in fact, may change to modify the practice in which the process is distributed and/or conducted. Since the practice of selling, growing, and distributing marijuana is so new, you can guarantee that these agencies will be an ongoing concern for any distributor of marijuana. This is their job, so expect visits, expect change.

These regulatory agencies have the right to enter your business at any time during the day or night, if you're open for business, even on the weekend. The marijuana industry is no different. When your state forms their regulatory divisions, there will be regulations, procedures, and requirements for operation. Follow them to a tee, to the best of your ability. Inspectors will visit unannounced; take them very seriously and correct any mistakes in a timely manner. As a new industry, procedures may change operationally, as the state fine tunes their division. Keep up with all updates and do everything by the book. Don't cut corners. If you are one of the lucky ones to obtain a state license to operate, respect the agency that governs you and take all the necessary steps to follow their guidelines. If you do not take them seriously, they will shut you down.

In all businesses, accounting is an important part of running your operation successfully. Having good records and keeping everything up to date will take a lot of time, but will also tell you a lot of good information. It makes sense as a good general business practice and keeps you prepared for when your state agency happens to ask you for any financial information. This is also another form of checks and balances to make sure no theft is occurring.

The medical marijuana dispensary business is not as easy as it is perceived to be. The fact is, the world is currently monitoring what is happening in states with legalized marijuana for recreational use. The result is stringent enforceable penalties for the dispensaries. How you conduct your business and the systems you put in place to monitor sales are extremely important.

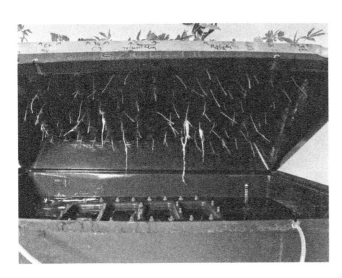

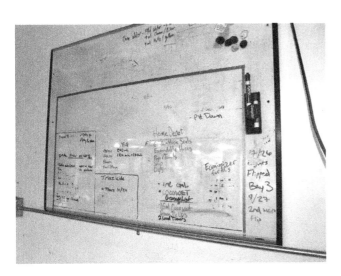

SECTION VII

EMPLOYEES

Employee Agreements

IN TODAY'S BUSINESS WORLD most companies hire individuals with the understanding that there are expectations and confidentiality that come with employment and must be addressed before they begin working for your company.

Over the last twelve months, the marijuana industry has exploded with job opportunities, bringing a new type of hire into this growing business. A talent war has broken out on who can hire the best gardener or "grower," which is a critical part to your organization. Now that marijuana is legal in a couple of states, gardens are expanding and your master grower is now handling your million-dollar harvest, so you need a good gardener. This rapid expansion in the industry is bringing opportunities to talented growers. Many are being lured by other business owners for higher salaries and a piece of the action. Yes, ownership. Marijuana businesses are increasingly resorting to litigation—some of it extraordinarily unpleasant—to prevent their gardeners and growers from moving to their competitors or finding a better opportunity and leaving them hanging. This industry is so new that there aren't many resumes—most of a grower's history is from illegal gardening activity. When you find a good gardener, you need to try to keep that individual. Many of these growers have talent in gardening but don't understand production, which is a very important part of your business.

The result is that many businesses have no choice but to come up with contracts or non-compete clauses for their employees. This business presently processes large amounts of cash along with growing a very expensive harvest of a prized crop. The employees you hire take on a very important role and are extremely important to the success of your business.

You might be wondering about trade secrets and growing techniques and the importance of protecting them. There are hundreds of different types of marijuana. Many growers have crossbred and cultivated different grades through genetic engineering that are considered their top performers, separating theirs from their competitors. You can compare these strains to a fine vintage of wine.

These crossbreeds may have been years in the making; the seeds may have come from different parts of the world. The way that this product is grown may be considered state of the art to this grow facility. These factors are considered "confidential information" and "prevention" for workers (including those who have not signed non-compete agreements) from moving to a competitor on the grounds they are taking trade secrets with them. The marijuana plant under the eyes of contract law is considered a "work product." This means it is protected from disclosure to outside sources.

A well-considered, written employment agreement ensures that employees know what you expect from them and what their duties are, which protects both of you. If a dispute does arise, you can refer to a signed copy of the employment agreement, or details of the collective agreement, under which they were employed.

With a well-written contract, settling disputes regarding employment becomes a much simpler and less expensive proposition for both sides. As with any contract, if there is a dispute the contract can simply be reviewed to confirm the rights and responsibilities of each party. If the contract is not being upheld by the employer or employee and it can't be resolved by discussion or negotiation, then a lawsuit may be filed. Of course, a central reason for a good contract is to avoid litigation. When there is a written agreement to refer to, the decision of who is right or who is wrong may be decided quickly as a matter of contract law, rather than as a protracted matter of "he said/she said." Although many people may believe the marijuana industry is run by a bunch of stoner type hippies that know nothing about business, that is far from the truth. Regardless, employee and employer having a signed contract is an absolute necessity.

THEFT

The course of action on stealing, or the misappropriation of funds, must be included in the employee agreement. The employee must understand your policy and the consequences that will occur, from immediate termination from their job to reporting them to the police, as well as the charges you will press. Legal fees that they will be responsible for should be included as well. This must be in **bold** letters in the agreement and employees must understand there is zero tolerance regarding these matters. Stealing is a crime and your place of business will not tolerate criminal activity.

This contract should be signed by the employer and the employee. If you're the owner, store a copy in a safe place and tell the new employee to do likewise. These contracts are extremely important and should be taken very seriously. At the end of this section is a sample of an employment contract that can be used as a template, but must be reviewed by your attorney. Every state has different regulations and this contract may need to be altered to fit the laws of your state. There is no guarantee that this contract will be enforceable in a court of law, but it makes your employee think twice about stealing trade secrets or stealing product or money.

LAWS EMPLOYEES SHOULD KNOW

You have worked long and hard to get your marijuana business up and running. It has been a struggle finding the necessary funds to maintain and grow your business. You have earned your master's degree in the arduous legal processes necessary to maintain your business, mostly by making many very expensive and time-consuming mistakes, but you have finally gotten to the point that your marijuana business is making money. You at last can see the light at the end of the tunnel.

You have gone through the laborious process of hiring who you think are very good employees. You did your own background checks, you called former employers, and you made your employees sign your employee agreement explaining what they are expected to do, as well as the ramifications of breaking and/or stealing and everything else that goes along with working in your business.

What happens next is the most mind-blowing thing that any business owner can go through. You find out, not from another employee, but from the police that one of your star employees has been selling out the back door. The police didn't call you; they came to your location, surrounded the building, and raided your business.

Police in Breckenridge, Colorado, arrested a dispensary worker for unlawful distribution. According to a report in *Summit Daily*, a dispensary worker was arrested after cops saw him selling marijuana on the street and then found him with more than four ounces of cannabis in his pocket. The seller allegedly told cops he was selling marijuana that he purchased from his employer. To make matters worse, he admitted to selling marijuana to a friend in college across the state line.

This infraction is not to be taken lightly. Expect your place of business to have raids if you haven't already. They will be conducted "where there is probable cause that the premises were involved in illegal and large-scale trafficking of marijuana."

"When suspected criminal networks violate federal laws, those involved will be prosecuted." Keep in mind that, because of the newness of this business, you will be guilty until you prove yourself innocent! You will be fined and most likely shut down. There is also a possibility that you may find yourself in a very expensive legal battle to keep yourself out of jail.

What can dispensary owners learn from this? Make sure your employees know the law. Tell them from the get-go that selling out the back door won't be tolerated. And ensure they understand it's a fireable offense. Make sure that this is written in your employee agreement.

This might sound obvious, but some employees clearly don't think it's that big of a deal. And believe it or not, they could be unclear on local laws and regulations, especially in a lax state like Colorado. And as to the chance this employee was acting with permission or even explicit instructions from his employer? There's no quicker way to get a visit from the feds.

HIRING EMPLOYEES

Hiring your employees happens in different stages. The first hire for the operation will be your main or master gardener. This will be your most important employee. While the grow is under construction, your gardener will be planning with you, getting everything ready for when the city and state gives you the green light to grow. Since this is such an important position, here are some tips when looking for the right employee. This being a new industry, a lot of your gardener's experience will come from growing illegally. Many of them will have the "artist" mentality, raving about growing six to twelve plants and making them masterpieces. This sounds great, but how are their "works of art" when that person is growing eight hundred plants? How do they handle rotating your harvest? Production schedules? Pesticide regimens? Nutrients used?

With that in mind, for your first hire, work side by side with your gardener, gaining knowledge every step of the way. In case of emergencies, you become the backup gardener. It's good to know every aspect of this business.

With the industry being so new, it's hard to find a manager/master gardener that understands production and the science of the marijuana plant. Usually you will need more than one gardener to run your grow; each one may have some strengths that the other lacks. Look for someone who:

- Is willing to share knowledge.
- Is flexible on hours.
- Understands the plant.
- Understands general production methods.
- Is open to new ideas.
- Has previous experience.
- Is a team player.
- Has a college degree in botany or horticulture.

As you build your organization, you will have a team of growers, each one adding to your formula in creating the perfect garden. Learn from everyone; there are one hundred different ways to grow marijuana—all of them correct—but one way may be better than the next.

Now that your garden is underway, you will soon have to hire personnel for the dispensary. This type of person should be detailed, organized and have good customer service skills. A lot of money goes through the dispensary, so they should have above-average mathematical skills, as they most likely will be handling money and a cash register. One of the other job responsibilities will be weighing out your product. You want to make sure that the employee understands what an eighth or a quarter is and the equal weight in grams. A quick way to lose money and product is by giving out wrong dosages. Experience will be very limited; review the resume and look for stability and length of stay at previous jobs.

Below are general recommendations and rules you may want to follow when hiring your employees.

Although age twenty-one is the legal requirement, it should be a bit beyond that, but not only for having had the time to gain more skills. Neurologists have discovered that the frontal lobe portion of the brain is the one that controls judgment and emotions, comprehends consequences, controls empathy and impulse behavior, and gives flexibility in thinking processes. However, the frontal lobe is not completely developed until the age of twenty-five. Adding four years at the very minimum to the legal age of your prospective employee is highly recommended.

- Consider whether you can outsource tasks to consultants or freelancers before hiring someone on staff.

- Referrals from friends, advisers and industry colleagues are often the most efficient way to find new employees.

- Require at least three references and call them.

- Check with the candidate's former employer.

When you reach the point when it is time to begin hiring employees for your marijuana store/growing facility there are mandatory steps you must take in order to be in compliance with the city, state and federal agencies. As stated, these are requirements, not options. You can access the following website to obtain the necessary forms: www.irs.gov

1. You must verify that each new employee is legally eligible to work in the United States. They must produce two forms of identification. It's a good practice to make photocopies for their personnel files. Have the employees you hire fill out Form I-9, Employment Eligibility Verification.

2. You are required to get each employee's name and Social Security Number (SSN) and to enter them on Form W-2. This requirement also applies to resident and nonresident alien employees. You should require your potential employee to show you his or her social security card. You may, but are not required to, photocopy the social security card when the employee provides it. Record each new employee's name and social security number from his or her social security card.

3. To know how much income tax to withhold from employees' wages, you must

have a Form W-4, Employee's Withholding Allowance Certificate, on file for each employee. Ask all new employees to give you a signed Form W-4 before they start work. Make the form effective with the first wage payment. If employees claim exemption from income tax withholding, they must indicate this on their W-4. The amount of income tax withholding must be based on filing status and withholding allowances as indicated on the form. A Form W-4 remains in effect until the employee gives you a new one. If an employee claims exemption from income tax withholding, they must give you a new Form W-4 each year. If an employee gives you a Form W-4 that replaces an existing Form W-4, begin withholding no later than the start of the first payroll period ending on, or after the 30th day, from the date you received the replacement Form W-4.

4. Criminal background check: Because this is a legal marijuana business, you must make sure anyone you hire has a criminal-free background. At the present time, a legal marijuana store is a cash-driven venture and you will be trusting an employee with large amounts of cash. You must be able to trust who you hire. There may be a small fee attached to this process, but a criminal background check is a must. In Colorado, this is a mandatory requirement.

5. Colorado requirements: Currently, the State of Colorado requires a potential employee to obtain a MMED (Medical Marijuana) badge. Colorado law states you cannot owe any student loans or child support, have no controlled substance related felony, have any felony jail time in the past five years, have any missing payments to any federally funded subsidized institution, have incomplete tax records, have any revocation of caregiver authority and, yes, have no overseas assets. Application forms can be downloaded on the following website: www.colorado.gov

6. Credit check: This is not necessarily a requirement, but almost all employers that deal in a cash business run this report on potential employees. This will help you determine if someone is vulnerable to the temptation of stealing to pay their debts. The state of Colorado requires this.

As an owner/employer you are responsible for several federal, state, and local taxes. You must withhold federal income tax, social security and Medicare taxes, and Federal Unemployment Tax Act (FUTA) taxes. You are required to make withholding payments to each of those agencies. You are also responsible for carrying Worker's Compensation insurance. You do not want to risk losing your business should an employee get injured on the job.

As an employer/owner, make sure that you have crossed all the T's and dotted all the I's before you schedule an employee to work in your store.

FIRST IMPRESSIONS

The legal/Medical Marijuana business is one of the fastest growing ventures this country has seen since the explosion of Silicon Valley in the 1980s. It is imperative as an employer that you hire a staff that is as knowledgeable and experienced as possible. You cannot afford to hire someone who just looks the part; they have to walk the walk and talk the talk.

The saying, "You only get one chance to make a first impression" was and will always be true. A customer entering your store for the first time will always take note of your employees' appearance and demeanor. So what they wear and how they present themselves is very important. Are they greeted with a warm smile and friendly voice? If so, then their first, albeit unconscious, response is, "I'm in the presence of a professional, an expert in her field. I'm not only in good hands, but the respect here will be mutual." So, here are some suggested guidelines when choosing who to hire to represent your business:

PHYSICAL APPEARANCE/EMPLOYEE EXPECTATIONS:

- Men: Clean, well-groomed hair within a reasonable length. No buzz cut necessary, but you should be able to see his eyes.

- Women: Clean, well-groomed hair. Moderate make-up.

- Men: For security reasons, no outer garments. A clean shirt or a tee-shirt with the store's logo. Clean, pressed pants or jeans. Jeans should not have rips, cuts, patches or tears.

- Women: Same standard, tasteful attire, no excessive jewelry, conservative cleavage.

- Tattoos should be covered and piercings removed during business hours.

- Wear a visible, legible, current badge.

- Clear eyes and a sharp mind.

- Recreational usage, smoking, or consuming edibles is not permitted during working hours. **EVER!** This would be like a bartender/cocktail waitress drinking on the job. It is absolutely against the law.

- Must be over twenty-one.

- Bud Tender and Cannabis Consultant are professional titles for your staff.

- Your employees are your gatekeepers, your representatives, and they should be trained and treated as such.

- Employees should always stand up and greet your customer in a friendly and professional manner.

- Be well-spoken with a calm, professional demeanor and excellent listening skills.

- Employees should be able to gauge the level of marijuana education of each customer, so they can be as much of an educator as the customer requires and *asks* for, but never offers advice without solicitation.

- Employees should have personal and media knowledge of medical marijuana success stories; i.e., recall of a loved one who could have avoided suffering. If a prospective employee has no reference, a brief but powerful DVD should be shown as a training module, giving real examples.

- Your employees will be/should be eager to help your customers by exhibiting patience, compassion, sensitivity and genuine interest.

- Have brochures and timely periodicals such as *The Hemp Connoisseur-Colorado's Premier Guide to Cannabis* available and on hand. Employees should be educated and be able to speak informatively about the business of marijuana.

Hiring the right employees is as important as the inventory your store carries. One complements the other. Accomplish this and the customer's first impression will always be a positive one.

EMPLOYMENT AGREEMENT

(Sample for state of Colorado. Your attorney can advise how to customize the content for your state.)

Registered Business Name: _____

Address _____

This Employment Agreement is in effect as of (date and year) _____

between (Store/Growing Facility name) _____, a legal marijuana business with its principal

location at: _____

(Hereafter referred to as the **"Store/Growing Facility"**)

and the employee (full name) _____

(Hereafter referred to as the **"Employee"**)

who resides at (address): _____

Background

A. The **Store/Growing Facility** is of the opinion that the Employee has the necessary qualifications, experience, and abilities to assist and benefit the business.

B. The **legal business name**_____ desires to employ the Employee and the Employee has agreed to accept and enter such employment upon the terms and conditions set out in this Agreement. In consideration of the matters described above and of the mutual benefits and obligations set forth in this Agreement, the receipt and sufficiency of which consideration is hereby acknowledged, the parties to this Agreement agree as follows:

This Employment Agreement Does Not Constitute an Employment Contract

1. The Employee understands and agrees that this Agreement is not an employment contract. Nothing contained in this Agreement shall give the Employee any right to continue being employed by the **legal business name**_____ for any particular length of time, or limit in any way the right of business to terminate employment, if necessary.

Commencement Date and Term

2. The Employee will commence permanent full-time/part time employment with the **legal business name**_____ on _____ day of (month) _____, (year) _____, the "Commencement Date."

3. The Employee must successfully complete a probationary period of thirty (30) days of work (the "Probationary Period"), beginning on the Commencement Date. At any time during the Probationary Period, as and where permitted by law, the **Store/Growing Facility** will have the right to terminate employment without any notice or compensation to the Employee other than wages owed for hours of work already completed.

Job Title and Description

4. The **Store/Growing Facility** agrees to employ the Employee as a:

○ Receptionist   ○ Maintenance Personnel
○ Cannibus Consultant   ○ Gardener
○ Assistant Manager   ○ Assistant Gardener
○ Manager   ○ Grower
○ Security Personnel   ○ Bud Trimmer
○ Other: _____   ○ Bookkeeper/ Accountant

The Employee will be expected to perform the following job duties related to the dispensary:

○ Greet customers
○ Attend to and meet all the needs of customers
○ Clean workspaces
○ Assist other employees when needed
○ Maintain professionalism with staff and customers
○ Answer phones

Job duties related to gardening are based on agricultural skills and all responsibilities based around the field. These include watering, grooming, cloning, transplanting and maintaining a sanitary workplace.

5. The Employee agrees to be employed on the terms and conditions set out in this Agreement. The Employee agrees to be subject to the general supervision of and act in accordance with the orders, advice, and direction of the **owner or manager of the facility**.

6. The Employee will perform any and all duties that are reasonable and that are customarily performed by a person holding a similar position in the industry of the **Store/Growing Facility**.

7. The **Store/Growing Facility** cannot unilaterally and significantly change the Employee's job title or duties. The **Store/Growing Facility** may make changes to the job title or duties of the Employee where the changes would be considered reasonable for a similar position in the industry or business. The Employee's job title or duties may be changed by agreement with the approval of both the Employee and the **Store/Growing Facility**.

8. The Employee agrees to abide by the **Store/Growing Facility** rules, regulations, and practices, including those concerning work schedules, vacation, and sick leave, as they may from time to time be adopted or modified.

Duty of Loyalty

9. The employee acknowledges that he/she owes a duty of loyalty to the **Store/Growing Facility**, and during his/her employment with the **Store/Growing Facility**, will use his/her best efforts to serve the interests of the **Store/Growing Facility** and will not take any action which would be harmful to either.

10. While employed by the **Store/Growing Facility**, the Employee will not promote the services or products of any person or entity that is or will be in competition with either the **Store or Growing Facility**.

Duty to Devote Full Time

11. The Employee agrees to devote full-time efforts to the employment duties and obligations as described in this Agreement.

Employee Compensation

12. Compensation paid to the Employee for the services rendered by the Employee as required by this Agreement will include a wage at the rate of $ _____ (USD) per hour as well as any compensation paid for overtime hours.

13. Compensation will be payable (circle one) **weekly/biweekly** or monthly while this Agreement is in force. The **Store/Growing Facility** is entitled to deduct from the Employee's compensation, or from any other compensation in whatever form, any applicable deductions and remittances as required by law.

14. The Employee understands and agrees that any additional compensation paid to the Employee in the form of bonuses or other similar incentive compensation will rest in the sole discretion of the **Store/Growing Facility** and that the Employee will not earn or accrue any right to incentive compensation by reason of the Employee's employment.

15. In cases where overtime hours are worked in a period, overtime will be paid as required by law.

16. The **Store/Growing Facility** will reimburse the Employee for all reasonable expenses, in accordance with the **Store/Growing Facility** policy as in effect from time to time, including but not limited to any expenses incurred by the Employee in connection with the business. Expenses will be paid within a reasonable time after submission of acceptable supporting documentation.

17. If the Employee is entitled to a commissioned salary as part of his/her total compensation package, the commission will be a set split of _____ per _____. This split is subject to change by the **Store/Growing Facility** if said split is no longer suitable or profitable to the business. Any and all changes to the commission split will be discussed with the Employee, and the **Store/Growing Facility** and Employee will reach an agreement on a commission split suitable to both parties.

Place of Work

18. The Employee's primary place of work will be at the following location:

_____

Store/Growing Facility Hours

19. The **Store/Growing Facility** hours are from (time) _____ to (time) _____, from (day) _____ to (day) _____. These hours are suitable for the businesses customers and may not reflect a typical forty-hour work week. The Employee will be responsible for arriving at work on time at_____ and working until _____, from (day) _____ to (day) _____. Any changes to these work hours and days must be discussed by the **Store/Growing** Facility and the employee ahead of time and with enough prior notice to allow the **Store/Growing Facility** and employee to make necessary adjustments to arrive on time for the following workday.

Employee Benefits

20. The Employee will be entitled to only those additional benefits that are currently available as described in the **Store/Growing Facility** employment handbook and manuals or as required by law.
Please make sure if #20 is included in your employee agreement, you have a handbook ready.

21. The **Store/Growing Facility** discretionary benefits are subject to change, without compensation, upon the **Store/Growing Facility** providing the Employee with sixty days' written notice of that change and providing that any change to those benefits is taken generally with respect to other employees and does not single out the Employee.

Sick Leave

22. In the event the Employee becomes ill or injured and is not able to work, the Employee must notify the **Store/Growing Facility** as soon as the illness or injury becomes apparent. The Employee is entitled to _____days of paid sick leave, or the number of days required by law, whichever is greater. This only applies to full time employees.

Vacation

23. The Employee will be entitled to two weeks of paid vacation each year during the term of this Agreement, or as entitled by law, whichever is greater. Optional—under owner's discretion
24. The times and dates for any vacation will be determined by mutual agreement between the Store/Growing Facility and the Employee. Optional—under owners discretion

Termination

25. Upon termination of employment, the **Store/Growing Facility** will pay compensation to the Employee for any accrued and unused vacation days.

Theft

Any employee caught in the act of stealing or the misappropriation of funds will be immediately terminated and prosecuted to the fullest extent of the law. The employee must clearly understand that theft is both a serious criminal offense and a civil tort. A person convicted of employee theft may receive jail time, heavy fines, restitution, and more. *Your employees should know you won't hesitate to press charges.*

Commission

26. If the Employee is compensated entirely by a commissioned salary, it is possible to take vacation days, although it may not be reasonable for the **Store/Growing Facility** to pay the Employee for vacation time. Vacation compensation for the Employee will be handled as follows: _____

_____

_____

Option - under owner discretion

Noninterference and Non-solicitation

27. During employment with the **Store/Growing Facility** and for a period of one year following the termination of employment, the Employee agrees not to attempt to influence or to encourage any other person who is employed or engaged by the **Store/Growing Facility** (whether as an employee, independent contractor, or other) to terminate his/her own relationship with the **Store/Growing Facility**.

28. During the one-year period following the termination of employment with the **Store/Growing Facility**, the Employee will not, directly or indirectly, whether on his/her own behalf or on behalf of any other person or entity, hire or attempt to hire for employment, or participate in any business activity with, any person employed or engaged by the **Store/Growing Facility** (whether as an employee or independent contractor) during the period that person remains employed by the **Store/Growing Facility**.

29. The Employee agrees not to solicit or assist others in soliciting any marijuana related business, directly or indirectly, from any of the **Store/Growing Facility** customers, even if the Employee is participating in a business outside of the **Store/Growing Facility** market area. In plain speech, the Employee will not poach customers from the **Store/Growing Facility** to benefit him/herself or others.

30. Following the termination of employment with the **Store/Growing Facility**, the Employee agrees not to promote him/herself as having been associated with the **Store/Growing Facility** without the **Store/ Growing Facility** express written permission. The Employee understands this provision does not prohibit the Employee from identifying the **Store/Growing Facility** as a former employer on a résumé or employment application, or as part of the necessary procedure.

31. The Employee understands that **Store/Growing Facility** employees may develop a personal relationship with some of the businesses customers. The Employee also understands that this noncompetition section is aimed at protecting the interests of the **Store/Growing Facility** in preserving the **Store/Growing Facility** relationships with these customers beyond the period of the Employee's employment with the **Store/ Growing Facility**.

32. While the Employee is employed by the **Store/Growing Facility**, he/she agrees not to compete with directly or indirectly or become associated with any business competitive with the **Store/Growing Facility**. Within this section, "compete" means to participate in any business activity which is similar to the business activity the Employee performs during employment with the **Store/Growing Facility**.

33. For a period of **one year** following the mutual termination of employment with the **Store/Growing Facility**, the Employee agrees not to compete with the **Store/Growing Facility** directly or indirectly, whether as owner, employee, consultant, or other, or to become associated with any business competitive with the **Store/Growing Facility** indirectly or directly, within the **Store/Growing Facility** market area. Within this section, "Market Area" consists of the area within a ten (10)-mile radius of any of the locations of the **Store/ Growing Facility** in which the Employee has worked. The distance of the mile radius must be reasonable, since the industry is new and limited.

34. The Employee confirms that if employment with the **Store/Growing Facility** terminates for any reason, the Employee will be able to earn a livelihood, due to his/her sufficient experience and capabilities, without violating the terms of this Agreement. The Employee understands that his/her ability to earn a livelihood

without violating the terms of this Agreement is a material condition of employment with the **Store/Growing Facility**.

35. The Employee represents and warrants that he/she is not subject to any other agreement containing a noncompetition provision or other restriction with respect to (a) the nature of any services which he/she will perform in the course of employment with the **Store/Growing Facility**, or (b) the disclosure or use of any information which directly or indirectly relates to the nature of the business of the **Store/Growing Facility** or the services to be rendered by the Employee during the period of employment with the **Store/Growing Facility**.

Conflict of Interest

36. During the term of the Employee's active employment with the Employer, it is understood and agreed that any business opportunity relating to or similar to the Employer's actual or reasonably anticipated business opportunities (with the exception of personal investments in less than 5% of the equity of a business, investments in established family businesses, real estate, or investments in stocks and bonds traded on public stock exchanges) coming to the attention of the Employee is an opportunity belonging to the Employer. Therefore, the Employee will advise the Employer of the opportunity and cannot pursue the opportunity, directly or indirectly, without the written consent of the Employer, with the guarantee from the Employer that consent will not be unreasonably withheld.

37. During the term of the Employee's active employment with the **Store/Growing Facility**, the Employee will not, directly or indirectly, engage or participate in any other business activities that the **Store/Growing Facility** in its reasonable discretion, determines to be in conflict with the best interests of the **Store/Growing Facility** without the written consent of the Employer, which consent will not be unreasonably withheld.

Nondisclosure of Confidential Information

38. The Employee recognizes that the **Store/Growing Facility** Confidential Information is considered confidential and constitutes trade secrets unique to the **Store/Growing Facility**. Confidential Information includes customer lists, price lists, rate structures, customer service records, payroll information, sales and profit data, marketing strategies and information, and any other information of a technical, financial, or business nature now or hereafter existing or developed that is unique to the **Store/Growing Facility** and/ or provides **the Store/Growing Facility** with a competitive advantage in the marketplace. Confidential Information does not include any information that is generally known by or available to the public.

39. The Employee acknowledges and agrees that the **Store/Growing Facility** Confidential Information was and will continue to be acquired and compiled by the **Store/Growing Facility** at great effort and expense and is the property of the **Store/Growing Facility**. In addition, the Employee agrees that this Confidential Information is valuable, special, and unique. The Employee understands that the Confidential Information could be adapted for use by other businesses competitive with the **Store/Growing Facility**, if it were presented to or made accessible to those businesses. *Optional—breaks down #38.*

40. The Employee acknowledges that the **Store/Growing Facility** operates in a competitive environment and therefore the Confidential Information is valuable. The Employee is aware that material and irreparable injury would be done to the **Store/Growing Facility** if the Confidential Information were disclosed to third parties, particularly competitors or potential competitors.

41. The Employee understands that it will become necessary to disclose to him/her the **Store/Growing Facility** Confidential Information as part of employment with the **Store/Growing Facility**.

42. The Employee agrees to treat all Confidential Information in a secret and confidential manner at all times during and after his/her employment with the **Store/Growing Facility**, and he/she will comply with the businesses procedures for maintaining the secrecy of the Confidential Information. The Employee agrees not to make use of or disclose any Confidential Information, directly or indirectly, for any purpose whatsoever, to any person or entity outside without specific written authorization from the **Store/Growing Facility**, either during employment or after employment with the **Store/Growing Facility** terminates.

43. The Employee vows to use the **Store/Growing Facility** Confidential Information only as necessary and proper in the context of performing the duties of an employee of the **Store/Growing Facility**.

44. The Employee understands the obligations of confidentiality do not apply to any information which is now published or which subsequently becomes generally publicly known, unless the information became public as a direct or indirect result of the Employee's breach of this Section.

45. Following the termination of his/her employment with the **Store/Growing Facility** for any reason, the Employee agrees not to take any of the **Store/Growing Facility** property or any of its Confidential Information with him/her in any form, whether as an original, a facsimile, a copy, or an extract or summary of any kind, and he/she will return to the **Store/Growing Facility** any property and any materials containing or constituting Confidential Information which the Employee may still possess. As a prior condition to receiving any final compensation, the Employee will execute a sworn statement vowing that he/she has complied with the provisions of this Section.

Enforcement of Agreements

46. The Employee understands that breach of any of the covenants in this Agreement is a material breach and will cause the **Store/Growing Facility** great and irreparable harm. Consequently, in the event that the Employee breaches or threatens to breach any of the provisions of this Agreement, the **Store/Growing Facility** will be entitled to equitable relief, including but not limited to a temporary restraining order, preliminary injunction, and permanent injunction, in order to protect the rights of the **Store/Growing Facility** and prevent or restrain any such breach by the Employee or his/her partners, agents, representatives, employers, employees, and/or all persons directly or indirectly acting for or with the Employee. Such injunctive relief shall be in addition to and not in lieu of monetary damages to which the **Store/Growing Facility** may be entitled under the law.

47. Nothing in this Agreement shall be construed as prohibiting the **Store/Growing Facility** from pursuing any remedies available to the **Store/Growing Facility** for such breach or threatened breach.

48. The Employee understands that each breach by him/her will constitute a separate cause of action for which the **Store/Growing Facility** may collect damages cumulatively.

49. In the event that the **Store/Growing Facility** seeks to enforce any of its rights contained in this Agreement through legal proceedings due to a breach or a threatened breach of this Agreement by the Employee, the employee agrees to reimburse the **Store/Growing Facility** for all reasonable costs, expenses, and counsel

fees incurred by the **Store/Growing Facility** in connection with the enforcement of its rights under this Agreement, whether or not litigation is commenced.

50. A claim or cause of action by the Employee against the **Store/Growing Facility**, whether based on this Agreement or otherwise, shall not constitute a detriment to the Businesses enforcement of any or all of the covenants under this Agreement.

51. If any of the provisions of Sections 3, 4, or 5 of this section of the Agreement should ever be adjudicated to exceed the time or geographic limitations permitted by applicable law, then such provisions shall be deemed reformed to the maximum time or geographic limitations permitted by applicable law and public policy.

Complete Understanding

52. This Agreement contains the entire understanding of the parties and all prior agreements or promises pertaining to the subject matter of this Agreement merge with this Agreement. This Agreement may not be altered, amended, or modified without the written consent and signature to the new version of the Agreement by both parties.

Conclusion

53. The covenants contained in this Agreement shall be construed as separate covenants, covering their respective subject matters, with respect to each of the separate cities, counties, and states of the United States, and each other country and political subdivision thereof (each such city, county, state, country, and political division being referred to in this Agreement as "Jurisdiction") in which the **Store/Growing Facility** transacts business.

To the extent that any covenant is adjudicated to be invalid or unenforceable with respect to any one or more of such Jurisdictions, (a) such covenant shall not be affected with respect to each other Jurisdiction and (b) such invalidity or unenforceability shall not affect any other covenant of this Agreement which can be given effect without the invalid or unenforceable covenant.

In witness whereof, the parties hereto have caused this Agreement to be executed:

Legal Business Name: _____

Witness: _____

Witness's Title: _____

Witness's Signature: _____

Employee's Name: _____

Employee's Address: _____

_____

I acknowledge that I have carefully read the above Agreement in its entirety and have had the opportunity to ask questions of the Store/Growing Facility and my chosen attorney, should I choose to do so, about this Agreement. I certify I fully understand and voluntarily agree to each provision of this Agreement.

Employee's Signature   Date:

_____   _____

The above Agreement is a guideline to be used for the sole purpose of the Store/Growing Facility in employee hiring. This Agreement has been prepared by the Marijuana Business University. This Agreement is not to be used in a court of law, unless upon the advice of a licensed attorney. Said publisher, Ready, Set, Go! will not resolve any damages and/or lawsuits that arise as a result of the Store/Growing Facility and Employee signing this Agreement.

A Great Gatekeeper

HOW MANY TIMES HAVE YOU WALKED INTO A PLACE OF BUSINESS and were not greeted by someone? It may have been a clothing store, restaurant, doctor's office, or a beauty salon. How does that make you feel?

Do you find yourself wondering if you should leave? Is the place open for business? You don't know if you should sit or stand or yell hello to see if someone is going to help. The importance of a gatekeeper is crucial to your business.

Historically, the gatekeeper has had many job titles, such as receptionist, secretary, or salesperson. What matters most is not the title, but that you realize how critical this person is to the success of your business.

This is the first person your patient/clients meet when they walk into your dispensary. He or she is the first person who speaks on behalf of your company when a potential client comes in or an existing one calls to make sure the right medicine is in, or a distributor calls for assistance in placing a product order. In essence, this person speaks for you and is an extension of you and your businesses brand. They are responsible for greeting and checking in your customers, and so much more. Their role is crucial to the success of your dispensary.

Your business can live or die by the person who first greets your customers.

HIRING EMPLOYEES

When hiring, have you thought about the personality and character of this individual? Are you certain this person is outgoing and enjoys being around people? There are certain things you should look for when hiring this person.

Listed below are several key items to keep in mind when you are interviewing for your gatekeeper:

- Basic understanding of the marijuana industry and terminology.
- Open to working in a field that is controversial.
- Have an understanding of people's needs if they have a medical condition.
- Appearance is very important.
- Should have basic research skills.
- Outgoing, "people person."
- Should understand and be able to use all office equipment.
- Handle all phone calls.

167

- Desire to take charge.

- Understanding and ability to use the dispensary's software.

- Sales background.

- Willing to work full-time, including weekends.

- Capable of being your right-hand person.

- Capable of handling money.

- Trustworthy.

- Willing to manage.

When hiring your gatekeeper, be sure to ask:

- What type of computer skills do you have?

- Have you ever deposited money at a bank?

- Have you done credit card processing before?

- Are you able and capable of opening and closing the dispensary?

- Can you work weekends?

- What type of phone skills do you have?

- Do you understand and follow time management?

- Can you take a tough phone call?

- How do you handle people who are rude or upset?

- What kind of sales experience do you have?

- Do you understand the dangers of the job and procedures to follow if there is an emergency?

The most important factor with this hire is to make sure that person is a good communicator.

High turnover is often caused by not having the "right person for the right position." Often, dispensary owners or managers are hiring, but not taking the time for a proper interview due to an immediate opening at the front desk. To find the right person, get focused, get organized, and get prepared for the recruiting and interview process. First, you should plan on finding and interviewing several candidates, not just one or two.

The best way to recruit for this position is to find someone that already has good organizational and customer service skills. Keep your eyes and ears open for your next front desk person through your own customer service experiences. When it's time to interview, tailor the interview questions around the important duties of a front desk hire and break out this book for some reminders. Remember, the front desk is the first impression, the last impression, and often the *lasting* impression of what your customer remembers.

The people who "wow" you should work for you. Don't wait until you need someone! Interview often, even if you don't have an opening! This will improve your interview skills, keep qualified people on file, and also give you a backup plan if someone suddenly leaves.

A great resource in finding qualified help is to put an ad on Craigslist. Use keywords that people can identify with, such as dispensary, budtender, trimmer, manager, (not receptionist).

During the interview, make sure to explain all the sales responsibilities the front desk team has (listed above) and see how comfortable that person is while sitting in a chair to be interviewed. Are they fidgety? Shake their hand. Is It clammy? Do they interrupt you in a sentence so they can speak? This is a clear indication that this person is uncomfortable and nervous and may not be the person for you.

One interview technique involves handing your pen to the person you are interviewing. Using this performance-based interviewing technique will allow you to see how well they can describe the features and benefits of the pen and offer the sale of the pen to you. Plus, you'll be able to test and see how brave their sales skills really are! You will find, or eliminate, many candidates with this simple exercise. Try it!

Train, Track, and Reward

THE KEY TO RUNNING A SUCCESSFUL FRONT DESK is keeping your gatekeeper apprised of new laws and regulations that must be followed, as well as the owner's beliefs and expected business tactics. Without training, you can't expect this person to run and manage a successful front desk operation. Below are some of the key guidelines to running a dispensary front desk:

- Always be clean and organized.
- Make sure staff looks professional.
- Always have a smile.
- Always greet the patient by their first name and give them a big "hello, nice to see you."
- Make sure to ask patients how their service and experience was.
- Make sure you ask which products they would like to purchase. If they are purchasing products, ask if they understand how to use them.
- When products are sold, always ask if there is anything else they need; make suggestions.
- Have a proper POS system to run all your books, product sales, inventory, expected taxes, etc.
- Always keep track of records and receipts. Staying on top of things and not letting things go until tomorrow is key to front desk success.
- Keep up with all social media, such as emails, Facebook, Twitter and all the marijuana reference sites, such as www.*weedmaps.com* or www.*leafbuyer.com*.
- Most important: STAY CURRENT WITH ALL STATE AND CITY REGULATIONS.

―――

Each front desk professional should be trained on the products you offer. The ultimate way to train your front desk team is to have your vendors meet with them and educate them in their products. Create a thirty-day service training commitment for a new team member at the front desk. Make sure the budtenders and the front desk team member stay focused on your customers' needs about the products being sold. The front desk team member should take notes on the features and benefits of the products, how they affect the body, potency expectations to the customer, and recommended use. Finally, the team member should ask how they presently use the medication and recommend a proper dose. Remember, they are just budtenders, not doctors, and they can only recommend what they feel would be the proper dosage. It is up to the patient to handle his medicine as he would from a pharmacy.

Your front desk person should also be well scripted and well trained in what makes your dispensary "different" from the competition. Whether your dispensary is three thousand square feet or eight hundred square feet, a dispensary tour is a critical place to start with a new client. Your tour can take a customer on a walk through your dispensary, pointing out the wide range of products and medicine that you offer.

Implementing a goal and reward system is essential for motivating, tracking, and coaching the individuals on your front desk team. Each goal should reflect the principles and targets of growing the dispensary retail business through the front desk. The goals should be customized according to your current business trends, but be high enough to establish proper growth of your dispensary based on daily, weekly and monthly sales.

Implementing a goal system also requires the follow-through of a reward program. Rewards should be given monthly according to the accomplishment of the goals. They could be monetary or medicine, depending upon whether the front desk person has a prescription card. Usually they do, so you are able to reward your staff and save them money.

Dispensary owners or managers need to plan thirty-minute weekly or biweekly meetings with each individual on the front desk team. Review tracking and make suggestions on scripts or actions to teach front desk team members how to hit goals.

If you have regular dispensary team meetings (and monthly meetings are recommended for a healthy, strong team culture), don't forget to recognize the front desk efforts and successes at those meetings. You can refer to the tracking sheets to quantify the efforts the front desk has made in building the dispensary business. Acknowledge individual goals achieved and pass out rewards at the meeting.

Positive End Results: For You, Your Employees, and Your Customers

MARKETING, ADVERTISING, AND WORD OF MOUTH bring valuable people into your business daily. It takes an investment of time, energy, and money to market the dispensary, build your brand, and secure loyal customers. Once you have a new client, your team does their very best to give great customer service and cultivate and maintain a relationship. So why do so many dispensary owners hire someone without the background and skills to run and manage the front end of their business?

Most of the time, it's about the money and not thinking of the full scope of responsibilities at the front desk. Please keep in mind that you get what you pay for. Yes, this person will increase your overhead, but he or she will be worth it if you find the right person. It will also take time to train this person, but let's look at the upside. Your gatekeeper should grow into your right-hand person. In time, this is what they should be expected to do for you and your business:

- Answer phones.
- Develop patient relationships.
- Answer routine patient questions.
- Order supplies.
- Handle all credit and cash transactions.
- Input all new patients into the system.
- Manage all calls and vendors.
- Maintain and update all monthly required reports for the city and state.
- Maintain office supplies and toiletries.
- Handle all software updates and changes.
- Initiate and assist in product sales.
- Educate patients on products.
- Keep patients happy while waiting.
- Greet patients in a warm and friendly manner.
- Thank your clients when they arrive and when they leave.
- Allow you to oversee other parts of your business.

- Deal with routine matters.
- Process mail.
- Maintain and keep track of inventory on all levels.
- Order inventory when needed (if this is within the scope of his or her job).

As an employee grows into his or her position, the hours that you would normally spend doing the above-mentioned items should decrease dramatically. The freed-up time should be spent doing things that normally get put on the back burner, such as spending time in your garden and giving your patients great service while strengthening your relationship with them. The marijuana business is not easy. The hours are long and arduous and your success will be based on the people you hire. The front desk person should develop into a key person as your business continues to grow.

It's important to have continuous training and employee development. Either send your key people to marijuana trade shows or arrange education classes in your dispensary through your distributor or software company. Management and/or business classes at your local high school or college can also assist in developing key people in your dispensary. As the marijuana industry continues to evolve, the need for education of your staff will also continue to grow. Seminars and trade shows are starting to pop up all over the county. Having your gatekeeper attend these seminars would be money well spent.

The key thing is to stay focused on your goals— better serve patients, develop strong relationships with your clients and educate them professionally on services and medication. The right gatekeeper will make this possible.

SECTION VIII

THE GROW FACILITY

Grow Facility Checklist

THE FOLLOWING CHECKLIST will help make sure you have the essentials you will need for your grow facility.

- ○ Work gloves, shoes, aprons, hard hats
- ○ Protective eyewear
- ○ MSDS sheets
- ○ Cabinets, shelves
- ○ Plants
- ○ Nutrients, soil
- ○ Hoses, buckets, irrigation system, irrigation lines
- ○ Storage tanks, pumps
- ○ Flowering tables
- ○ Potting buckets
- ○ Hoods, ballasts
- ○ Adjustable light hangers
- ○ Grow light system
- ○ Drying racks, drying and curing containers
- ○ General bathroom and cleaning supplies
- ○ General office supplies, computers
- ○ Work tables
- ○ Cloning area with several growing methods (aero cloner)
- ○ Trim room, trimming machine
- ○ Certified scales
- ○ Curing nets
- ○ Safe
- ○ Security alarm system
- ○ Air conditioning system, ventilation, Canam filters
- ○ Waste cans

○ Light hanging grid system
○ Brooms, shovels, hand tools

Building Permits to Start Your Grow Facility

BUILDING PERMITS are the way counties, towns and municipalities enforce their building codes in order to ensure that all buildings meet minimum safety and structural standards. They are updated every few years as new building methods and materials are introduced. Subsequently, town ordinances, safety requirements and materials may also be new and restrictions may differ in each area. As of now, there is no standard permit process from state to state regarding marijuana grow facilities and dispensaries.

Here is a general overview of the process and some suggestions for making it run smoothly and quickly. While the municipalities are adapting to the new marijuana business model, they will be subject to changes from the state. These changes and modifications will be passed on to the inspectors, then to you. Expect delays, because the approval process can and will be an arduous task. This is also an expense you should account for when creating the costs in your business plan.

Difficulty: Hard

Time Required: The entire process from inception to an occupancy permit could be days to months. It really depends on a few factors:

- Your contractor and the building code inspectors.

- Timing will be crucial and making sure your paperwork is in proper order will result in a quicker turnaround and approval process.

DO YOUR HOMEWORK

1. Determine which type of permit you will need. If you are just doing minor repairs and painting/wallpapering/floor coverings for your building, you may not need a permit. For more complex types of construction, you will certainly need a permit. This would include new construction, additions, remodeling, tenant improvements, and changes in use, e.g., a change from an office to a professional retail use.

2. Read all you can about the building codes, zoning restrictions, and related local ordinances for the type of construction you will be doing. Even if you are planning to have a contractor do the work, be sure you know the restrictions and requirements. For example, be aware of setback restrictions—how close to the end of the property a building can be located. You don't want to start construction

and find out that your building is too close to the sidewalk or road! Also be aware of height restrictions for buildings, railings, and other structures.

3. Find a general contractor and draw up plans. If changes are being made to plumbing, electrical, and/or sewer/septic, additional permits may be needed. If you're doing the general contracting yourself, you will need to draw up the specifications yourself. You will also need inspections to show the municipality upon completion.

4. Prepare drawings and schematics and make several copies; the number you need may depend on the requirements of your locality. All drawings must be signed by a licensed contractor/architect. If your changes are minor, this requirement may not be necessary. If you are using a contractor, the contractor will arrange for the signatures on the drawings and schematics, such as plumbing, electrical, etc. You may also have to prepare land use and landscaping drawings and a general site plan, depending on the size and complexity of the changes.

5. If you need exterior signs, check your municipality's restrictions on size and placement before you order the signs. Some towns heavily regulate sign size, content, and placement, while others do not.

HOW TO GET A BUILDING PERMIT

Building permits are relatively easy to obtain. Call your city or town building department or check your town's website. If you live in a very rural area, contact the governing body that includes your rural area and find out who you should talk to.

WHAT TO PROVIDE YOUR CODE ENFORCEMENT OFFICER

It really depends on your municipality. Most towns require you provide a drawing and an estimate of the cost for the work that is going to be done in order to set up the production of your grow facility. Your drawings could be hand-sketched or could be a more formal architectural drawing, depending on the complexity of the project. The code enforcement officer can provide you with the requirements of your local municipality so you can get approval to operate as an ongoing business. Many times it is a simple two-part form. The applicant keeps one part and the code enforcement office retains the second part. The form will include information relevant for the town, a very brief description of your remodeling project, and a ballpark estimate of the cost of the project. If you are working with a contractor, the town may require that you attach a proposal from said contractor.

Remember, the code enforcement officer is your friend, not your enemy. You can call on your town's code enforcement officer anytime, not just when you are building something. They have the knowledge and expertise to help answer many of the remodeling questions you might have. Their salary is normally paid through your property taxes, so it's like free advice. Don't hire an extra consultant. Ask your code enforcement officer first.

The cost of the permit can be very minimal, depending on the work you are having done. For example, a permit in one town for a significant remodeling project costs approximately $100. The cost of a permit in your town may be based on the estimated cost of your project. The permit may be valid for as long as one year. Once you obtain the permit, tape it to your entry door or a window facing the street. This public display lets any neighbors or passersby know that you have obtained the necessary permit for the job you are doing and that the town you live in is aware of your remodeling project. Also, anyone who is interested can contact the code enforcement officer to find out the scope of your project.

What happens if your project runs long and you reach the expiration of your permit? Contact the code enforcement officer and ask for a renewal. If your project has experienced delays, the code enforcer may require you to apply for a renewal. The renewal cost is normally $25 and, again, this cost can vary from state to state, city to city.

The code enforcement officer in your town is there to serve you. Utilize his or her services for a safe, successful construction of your new business facility.

CONTRACTOR ASSISTANCE: WORTH IT!

As you can well imagine, building a dispensary and or grow facility will not be an easy undertaking. There is almost an infinite number of different circumstances where it might be required that you have a variety of building permits—it is literally impossible to list them all. Hiring the right contractor, one who is familiar with the necessary paperwork and permit processes in the town where you are opening your new business, will streamline the process. When you are hiring a contractor, there is going to be a part of the process where you both sign a contract. In that contract you should have it outlined that the contractor is responsible for obtaining and maintaining any and all required building permits, and that the failure to do so is going to result in the contractor footing the bill when it comes time to pay the fines.

Finally, before paying the contract, you should ask for a copy of any required inspection results. Making sure that everything is up to code is going to save you a huge headache, time, frustration, and added expenses later on when you try to open or expand your business. Because the marijuana business is so new, it is wise to have the local inspector and municipality on your side and in favor of your business. This will only help you down the road. Follow the guidelines, do your homework, get to know your inspector, and abide by the municipality's rules and regulations.

Regardless of your initiative, or your timing, or your finances, unless you're committed to navigating the labyrinth of statutes, regulations, and ordinances governing the licensing and operation of a medical /recreational marijuana grow facility and dispensary, you will not succeed.

Curing Your Harvest

THERE ARE MANY METHODS TO DRY AND CURE PLANTS, and how marijuana dries depends on the strain. Some dry tight and hard, others dry soft and fluffy. There are many ways of drying your plant and each has its good points and solid methods. The following tips are for the "trimming dry" method:

- Create an adequate indoor drying space and equip it with racks similar to what tobacco farmers use to dry their crops. These racks hang from the ceiling and are very easy to install. They are made of a fine, silk-like material with holes that allow airflow to all of your marijuana plants. There are usually four to five tiers (shelves) to accommodate drying large amounts at one time. They are about five feet around so you will need some space to adequately allow proper ventilation.

- Keep the humidity between 50-60 percent. Keep the temperature at about 60-70 degrees F. (15-21 degrees C.). The room should be relatively dark, because light, especially direct sunlight, degrades THC.

- Remove all fan leaves before you hang your plant. Removing large leaves and stems upon harvest saves time. This is what most growers do, because fresh, supple leaves are easier to work with than dry leaves. But the large fan leaves do serve an important purpose during the plant's growth. They serve as photosynthetic factories for the production of sugars and other necessary growth substances. Most cannabis plants begin to lose their larger leaves when they enter the flowering stage, and this trend continues on until senescence (death of the plant). At the time of harvest, these leaves are trimmed and discarded. Some companies buy fan leaves to produce product, but pay such a small amount (on a competitive market) that it does not pay to separate them.

- Hang your plant upside down in a cool, dark place and let it dry until the buds snap off cleanly (as opposed to just bending) when you put pressure on them. Rough handling and friction from fondling hands will bruise and knock off resin glands. Even with proper drying and curing, brutal handling of harvested marijuana will diminish THC content.

- Depending on the size of the drying room, you may break down the plant by branches and then hang it for drying. Try to keep plants from touching each other to avoid uneven drying and mold.

- Let the plants hang for about three days or until the outsides of the buds begin to feel dry. When you gently squeeze the buds, you should be able to feel that they are still soft and moist in the middle.

- Once the drying process is complete, remove all the buds from the plant, then clip and manicure the remaining leaves. Remove all of the remaining true leaves from all of the branches. There's no right way to do this—a firm tug on each leaf stalk might be one person's preferred method, while clipping might be another's. The leftover leaves are referred to as "overtrim," or "shake." This is a great source for making extracts such as wax, shatter, and oil for vapor pens. Bubble hash is another byproduct that can be made. All of these byproducts can become an extra revenue stream for your business. The dispensary section of this book gives more details about retail products. Place the buds in an air-tight container and leave them in a cool, dark place. Ideal curing time is over a month, but many of you may not have that luxury. Good curing takes about two weeks. Open the container once a day for six to twelve hours, depending on how fast you want to cure, and let it get some air ventilation. Make sure you release any moisture. Each day, check your product and bag it properly when you feel it is finally cured.

The "trimming wet" method is handled differently. Here are some tips for this style of trimming:

- Cut the plant from its "rootball" and hang it upside down next to the trimmer in the "trim area."

- The trimmer must remove all fan leaves first.

- Take your shears and break apart the plant in branches. Set these branches in a basket for easy access to trim.

- Take one branch at a time, clip off the bud and trim the "sugar leaves." A sugar leaf is the leaf coming from the bud that will look like it has "sugar" on it. They are usually found directly under the bud. Make sure you have a tray below your trimming spot to catch those leaves. They will be used for other products mentioned above.

- Now that you have trimmed all the leaves off, you are ready to begin the curing process. Place the product in nets for three to five days, depending on the density of the product. Make sure the room has good fan circulation and low humidity. We recommend that it is in a secure part of your facility.

- After this time period, you are ready to transfer the product into an airtight container for final curing. The time period for curing varies, depending on the strain.

- A good way to tell that your product is ready is when the stem on the "bud" snaps. If it bends and does not break, then it's not ready.

NOTE

Drying and curing cannabis properly will yield the most THC-potent smoke. When dried and cured improperly, potency can diminish substantially. The level of THC in a plant is determined by its genetics. Proper drying and curing will keep the THC level as high as genetically possible.

The Growing Cycle

AS HARVEST TIME APPROACHES, begin reaching into the live plant and removing all the dead and dying big fan leaves from the branches. A gentle tug, sometimes firm, is all that's required. During the last month or so of a plant's development, gardeners/growers remove the big "fan leaves" as they begin turning yellow. Cleaning these leaves, especially at the bottom of the plant will give a better opportunity for the lower buds to get better sunlight and grow bigger.

Most new gardeners/growers tend to harvest their plants too early because of excitement or not understanding when the product is ready. Your buds will gain about 25% of their final size in the last two weeks, so it's important to try to be patient and wait until the right time. Buds that are harvested too early usually have low THC content because the trichomes have not developed enough. As the buds mature, they start producing chemicals which will create the type of medicine patients are looking for.

There are many methods of production, but your garden size may dictate how you grow and maintain your plants. In a small garden, you may not have the luxury of growing your vegetative plants to great heights because of your rotation process. These factors have the greatest impact on total time it takes to factor in plant life and rotation:

- Plant strain (strain has the biggest impact on growing time)
- Desired yields (do you want to grow a few grams, a few ounces, or a few pounds?)
- Growing method (differing grow methods/setups can add or subtract a few weeks)

For most plants from seed to harvest, you should expect approximately fifteen weeks.

One thing is for sure, maintaining your plant, manicuring it properly and paying attention to detail should lead you to some good, healthy plants. Below are some tips to look for when a plant is ready for harvest:

- There are many methods to determine the right time to harvest your plant. Basically, you want to harvest when 50-75% of the white pistils/hairs have turned amber/brown.
- Another way to tell is when the trichomes (also known as crystals or resin glands) are either all white/milky or half white and half amber.
- Look at the leaf structure; they should be wilting because of nutrient deficiency. You should be "flushing" the plant at this point, which simply means to water it deeply.

After watering, use a shovel to dig into the soil (away from the root system), to see moisture levels three to four inches below the surface. If it's dry at this depth, your plant's roots are not getting enough water.

- Dry soil is by far the most common cause of plants wilting.

- The buds should have a popcorn look with hairs sticking out of it.

Here is the number one question asked about growing marijuana: How long does it take to grow? On average, a grow cycle from seed to harvest will run 4 months with a curing cycle of another 2-3 weeks.

Here is a breakdown to give you an idea of what happens during those 4 months.

BIRTH OF A PLANT

From a seed, it will take 5-10 days for it to germinate. From that point, it is transferred to ½ gallon pot for a 2-4 week period while the roots take hold. Now it's time for another transfer to either a 5 or 10 gallon pot, all depending on the structure of your garden. The time factor for this stage is another 2-4 weeks. This all depends on how long you have the luxury to grow your vegetation plants. Growing a "larger vegetation plant" will in general give you a larger yield. You need to look at how quickly you need to turn your product. Once you feel your plant is ready to go into flowering, add another 60 days before you can start harvesting. Now you have an idea of the time frame to harvest plants. Ten gallon pots will give you 4 plants per light, where 5 gallon pots can give you 6 plants per light.

All of the tips listed above will help you maintain your plants and will better educate you on when they are ready for harvest.

GROW LIGHTS

Grow lights are one of the most essential elements in your grow facility; these lights are responsible for the growth, aroma, quality and quantity of your harvest. Grow lights are not going to be cheap, no matter which type you choose. Even if you install them yourself, which is not recommended unless you are an expert in grow lights, the cost will be substantial. Hiring the right gardener/grower who is well educated in the grow light system is an investment that will pay dividends far down the road.

Each light produces different results, so your gardener/grower must be diligent in doing their homework. Together you can make a sound business decision about which grow light source to use.

There are more than three types of lighting used to grow marijuana indoors:

- **LED:** Light-Emitting Diode is a two-lead semiconductor light source that resembles a basic pn-junction diode, except that an LED also emits light. LEDs can be adjusted to fit a particular light spectrum. Produces four crops per year.

- **Induction:** The internal electrode-less lamp, or induction light, is a gas discharge lamp in which the power required to generate light is transferred from outside the lamp envelope to the gas inside via an electric or magnetic field. Produces four crops per year.

- **Sunlight:** Natural source of heat and light in a greenhouse structure. Alternate light must be employed on cloudy days and can produce more than one harvest with assisted lighting. You can create a combined artificial environment with natural lighting and save on energy consumption.

Under artificial light (sodium halide, lep, lec and other new technologies) the plant typically remains under 16-20 hours of light and 4-8 hours of darkness from germination until flowering. This process is used while the plants are in the vegetative stage. When the plants go into the flowering stage, the timing is 12 hours on and 12 hours off; however, times vary for the actual harvesting time cycle of different strains. There is an ongoing debate over the importance of the "dark period," which has yet to be resolved. It has been shown that, when subjected to constant light without a dark period, most types of flora, including Cannabis, will begin to show signs of decreased photosynthetic response, lack of vigor, and an overall decrease in vascular development. Photosynthesis is the process by which plants and other things make food. It is a chemical process that uses sunlight to turn carbon dioxide into sugars the plant can use as energy.

NOTE

High-pressure sodium lamps are used both indoors and outdoors. Many plant enthusiasts and greenhouse owners opt to have high-pressure sodium lamps installed because the spectrum of light emitted by them is known to encourage plant growth.

Ensure that your contractor/architect creates a space that has adequate room to install the required lighting. Make sure that the plant leaves are all strongly lit and receiving enough light. You will need a high pressure sodium bulb for the initial growth and a different duration for the light cycle: 18 light/6 dark for the vegetation and 12 light/12 dark during the flowering stages.

SETTING UP YOUR GROW LIGHTS

- Your light fixtures should start out a little higher than the height of your pots, leaving room so they can be raised to be above the final height of your plants. There are various ways to set up or hang the lights and you will need to do what works for your grow area. The simplest method is to either hang them from a bar or clamp the lights onto a rod that is suspended at the proper height. Remember any excess light that doesn't hit your plants is wasted light and will increase the cost to your energy bill.

- Make sure your lights are producing at least the minimum, and preferably the ideal, amount of lumens per square foot. A lumen is a unit of the total amount of visible light emitted by a specific source. Therefore, it's helpful to talk about how many lumens a source emits, as well as how many lumens your growing operation needs. On an average day, the sun emits about 5,000 to 10,000 lumens per square foot.

- The absolute minimum needed to grow average-sized plants is around 3,000 lumens per square foot. The actual amount of lumens that reach the bottom of your plant will fluctuate depending on the distance of the light source and the reflectivity of the surroundings.

- The ideal amount for a standard grow operation is somewhere between 7,000 and 10,000 lumens per square foot.

- To figure out how many lumens per square foot you're working with, simply divide the total lumens by the total square feet of your growing space. Say you're working with two 300-watt CFL*, each with 40,000 lumens, in a 3' x 3' area. Your total lumens are 80,000 and your total square footage is 9', so 80,000 ÷ 9 = 8,888 lumens per square foot.

  *CFL is compact fluorescent light bulb, an energy-saving, long-life fluorescent light bulb that fits into a standard light bulb socket. The tube is filled with a gas that emits light when an electrical charge is applied.

Be careful that you don't burn or overheat your plants with your light source. Having sufficient light will help your marijuana grow tall and healthy. The ideal temperature for your grow operation is somewhere between 72° F and 78° F (if you have CO2, these temperatures are 5 degrees higher) with 90° F being the maximum temperature the plant will tolerate. If your temperature is anywhere below this, consider adding a small heater to generate additional heat. If your temperature is anywhere above this, a fan and additional ventilation may need to be added to help provide the perfect growing conditions.

A timer to make your lights go on and off when you want is a necessity. You can get a cheap one for $5 or spend up to $30 getting a nice digital one. You don't necessarily need one to start, but you will need one by the time the plants begin to flower at about one month along. A higher quality timer can be incorporated into the "hard wiring lines" to your lights during buildout. This small investment will ensure that your lights turn off and on properly. It only takes one week to damage your harvest if just one of your lights stays on while the plants are "sleeping."

Proper ventilation is absolutely necessary for vibrant plants. If your grow room is in a small space, there's not much more that you can do other than use an oscillating fan to keep the temperature below 80° F. In a larger space, however, adding a duct system is efficient for many growers.

COSTS FOR YOUR GLOW LIGHT SYSTEM

The majority of growers are turning from induction lighting to LED. Do your homework before you make this decision and while figuring this cost into your business plan. The following grow light information was courteously provided by BlackDog LED—www.BlackDogLED.com.

Have you ever wondered what the total cost of setting up and running a traditional High Intensity Discharge (HID) garden is compared to a garden set up with the newest Light-Emitting Diode (LED) technology? We wanted to know exactly what an LED grow light versus HID would look like, so Black Dog LED ran the numbers. The short answer is that using LED lights becomes less expensive quickly. Black Dog LED compared an HID-lit garden that used two 1000w Metal Halide (MH) bulbs for vegetative growth and two 1000w High Pressure Sodium (HPS) bulbs for flowering versus a garden lit with two Black Dog LED Platinum XL lights.

For the sake of simplicity and to make sure this applied to everyone, we only included the cost of bulbs, ballasts, sealed reflectors, and fans/ducting in this research. We did NOT include the cost of air conditioning for the HID garden because this will vary from slightly expensive to very expensive depending on climate and time of year. If we had included air conditioning, it would make LED grow light versus HID lighting even more cost effective in less time.

Review the following graphs and then make your own informed decision as to which grow light system is best for your facility.

Scenar-ios	HPS Bulb Change	MH Bulb Change	LED Bulb Change	Veg. Hours On/Off	Flower Hours On/Off	Initial Cost	Cost at 12 Months	Cost at 24 Months	Cost at 48 Months
Black Dog LED	N/A	N/A	None	20/4	12/12	$3,458	$4,341	$5,225	$6,991
Optimal	6 Months	12 Months	None	20/4	12/12	$2,305	$4,619	$6,933	$12,039
Econom-ical	12 Months	18 Months	None	20/4	12/12	$2,305	$3,881	$5,935	$9,566

BLACK DOG LED PLATINUM XL RUNNING TOTAL

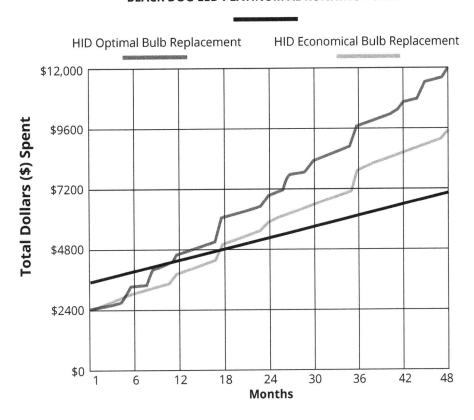

HID Optimal Bulb Replacement   HID Economical Bulb Replacement

Soil and Your Marijuana Plants

GETTING INVOLVED WITH THE MARIJUANA INDUSTRY and finally getting approval from the state and city council to open was a momentous task. You are now ready to set up your indoor garden and plant your prized crop. Your first thought is to run down to Home Depot, rent a truck, and get some soil to start the task of planting your marijuana right?

When it comes to potting plants, dirt is dirt, right? Actually, this common misconception can result in the poor health and inferior quality of your indoor plants. Knowing the correct type of soil for your marijuana plants, along with the proper soil preparation, is the key to gorgeous, healthy, marijuana crops. Big, healthy crops mean big profits, so choosing the correct soil is just another process you must learn in the marijuana business.

SOIL FACTS

Most bagged soil mixes are peat-based mixes, often made with reed or sedge peat, and pH adjusted with lime. They are rich and loamy fresh out of the bag, and often they are enhanced with fertilizer or water-retention crystals. If you've been gardening for a long time, though, I'm sure you've noticed that plants rarely thrive in these kinds of soils for very long. Instead, after a growing season—or maybe even two—the plant no longer grows as fast or looks as vibrant. With some poorer quality bagged soils, plants are lucky to survive a few months. Quality marijuana plants need quality soil.

The soil will be in many respects both the home and the food for your marijuana plants, so it should be taken seriously. Many veteran growers develop their own mixtures of raw soil, nutrients and absorptive material, but when you're starting out, it's best to find some commercial potting soil.

Soil character is specified by the ratio of three elemental components: nitrogen, phosphorous and potassium, usually written N:P:K. Marijuana likes to grow in a soil that is rich in nitrogen, so find a soil with a higher N value and lower P and K values. A typical good ratio is 20:10:10. The growing requirements of marijuana are nearly identical to the growing requirements of tomatoes. If you are purchasing growing supplies from a store in which the staff is not knowledgeable in cannabis growing, you can ask for advice regarding growing tomatoes to the same effect.

Many people prefer using organic soil for growing marijuana, but as long as it has the appropriate N:P:K ratio, good acidity, and enough plant food to feed the plant for three months, it should work fine. Another ideal characteristic is if the soil protects against over and under watering. Some soil manufacturers include materials that take care of this. While it is still very important to control your watering, this will help provide you with a margin for error.

For a slightly more advanced choice, you can go with a good organic soil medium and carefully mix in some organic nutrients for a proper growing environment. If you decide to go with this organic soil and nutrient solution for your marijuana grow, make sure you carefully follow the nutrient mixture and watering schedule. Thinking "more is always better" will result in you burning your plants and possibly compromising your marijuana harvest. The benefits of using these more advanced methods will be a possibly more robust harvest. The drawbacks are more work and more margin for error.

Organic soil is the most common soil used by indoor growers today, but their supply can be limited or difficult to order, and may be more expensive than organic soils.

One last word on soil: there are as many recipes for the perfect soil as there are cannabis growers. You can find enough variations of peat moss, Perlite, vermiculite, bat guano, bone meal, kelp, ash, worm castings and buried dead fish carcasses to write a small novel. The fact is that optimizing your grow soil to this degree is going way beyond the work versus reward ratio. Start out small and basic and then decide to work on highly optimizing your soil in your own small increments.

> **GROWING TIP**
>
> **Organic gardeners use their own compost prepared from a mixture of chicken, cow or other manure and household food waste, leaves, lawn clippings, dog hair, and other waste products, including urine, which is high in nitrogen.**

Reasons why cannabis is most often grown in organic soils:

- The soils produce a rich, earthy flavor with noticeable differences.

- The taste and flavor is unique, pungent, and prevalent. THC crystal content is always high.

- Those two facts reduce the growing work load. Organic marijuana is more resistant to disease.

The cannabis burns clean when grown with no pesticides in an organic environment. The taste and flavor tends to be unique, pungent, prevalent and flavorful. The THC crystal content is also higher.

ADVANCED NUTRIENT OPTIONS

Now that you have your high-quality organic soil, you are going to have to also add some high-quality organic nutrients to your watering schedule. Again, FoxFarm, for example, provides a good choice for high quality nutrients needed to grow marijuana (TGA, Nectar of the Gods #4). They have a three-step organic-based fertilizer and plant food liquid nutrients system. To use these products, simply mix with correct ratio of water and use for your watering cycle in every other plant watering. Have one watering jug filled with clean water, while the other contains the proper nutrients mixture. Each type of nutrient should be added at different ratios during different weeks of the plant's development. Also, be sure when adding nutrients to the water that you never mix any two nutrients together, even if they both should be used at the same time. Always add the nutrients to the water separately. Do not mix nutrients together in their pure forms—they must be diluted or nutrient lockout can occur.

The Grow: How to Get Started

THERE ARE THREE TYPES OF GARDENS TO CONSIDER when cultivating your product.

1. An indoor garden.
2. A greenhouse.
3. Outdoor growing. Yes, a few jurisdictions may allow this.

The first two methods are the most common, but a few municipalities do allow growing marijuana outdoors. Our focus will be geared more toward the indoor garden, where you completely control the environment. You control water, light, temperature, ventilation, humidity, carbon dioxide, and soil nutrients to provide your plants with optimum conditions. While outdoor seeds are generally limited to one growing season, indoors you can create a semitropical climate that will support multiple harvests. Understand that increased plant activity, from planting and propagation to cultivation and harvest, results in increased maintenance. The reward for your extra work, however, can be a greater yield in less time and space than a traditional outdoor garden.

When growing marijuana indoors, you are attempting to recreate a natural environment that your plants are going to need to thrive. The following are things that you should consider throughout construction and setup of your grow operation.

Once you create a great environment, you should be able to grow in outer space!

CHOOSING YOUR SPACE

In previous sections, we mentioned how to find your indoor grow space and where you might have to look. The amount of space you want to take may dictate the amount of capital you have to spend and limit how much you can produce. This is also a very large commitment as far as rent. Planning is very important and your financial means will play a big role in your survival in this new industry. These decisions in the beginning are very important.

What size grow facility do you start with? From what we talked about before, your electrical power and AC tonnage are important decisions in choosing the right location, as well as your rent. The real question is, what size square footage do I take? How much can I afford? How deep are my pockets? The garden startup is very expensive and the difference in a few thousand feet can mean hundreds of thousands of dollars of capital outlay. Discussions in this book are for grow facilities in the 2,500 to 10,000 square feet range. If it is anything larger than 10,000 square feet, there may be other requirements from your local municipality that you must comply with, such as where the facility can be located, odor regulations, etc.

These larger facilities are definitely held to very strict, rigid standards. If operating one, you would want to make sure that everything that the state and local officials are telling you as a business owner would remain absolutely in compliance so that you can remain in business.

An indoor grow facility must be divided up to handle all levels of production, from seed to harvest. These areas include:

- Seed and propagation area
- Vegetation room
- Flowering room
- Trimming area
- Curing room
- Security section
- Storage area

NOTE

The state will have standard regulations impacting marijuana grow facilities, but the city can do what they want and make their own rules. The city can ban it or accept the state regulations. Therefore, your municipality will be the point of contact for this information.

Each one of the three different-sized areas listed above must allocate a certain percentage of area for effective production. Some listed above don't take much room but must be considered. We have divided and combined them into percentages:

25% - 30%	Vegetation, transplanting, cloning and mother plant area
65%	Flowering area
10%	Trimming, curing, security and storage

Some of these areas vary in percentages, all depending on the shape of the location. If there are tall ceilings, you may be able to rack certain areas and take advantage of the height. Breaking down the percentages will give you a basic idea of how much production you will be harvesting, which in turn will give you approximate revenue projections.

Look at the 65% flowering area and see how much room you would have:

Original Sq. Ft.	Percentage flowering	Flowering area
2500	65%	1625
5000	65%	3250
10,000	65%	6500

Now that you have established a flowering area, you can figure out how many lights you have to work with. The shape of your space will determine the exact number of lights, but for now you can use an approximate amount to see how much revenue can be produced. The distance between lights can vary depending on the growing method. The following chart illustrates how much product can be produced from an average number of lights.

YIELD PER MONTH AT A 60-DAY CYCLE		
Flowering area	**Number of lights**	**Yield per light at .5 lbs.**
1625	45	11.25 lbs.
3250	90	22.5 lbs.
6500	135	45 lbs.
		Yield per light at 1.0 lbs.
1625	45	22.5 lbs.
3250	90	45 lbs.
6500	135	90 lbs.
		Yield per light at 1.5 lbs.
1625	45	33.75 lbs.
3250	90	67.5 lbs.
6500	135	101.25 lbs.
		Yield per light at 2.0 lbs.
1625	45	45 lbs.
3250	90	90 lbs.
6500	135	135 lbs.

The above numbers indicate The above numbers represent running at full capacity. When you get started, you may be limited on how many plants you can grow. In many states "the caregiver model" is based on a patient deciding not to grow their own plants and allowing a dispensary operation to grow for them. Now the dispensary has the right to grow for the patient. In Colorado, most patients are allowed to grow six plants, so if a dispensary has one hundred patients, then they are allowed to grow six hundred plants in vegetation and flowering. It is important to check with your state and municipality and find out in the beginning if there are exemptions on how much you can grow to get started. If not, you are limited to how many patients sign over their plants for you to grow. In the beginning, patients will be limited because of the lack of doctors writing prescriptions for them. All of this takes time, from growing the plants to gaining patients, so having the proper capital is very important.

FACT

Beer and marijuana are cousins. Beer's hops are in the same family of flowering plants as marijuana.

Below are some revenue projections. Prices of marijuana will fluctuate depending on market conditions. In the beginning, with competition limited, it will be on the higher side. Prices are based on the Colorado industry to the end user over the last twenty-four months. These numbers will help formulate your business plan.

YIELD PER MONTH AT A 60-DAY CYCLE			PRICE / POUND (AVG. RETAIL PRICE)		
Flowering area	**No. of lights**	**Yield per light at .5 lbs.**	**$3,000**	**$4,000**	**$5,000**
1625	45	11.25 lbs.	$33,750	$45,000	$56,250
3250	90	22.5 lbs.	$67,500	$90,000	$112,500
6500	135	45 lbs.	$135,000	$180,000	$225,000
		Yield per light at 1.0 lbs.			
1625	45	22.5 lbs.	$67,500	$90,000	$112,500
3250	90	45 lbs.	$135,000	$180,000	$225,000
6500	135	90 lbs.	$270,000	$360,000	$450,000
		Yield per light at 1.5 lbs.			
1625	45	33.75 lbs.	$101,250	$135,000	$168,750
3250	90	67.5 lbs.	$202,500	$270,000	$337,500
6500	135	101.25 lbs.	$303,750	$405,000	$506,250
		Yield per light at 2.0 lbs.			
1625	45	45 lbs.	$135,000	$180,000	$225,000
3250	90	90 lbs.	$270,000	$360,000	$450,000
6500	135	135 lbs.	$405,000	$540,000	$675,000

These figures can give you an idea of the revenue you should be able to produce and can be used to base some informal cash flow projections.

Startup Costs for Your Garden

- Lease deposits: first, last and security
- Licensing: state and city fees
- Equipment: hoods, ballasts, bulbs, garden tables, wall fans
- Construction: air conditioning, electric, plumbing, grid system for light installation
- Startup supplies: nutrients, soil, etc.
- Ventilation system
- CO2 system
- Security system and safe
- Computer system
- Irrigation system
- Insulating and sealing your indoor environment
- Seed propagation
- Liquidity
- Employee expense

Now that you have put this all together, you will need to wait four months on average for the plants to harvest. In the meantime, you are paying rent and staff, so be prepared to have the capital to cover this in the beginning. You may be able to buy from other dispensaries that have surplus, but in the beginning it will be a waiting game, since everyone is starting their garden at the same time.

NOTE

Seeds and clones—there are many online companies where you can buy your starter seeds and clones. We recommend doing your homework. Buying and transporting seeds and clones from state to state is illegal!

A CLOSER LOOK AT YOUR STARTUP COSTS

    1. Lease deposits. Your first, last and security can add up. On a small scale, a lease is $5,000 per month. So immediately you are laying out $15,000 to sign the lease. Then there are architects plans, permitting and construction which will probably take six months to complete. Add another four months for your harvest and you have now paid $50,000 in rent before you have harvested a plant. Startup $65,000.

2. **Licensing.** State fees for a dispensary and grow start at $6,200 and the local municipality usually has the same fees. Startup $12,400 minimum.

3. **Equipment.** For a small garden with a forty-five flowering light operation, your lighting priced out is basic HPS lighting for this exercise. If you decide to use induction or LED lighting, the cost will rise significantly. Startup $30,000.

4. **Construction.**

   - **Air conditioning.** A simple formula to use is one ton for every four vented lights you are running. For a forty-five light operation, ten tons of AC (min.) is recommended for flowering, and another five tons for your vegetation and the rest of your space. This does not include an AC unit for cooling the lights. This will be needed in certain states. Total of fifteen plus tons. Startup $25,000.

   - **Dehumidifer.** Can be built into AC unit from the factory. Startup $2,500.

   - **Electric.** No telling what your location may have. Basing cost on previous experience. Startup $20,000.

   - **Grid system to hang the lights.** Your warehouse is usually too high to hang lights directly from the ceiling, so a grid system is put up to support all the ballasts and lights. Startup $4,000.

   - **Plumbing, irrigation system, and water storage tanks** $5,000.

   - **Drywall and miscellaneous construction** $5,000.

   - **Ductwork.** This is needed to keep all the lights cool. Startup $5,000.

5. **Startup supplies.** When you begin your garden you will need, pots, soil, flood trays, nutrients, cloning trays. There are one hundred different ways to grow and you will need supplies in the beginning to fit your growing needs. Startup $5,000.

6. **Ventilation system.** This is considered the ductwork discussed in construction.

7. **CO2 system.** Not much upfront cost, usually tank rental, regulators and some hosing. Startup $1,000.

8. **Security system.** You will need a system that has a lot of memory and cameras. It needs to be in a secure place. Startup $3,500.

9. **Safe.** Startup $1,500.

10. **Computer with internet capability,** $750.

11. **Irrigation system.** This is mentioned under construction.

12. **Sealing your environment.** This will be insulating your warehouse, sealing all cracks, blacking out all possible light leaks. Startup $1,500.

13. **Seed propagation.** Investing on good genetics to start your garden. Startup $2,500.

14. Liquidity. Have backup money ready to go. Banks won't finance your business. YOU ARE THE BANK!

15. Garden staff expense $20,000.

TOTAL STARTUP - $209,650

SECTION IX

THE "REALLY BIG SHOW"—YOUR DISPENSARY

Dispensary Checklist

THE FOLLOWING CHECKLIST will help make sure you have all the essentials you will need for your dispensary.

- ◯ Signs: Name, address of business, and hours of operation. All posted signs that meet regulatory requirements.
- ◯ Reception: Computer, phone, internet, fax machine, copier, desk, chairs, file cabinets.
- ◯ Clear glass buzz-in door. Many locations have bars on the interior of the entrance door.
- ◯ Décor: Photos, murals, posters, etc.
- ◯ General office supplies.
- ◯ General bathroom supplies.
- ◯ General cleaning supplies.
- ◯ Business cards.
- ◯ Display frames for all licenses and permits.
- ◯ Display cases.
- ◯ Locked refrigeration unit for edibles.
- ◯ POS system. Colorado requires Marijuana Inventory Tracking System (MITS), which tracks product from seed to harvest.
- ◯ Inventory: marijuana, hashish oil, extracts, wax, edibles, water pipes, glass pipes, papers, rolling machines, etc.
- ◯ Storage containers.
- ◯ Salves, tinctures, sodas, juices.
- ◯ Product containers, baggies, vials, child-resistant containers.
- ◯ Pricing board.
- ◯ Cash register.
- ◯ Safe.

NOTE

Your state may require that your dispensary have a consultation room.

○ Security system.
○ HVAC system.
○ Ventilation system.

The Name Game

SELECTING THE RIGHT NAME FOR YOUR DISPENSARY can make a real difference in attracting your ideal clientele—the kind with money to spend. The name you choose should reflect a number of things: who you are, what you believe in, the kind of products you sell. Above all, it should give a first-time visitor an idea of what to expect and encourage him/her to come inside and explore.

Your initial instinct might be to give your dispensary a jokey name, like Stonerz or Toker's Paradise. Keep in mind, though, that your customer base will be made up of all sorts of people, from seniors seeking relief for chronic pain to returning veterans suffering from PTSD. Your name should convey that your dispensary stands for more than just a good time; it represents healing, wellness, nature. Lean toward something professional—and inviting—that will appeal not only to the teenagers with fake IDs, but to a variety of buyers. Think Hemp, Green Health, Bright Leaf Cooperative. With these considerations in mind, here are some quick tips for choosing a business name that works for your small business venture in a web-savvy world.

CHOOSE A BUSINESS NAME THAT MAKES SENSE

Before you pick the first name that springs to mind, think about how your name will be used. If you are simply starting out as a small dispensary, it's very easy to just operate your business under your personal name. But if you anticipate being in business for the long haul, you might want to consider a business trade name that can develop with you. Also, depending on the name that you choose, there may be a point in time that you want to sell your marijuana business. If your business name was not well thought out and bears your first or last name or something reflecting a Cheech and Chong movie, the possibility and ask price may reflect you not being able to sell for "BIG" money. Here are some points to consider:

Imagine how the potential name will:

- Look (on business cards, website, advertisements, with a logo).
- Sound (ease of pronunciation).
- Be remembered (positive or negative connotations the name may evoke).
- Distinguish you from competitors (avoid trademark infringements).
- Easily incorporate into a company logo.
- Look on the sign outside of your dispensary.

- Look on shirts, hats, banners, the side of your truck or in a magazine ad or newspaper.
- Make a positive impression.
- Bring your brand to life.
- Affect your new landlord—will he turn you down because of the name you choose?
- Make the community feel about your business.
- Affect how law enforcement, tax officials, and other authority figures perceive your business' name.

You may want to avoid:

- Embarrassing spellings, abbreviations, profanities, potentially offensive undertones.
- Implied associations with organizations/people the business is not connected with.

CHOOSE A NAME THAT WORKS ON THE WEB

Since we live in an online world, take time to research whether your business name is Web ready. Consider the following:

- **Conduct a domain name search.** This will help you identify whether you can actually set up a website with a web address (domain name) that is clearly affiliated with your business. You can do a quick domain name search in the WHOIS database. You can also check GoDaddy.com to see if the name is available. It will let you know whether your preferred domain name, (e.g. www.herbalhemphh1.com), is available for use or not. If it is available, you can claim it as yours early in the business naming process, long before you get around to creating a website. If the domain name has already been claimed, you may need to revisit your name idea. Read *Tips on Choosing a Good Domain Name* from www.thesitewizard.com.

- **Is your business name email friendly?** For the purposes of setting up a business email, consider whether your chosen business name is memorable and easy to spell. You may even want to consider abbreviating your company name to an acronym for email purposes. Also, if you or future employees have long names, determine whether your email naming policy will include first and last names (johndoe@herbalhemphh1.com), first initial and last name (jdoe@herbalhemphh1.com) or simply first names (john@herbalhemphh1.com).

- **Is your business name social media ready?** In addition to checking the availability of your business name as a potential domain name, take time to conduct a search of Twitter and Facebook to ensure that no other businesses or brands are operating in the social networking world with the same, or a similar, name.

Naming a business is a lot like laying the cornerstone of a building. Once it's in place, the entire foundation and structure is aligned to that original stone. If it's off, even just a bit, the rest of the building is off, and the misalignment becomes amplified. Your name is the embryo of your company. What follows after your name is born is the creation of your business. A well thought-out name doesn't guarantee success, but it does give you the branding and much more to promote and build your organization. Let's take a look at some names that are good, bad, and ugly.

How should you go about choosing a name? First, find a quiet room, a thesaurus, and a writing pad, and section off a few hours of your day. Think about the feelings you want to evoke in people when they hear about your dispensary. Use the thesaurus to find related words or phrases.

Once you've jotted down a list, try experimenting with combinations of words and phrases. Say each one out loud. How do you feel when you hear them? Cross off any you don't love.

When you've narrowed down the choices to your favorite few, share them with family and friends. Gauge their gut reactions to each one.

Finally, check online for available domain names. You'll want at least a few options in case your top pick is already taken.

Remember: have fun with the process! You're branding a company that will be part of your life for a long time—a business you're excited to share with the world. It's a great place to be!

The Distinctive Dispensary

WHAT MAKES YOUR DISPENSARY DIFFERENT than others in your area is up to you. Everyone thinks they have the best ideas when it comes to being unique. The fact is, most ideas have been done already. Yes, being the best dispensary in town and having a great staff is very important, but how you market your dispensary to set yourself apart from others, attract new clients, and keep them coming back is one of the most important elements of creating a successful marijuana business.

How will you create the experience and the environment that people are looking for? Most are looking for a place that combines a multiple of different things: safety first, outstanding customer service, professionalism, and a vibe that makes them feel at home—or relaxed enough to make a large purchase. Your store should emanate an atmosphere where a customer can relax, unwind, and confidently enjoy the ultimate buying experience in the area.

In the beginning, you must determine what you can do to provide standout service that keeps your clients happy and coming back, yet doesn't cost too much. As your business grows, you will be able to spend more on the other ideas and marketing that will be a bit more expensive.

SIMPLE & INEXPENSIVE WAYS TO KEEP CLIENTS HAPPY

- Welcome clients when they come into your dispensary.
- Provide different types of magazines for your clients.
  - Suggestions: Magazines that are related to the industry, such as High Times. Once your industry opens up in your state, there will be new magazines that spring up. In Colorado, you have Chronic, The Daily Doobie, The Rooster, The Hemp Connoisseur, and The CM Report, just to name a few. Usually these magazines are given to you by the publisher to hand out for circulation and it costs you nothing.
- Remember important facts that you spoke with your client the last time they visited. Pick up where you left off.
- Know what your medical marijuana patients want and be sure their medicine is always there. This decreases the odds of them looking into another dispensary for their medication.
- Thank them for their business when they leave.
- Offer them a beverage like coffee, soda, or bottled water while they are waiting to enter the buying area. Depending on the state that you are located in, there may be

laws specific to how many people are allowed in the buying area at once. Therefore, having a relaxing waiting room is important.

- Have a relaxing waiting area for your clients where they can read or hang out while they wait to make their purchases.

- Make popcorn, either in a microwave or with a dedicated machine.

- Have an espresso machine or coffee bar area. (This is optional, all depending on the area where you're located).

The success of your business is in the design of your dispensary and the ease for the customer to have the ability to shop. There will be competitors in your area that may or may not take the design elements of their dispensary seriously enough to make a difference. The little things can make your dispensary stand out and separate you from the competition—the place that people talk about and want to keep returning to. Yes, it's about what you sell, but the overall experience and the ease of buying quality product is just as important.

STANDOUT IDEAS FOR YOUR DISPENSARY

Here is a list of things that you can incorporate into your place of business that will make you stand out.

- **A massage chair** that your patients can use to relax in while they are waiting. It's very therapeutic.

- **A fish tank.** The bigger the better, if you have the room. This is a great centerpiece. This gives a cool, relaxing vibe to your dispensary. Just remember that it will require maintenance. You can pay for a service or do it on your own.

- **Large bulletin board.** This should allow people to post events and business services they offer. Sports or entertainment memorabilia and artwork will give your dispensary a friendly feel.

- **A unique sculpture**, as long as it doesn't take up too much room.

- **Waiting area.** This area needs to be inviting and comfortable and have enough space for your clients to stretch out and relax.

- **Flat screen televisions.** These should be placed around the dispensary to offer your clients the ability to watch TV while waiting to make their purchases. Not just one, but several spread around the store.

- **In the reception area, have a glass and pipe display.** It will give the customer an opportunity to purchase something while they're waiting.

- **Water cooler.** Most clients like to have the ability to grab a water when on the go.

DÉCOR STYLE

When choosing furniture and trying to come up with a unique look, feel, or vibe for your dispensary, you have to think about what fits your customer population. Most will be middle aged, mid-forties, and professional. The average age will lower if you are in a college town. Trying to make your dispensary fit everyone's personality will be impossible. It comes down to what you think will make your customers happy and will give them an overall atmosphere that meets their wants and needs for the ultimate buying experience.

Some men like to exist in a cave-like atmosphere (hence, the man cave) with no more than a big burly chair and a giant flat-screen TV. For others, furniture, like nice big leather couches and mahogany, may be a way for them to feel masculine and express their success. When you bring these same things into your store, you are reflecting an image with which they want to be associated. If you are opening your dispensary in a progressive urban area where upbeat, contemporary style would be appreciated, then find ways to accomplish it by bringing in eclectic pieces of furniture, or maybe antique marijuana memorabilia for conversation pieces.

COMFORT

In this industry, there are many women who walk in to purchase product. It is important to exude a neutral, comfortable feel so it doesn't offend either gender.

SIZE MATTERS

No matter what type of furniture you pick, guys like big. In fact, the bigger, the better. Look for deep seats and real wide cushions on your reception furniture. If you plan on having a sports theme, make sure the upholstery is tough enough for guys to tackle the chair or each other while waiting to purchase. Guys will be guys, and if sports are on your flat screen TV, you just never know. Better safe than sorry.

KEEP IT DOWN

Inside your dispensary room, you will need to pump up the volume. You must invest in a nice sound system. To reduce neighbor complaints and enjoy better sound quality, you may want to invest in good acoustical ceiling panels when building out your space. Many retail environments may be in a strip mall. The last thing you want is your next door business neighbor complaining about noise or music being too loud.

VENTILATION

If you are located in a shopping center and share a common wall with another shop, make sure you have a good filtration system to filter out the smell of your product. If not, the store next door will smell like marijuana and you will begin to get complaints.

IT'S YOUR PLACE, MAKE IT YOUR STYLE

You will be spending many hours in your dispensary. The store will likely be open seven days a week. Your time spent there working should be not only enjoyable and comfortable for your clients, but for you and your staff as well. Remember, the most important aspects are to be different, be professional, and create a welcoming and comfortable environment for everyone—somewhere that, if you were the customer, you would want to frequent often to buy all your medical and or recreational needs.

Check-In Process

THIS SECTION IS ALL ABOUT THE SAFETY AND SECURITY of your employees and your dispensary. It will give you important information necessary for your receptionist to know when a potential customer wants access to your dispensary. The most important responsibility of your receptionist will be to check-in your customers. This person will be responsible for recognizing certain traits of a potential customer to ensure their safety and the security of your dispensary.

The way a potential customer appears will alert your receptionist to possible danger. For example, if a potential customer is wearing a hooded sweatshirt, a large, oversized jacket, and glasses that hide their eyes, they could possibly be someone looking to rob your dispensary. Your receptionist must be experienced and well trained enough to discern a possible threat and act accordingly.

Stay calm during a robbery:

- Breathe.

- Comply with their demands.

- Relax and try to stay focused.

- Listen as well as you can.

- Be on guard for the worst.

- Do not reach or make sudden movements.

- Do not be a hero.

- Give them what they want.

- Aim to remain calm and immediately seek help after the robbery.

If the potential customer passes the receptionist's screening, they can be buzzed into the reception room. If the customer is there to purchase either medical or personal use marijuana, the following steps should always, without fail, be followed. Not doing this by the book could cost you your license and your business. **Do not rush this process!**

1. The customer must produce a driver's license or photo identification.

2. For medicinal purposes, the customer must produce a current prescription card.

3. Personal use purchases require two forms of identification and the person must be twenty-one years of age or older.

4. Whatever the customer produces for identification, expiration dates must be noted.

5. Prescriptions must also have a valid date.

6. All identification must match the person submitting it.

Some states/municipalities require that your dispensary make copies of identification and prescription cards. If they require something above and beyond this, make sure you are up to date on your local ordinances and follow them to the letter of the law.

Dispensary Menus that Sell

ONE OF THE BEST WAYS to catch a potential customer's attention—before he or she has even set foot in your business—is by producing and distributing a menu. Typically created from a single letter-size sheet of paper, a menu provides a relatively inexpensive means of showcasing both your products and the personality of your dispensary. Its intent, of course, is to entice both new and returning customers into trying a variety of the products you offer, and to inspire brand loyalty in everyone who crosses your threshold.

The ideal menu should appeal to a wide range of budgets and interests. You'll want your clientele to include everyone from the big spenders to the more cost-conscious and, possibly, uninitiated, which makes a well-designed, easy-to-understand menu a must. Your customers, in turn, will want many options—and prices—to choose from, to know that they're getting the best value for their money, and to be sure they'll have a great experience whenever they visit your business.

Most of all, your menu should be a reflection of who you are and the values you represent. It should convince each potential client that your dispensary alone provides the highest level of quality, and that he or she can trust your expertise—and that of your staff—in finding the best products for his or her individual needs and budget.

Below is the outline to create a successful dispensary menu, from design and layout to price point.

PROFESSIONAL DESIGNERS

The best way to distinguish your brand from the ones that feature amateurish, stereotypical designs is to hire a professional. Consult a local printing company for recommendations on a graphic artist who can assist with the design and layout of your menu. Be sure to ask for the artist's portfolio to make sure your ideas will be in the right hands. Your hired artist will help you through the entire process, from creating the logo and layout, selecting colors, and printing. He or she can also assist in designing a professional website.

COVER AND LOGO

The first thing your client will see is your menu cover—and your logo should be the first thing he or she notices. You should also include your dispensary name (if not incorporated into the logo), street address, phone number, website, and email address. Be sure to include information about online bookings and gift card purchases, as well as linking via social media (Facebook, Twitter, Instagram, etc.). Everything should be set in good-sized, easy-to-read print.

SHAPE, SIZE, & COLOR

As noted above, the standard menu is letter size (8½" by 11") and, depending on the amount of information you need to lay out, either folded in half or made a trifold. Resist the temptation to get creative here; it'll end up costing you both money and production time.

REAL ESTATE

While building your menu, you must look at it as a piece of real estate. Every product on your menu is a tenant renting space—and you have to find the right space for each tenant. Certain spots on the menu tend to draw the reader's eye more than others, which of course makes those spots more valuable. In a trifold design, for instance, the upper right, left, and center are together considered the high-rent district. Be sure to put the products you'd most like to promote in this prime area, accompanied by clear images and well-written text.

CHOOSING PRODUCTS

As you decide which products you want to sell, and especially those you want to promote, be sure to collaborate with your staff. Which products do they use themselves? Which do they recommend to friends and family?

You should also let your farmers assist you in choosing products. They can tell you which, in their experience, have proven most profitable.

Do as much research as you can into the newest and most popular strains. You'll want to stand out from all the other businesses and be the first one in the area to offer the most current products. Listen to your customers, too, and find out what they'd like to see offered.

Remember, you should revisit your menu at least once a year with an eye to what you're still selling (and selling the most of), what's new to your dispensary, and what you're no longer carrying. Make your changes accordingly.

MENU AND WEBSITE

Your website should be cohesive with your menu. A coordinated look is one of the best ways to brand your facility. All your colors, pictures, and pricing should match—from the menu to the website, from advertisements to business cards—and your mission statement or message should always be visible.

Because your selection of products is likely to vary, it's a good idea to direct patients to your website for more specific details. This will help you extend the lifetime of your printed menus. Many of your patients may prefer to look up your online menu rather than pulling out a printed one, saving you time and money on reprinting.

PRICING

Correct pricing is essential to the success of your business. Your dispensary could get rave reviews for its knowledgeable staff of budtenders and variety of products, but if your prices are too high, customers will stay away. It's a sensitive subject.

Establishing price points, however, is simply doing your homework. Check out other local dispensaries and gauge their menu pricing. Speak to your farmers, who can give you an idea of the actual numbers that other local dispensaries are charging for their retail products. It's a small industry, so many of the farmers know each other and share information. Finally, get to know your clients and the area in which they live and work. This should help you establish the right pricing to meet the current market. People want value for their money, of course, but they don't necessarily need you to be the lowest price in town. If your patients feel that they're getting even more than they paid for, then you've offered both service and a product at a value.

COSTS AND HOW MANY MENUS TO PRINT

Printing the right number of menus will always be a guessing game. It would be great to stay so busy that you run out within your first six months—and then have to print more.

Your best bet is to use 1000 as the magic number for your first run. Get printing prices on 1000, 2000, 3000, and 5000 pieces. The per-piece cost goes down with higher quantities. Keep in mind, though, that if you order too many you'll be stuck with the leftovers. For your first run, we suggest choosing a lower quantity and adjusting for future printings. If, however, you plan to use the menus for marketing, you might go ahead and risk paying for more.

Keep in mind that special colors or foil quickly become costly. It may be that these extra details are worth the additional investment. Or it may be that a simple look is a better (and more economical) fit for your business. The cost per menu will also vary depending on paper grade and complexity of logos. Depending on your budget and the level of quality you're shooting for, you can spend as little as fifty cents or as much as two dollars per menu. Be sure to price the final menu proof with at least three reputable companies.

Remember, every customer should be given a menu, especially the new ones. Each menu should be accompanied by referral cards. That way, your loyal customers can both refer a friend *and* give that friend your dispensary menu.

Menu Products

WHILE YOU ARE IN THE PROCESS OF CREATING YOUR BUSINESS PLAN, take a moment and think about what kind of inventory you want your store to offer patients, and if you have a recreational license, customers. Besides the obvious choice of marijuana, there are many extracts and edibles that offer medicinal benefits and need to be considered in offering patients the right product and creating the right business model. There are a myriad of products your patients might want to purchase. Check out other dispensaries and see what they offer. Ask which items are the most popular, then decide which ones you want to consider as part of your inventory. Make note of the prices they are charging as well. This will also give you an estimate of what the startup inventory costs will be for your business plan.

INVENTORY THAT MIGHT BE CARRIED IN A TYPICAL DISPENSARY:

- **Flower or Marijuana:** This is your primary product and will have several different forms that you will sell. Regular marijuana, infused marijuana, shake, and joints, to name a few.

- **Concentrates:** The fastest growing part of the industry is extracts. These come in the form of oil, wax, shatter, and tincture, and all of them are made in different variations as far as the process goes. The manufacturing of the product usually carries a different license; in Colorado it's called an MIP (Manufacture Infused Product) license and has different requirements than a regular garden license. Hash oil for hand held "vapor pens" is the single fastest-growing item in the industry. If you cannot manufacture the product yourself, then find a reliable licensed lab that can make it for you. All of these products are manufactured from your plant trim (sugar leaves, not fan leaves). A lab may have their own garden and just sell you the product for a price or use your trim and either do the usual percentage split or a much lower price per gram. There is a large profit margin if you use your own trim.

- **Edibles:** Remember eating brownies in high school? It's not like these edibles made presently. Today, consumable products are used for medicinal purposes, and they come in a variety of forms. Besides the traditional brownie or cookie, you now can buy chocolate in twenty flavors, hard candies at different strengths, gummy bears, taffy, pixy sticks, coffee, tea, gum, mints, juices, sodas or even a chai tea. As a startup in a new state, there will be edible companies popping up everywhere. Many entrepreneurs are looking for a new opportunity, a new industry with unlimited growth potential. They start an edible company and the product stinks. Try to first look for edible companies that are already manufacturing in other states. Companies like Cheeba Chew and Dixie Elixirs have established track records. There is one important factor when buying an edible product: consistency. Infusing of the product needs to be processed in a consistent way. A regulated dosage in a product must be evenly spread throughout the item, so your patient knows how much they are taking while ingesting. Eating too much of a dose, can give you an undesired effect, like the room spinning or seeing things. These products are designed for medical purposes, so it's important that you are buying a reliable, consistent product that your patient can benefit from.

- **CBD:** Another important aspect of the edible market is an extract cannabinoid from marijuana and hemp called CBD, which is used for pain. Many products are made with this because of its medicinal effects and benefits it gives patients.

- **Ointments and Capsules:** There are products available such as salves, massage oil, lotions, and bath salts, all infused with minimal amounts of THC. Companies are producing extracts and placing them in capsules for consumption. Each capsule extract may give you a different effect, one for sleeping or one for energy. As this industry develops, more variety of extracts out of marijuana will evolve.

- **Glass Pipes, Bongs, Grinders, Rolling Papers, etc:** Most of this is self-explanatory, but today with all the concentrates, new products have arisen. Now you can find, oil rigs/pipes, vapor machines, wax pipes, dabbers (metal utensils for wax or shatter), plus hand held vaporizers.

- **Clones:** Some municipalities will allow you to sell clones to your patients; many grow on their own. Make sure you stock your shelves once spring arrives, as many patients grow outside.

All of these products give you the opportunity to cover a wide range of patients. Not only will you be helping people, but you will be making nice profit margins as well. My focus on the products is for the medical end, not recreational, because when a state opens with marijuana, it begins with the medicinal end.

Other products that may increase revenue if your location is big enough to carry:

- T- shirts
- Hats
- "Bud" calendars
- Cups and mugs with logos
- Residential grow books, videos, CD's
- Weed accessories such as holding containers, ashtrays, lighters, hemp wicks, scales, grinders, glass cleaners, incense, detox juices and even grow kits. The list goes on and on.

All of these products will give you the ability to handle many ailments that patients have and create a base for client retention. The actual cost of the startup inventory, depending on the size of your projected operation, can be expensive. An average order from one vendor can easily run a few hundred dollars. You may have to stock up, because all of these companies are just opening up as you are, and have startup hiccups such as delivery or production problems. You never want to run out of product for patients because you may lose them to another dispensary. One more point: make sure you have enough capital to handle inventory; no one gives credit in this business.

A Pleasurable and Informative Buying Experience

HOPEFULLY BY THE TIME YOU ARE READING THIS CHAPTER, you're licensed and getting ready to open your dispensary. You have done a lot of planning, filed many applications, and have prepared for this day. Now it's time to stock up and give your clients what they want. What do you carry? What do customers want? Who do you buy from? Where do you go from here?

By now your garden is harvesting and there will be several things that you will be producing out of your facility. Of course, your primary product will be the strains you cultivate. You should start your garden with a balance of sativa, hybrid and indica strains, approximately thirty to forty phenotypes. From this production, you will create other products. A lot of these are formulated from the trim (manicuring) of the plants—small leaves that are cut off the plant that contain THC. With these "sweet or sugar leaves," several different products can be produced.

These items include different types of concentrates:

- **Bubble hash:** a process of mixing dry "sweet leaves" with regular ice and washing through several layers of cheesecloth to create a fine grade of hash.

- **Keif:** a process of mixing dry "sweet leaves" with dry ice, separating the THC from the leaves. This is done through a fine cheesecloth bag.

- **Infused flower:** taking your flower and applying keif to it. This is done while the marijuana is fresh and newly trimmed. This gives the keif the ability to stick easily on the bud and creates a very potent form of marijuana.

- **Extracts:** these include oils, wax, shatter, budder and tinctures. This process usually requires a special license.

- **Edibles:** from extracts such as oil and budder, you can create a whole line of infused edible products.

From your garden, you have the ability to create many different products that will help patients and increase revenues.

If you do not have the ability to produce extracts or edibles, there will be many companies just starting to open that provide these products. Look for those that have been operating in other states with a track record. Here is a list of different types of edibles and extracts that you should look for:

- Cookies and brownies
- Infused "tootsie rolls"
- Soda
- Hard candies
- Soft gummies
- Tea and coffee
- Bath oils
- Salves
- Wax
- Budder
- Shatter
- Hash oil

All of these items will give you the versatility to help your patients with their ailments and give you the opportunity to sell more products and increase revenue.

If you have that special license, you have the ability to make all the products above. This will increase your margins and give you more opportunities to advance in different market sectors for this new industry.

Here are several of the best and most easy-to-follow secrets for you to use when selling merchandise to your customers:

Invoke Science: The best thing you can do is dress like a professional. Why not have staff wear a sharp black shirt or apron that says to the customer "I am a professional and I know what products, merchandise, or marijuana works for you, my customer?" The name of the dispensary should be displayed on the clothes you are wearing. This is a marijuana store—why not give the feel of it being a professional environment.

When you buy a cup of coffee from Starbucks, their employees are in uniform all wearing the same thing. We all know the success they have had. Branding is extremely important and the way you and your employees look will only help your customers realize the type of professional operation you have established.

Clinique came up with the best marketing idea ever created: put sales people in white lab coats. People are conditioned to respect what people in white lab coats have to say. A makeup or counter person in a white lab coat establishes that he or she is an expert. Of course, they have to be well versed in the products they're selling, but the image of knowledge is a surefire way to help sell products.

Why not have your counter person in a lab coat? Would that give a different perspective to your customers? Is there a doctor in the house? Depending on medical or recreational, it would certainly differentiate your dispensary from others.

Play the Expert: Play on the philosophy of the brands you're selling. Explain in detail the long list of proven facts about your products and have a list of any information or facts about using these brands. Outline the differences, strengths, strains, quality and what type of response your customer should have when using them.

Knowledge is the key in selling any merchandise. The more information your sales team demonstrates about the marijuana you grow and sell will only help you sell more. Edible information is also important for the first-time user or the novice; explain in detail the importance of understanding what may happen if you eat or ingest too much.

More Expensive Equals Better: Selling a product that is twice as much money as anything else suggests it's better than any other brand or strain, and symbolizes a certain status and reputation as being the best. The "if it's more expensive it must be better" mentality trick is one of the oldest in retailing, but it still works today. Many people feel like they want to try something special or something different, they've worked hard and they owe that much to themselves. This is the "feel-good-we-earned-it purchase."

Customers want to have the ability to splurge on something they normally may not buy. Why not put out a more expensive product front and center or an edible that costs a bit more than others. Make their purchase a special one!

The Nose Knows: This is a clever trick, but many retailers today pump certain smells into the air to put you into the buying mode. Certain department stores rely on fragrance to help sell bathing suits by having a coconut or beach-like smell in the swimwear department. Infant apparel gets a baby powder smell and lingerie gets a lilac smell.

In a dispensary environment, give your retail area the exact smell you need to encourage customers to buy. Burning incense may boost happiness, so it might make people more willing to buy. Or you can try a candle that smells similar to a particular product you're selling. Be careful about the scent being too heavy though, since that makes people with allergies or sensitive noses want to escape instead of stick around. The more pleasurable you make the shopping experience, the more likely your customers are to stay longer and buy more. How many times have you found yourself buying something that smelled so good you just *had* to have it?

Music to Your Ears: Most retail stores play music to keep shoppers relaxed, soothed, and happy. When customers are happy, they tend to splurge on things they may need less. Have you ever had the experience of staying longer than you wanted in a store because your favorite song started playing and you couldn't leave until it was over? Those extra two minutes could be all the time customers need to spot another product that interests them.

If you're catering to an older clientele, it makes sense to play music from their era. This will bring them back to happier times and remind them of their glory days in the past. If you cater to a younger generation, it makes sense to play music they listen to. If you're not sure what's hip these days or what appeals to the kinds of people who come to your dispensary, visit big name and boutique clothing stores where your clients typically shop and listen to the music playing there to get ideas. You can always go with soft, soothing elevator music. That tends to work on all generations. If all else fails, ask your clients what music they like and what's popular these days, then suggest that type of music to your dispensary's owner or manager.

Make It Shine: What do new cars and diamonds have in common? They're both shiny and they're both expensive. Those things are not coincidental and retailers know it. It's almost a physical response. Humans automatically assume something that gleams is fancy and valuable. That goes for the surfaces around and under the shiny product, too. If you want to be successful in retail, your counters and every surface that products rest on must gleam and shine. Give customers the impression your products are worth every penny you're asking them to pay.

If they see it, they will buy it. Dirty, dusty glass counters will inhibit sales. Crisp, clean counters are a must to assist in selling marijuana!

Make the Puzzle Fit: Whether you're working in a small dispensary or large one, make all the parts come together. If you're catering to old or new customers, let your customers see how the puzzle comes together. Pipes, bowls, rolling papers, and cleaners should all be in one section. You don't want them wandering around your store, trying to figure out how to get ready for a night on the town. Make it simple, keep it close, and make sure the price is right. Let the entire purchase fit in their budget and don't let them leave without having everything they need to have a good buying experience without having to shop at another dispensary. It's much easier for them to make a purchase if they can see the coordinated end result.

A Little Loyalty: Every good dispensary should design a loyalty or perk program to turn one-off customers into repeat retail clients. If you plan the program intelligently, then all it takes is printing up a batch of attractively-designed punch cards and investing a very small amount in a special rubber stamp or hole puncher. These days, you could even skip the paper cards and keep track of the loyalty program digitally. Whether you offer a free edible after a client buys ten, or a discount on a large marijuana purchase after a certain number of visits, it's a great idea to give the customer a freebie punch, stamp, or credit just for starting the program. That way, the goal of that free merchandise seems closer and easier to reach. Getting customers to think freebie in the future is nearly impossible, but if they see two down and eight or less to go, they're more likely to keep coming back and using the loyalty program.

Doorbuster: We all want a bargain. Big retailers have had doorbuster days for years. The day after Thanksgiving, Black Friday, has been a retailer's dream for as far back as I can remember. Recently, Black Friday is stretching into Saturday and Sunday to become a whole Black Weekend! Soon enough, we'll start calling the entire week after Thanksgiving, Black Week.
Why is it that customers are compelled to rush to the store to buy the same thing they could have bought the day before, a thing that may not even be rare or valuable? The art of shopping itself, the high of getting something perceived as valuable for a price that's perceived as low, is a big reason why customers go to doorbuster sales in the first place---and stores take advantage by turning sales into adrenaline-charged events.

Ever heard of Filene's Basement, the bargain department store? If you've been to Boston, probably so. For decades, Filene's hosted a yearly bridal gown bargain sale. It got to be such an event that one year, bargain-hungry brides-to-be snatched all the dresses off the racks in thirty-seven seconds, while TV news crews recorded and timed them!

Your business can also offer these one-day sales or doorbusters. Create a plan about how to organize an event, what products to discount, and how to get the word out—then present your awesome plan to your customers.

Let your customers know that you are planning an event; tell them you will be dropping prices on special items. Email them, call them, send a postcard, post it, text it, offer hors d'oeuvres and wine tastings, make it an extravaganza! There is no reason your event can't give your customers the same adrenaline rush the big stores do, with the same type of results.

CHECK IT OUT

Little secrets that will make you the retail genius of your dispensary:

- ○ Suggest a dress code for your sales team.
- ○ Remember to play music that suits your audience at all times.
- ○ Keep your counters, shelves, and products shining and clean.
- ○ Remember to make the puzzle pieces fit.
- ○ Design a loyalty program to get customers buying regularly.
- ○ Organize a doorbuster sale or bargain event to boost sales.

Chapter Resources:

"The Basement Through the Decades." Filene's Basement. http://www.filenesbasement.com/our_story.php

Halpern, Derek. "How to Turn New Customers into Repeat Customers (the secret is this one experiment)." Social Triggers blog. http://socialtriggers.com/get-repeat-customers.

Establishing Dispensary Merchandise Pricing

YOU OFTEN SEE OR HEAR RETAILERS' ADVERTISEMENTS that promise you "quality merchandise at a fair price." Just what is a "fair price?" As you enter the retailing arena, you will soon learn that there really is no universally accepted definition. Most of the time the answer is "It depends . . ." It depends on how much you paid for the merchandise, if you are growing your own product (the costs associated with cultivation will affect the price point you charge), who you bought it from, what your competitors are charging, your overhead expenses, your sales volume, and a hundred other variables.

How you establish prices for your merchandise will be one of the most important decisions you will make, since it directly affects that all-important variable, profit. You must strike a delicate balance, setting a price that is high enough to allow you to achieve a reasonable profit margin, yet low enough to keep your merchandise affordable and competitive. There are many outside influences that affect profitability and a retailer's bottom line. If you think selling marijuana in your dispensary is not being a full blown retailer, you are wrong. Retailing is retailing, no matter what you are selling. Setting the right price is a crucial step toward achieving that profit. Retailers are in business to make a profit and so are you, but figuring out what and how to price your marijuana products may not come easily.

Before we can determine which retail pricing strategy to use to set the right price, we must know the costs associated with the products. Two key elements in factoring product cost are the cost of goods and the amount of operating expense.

The cost of goods includes the amount paid for the product, plus any shipping or handling expenses. The cost of operating the business, or operating expense, includes overhead (rent, utilities, insurance), payroll, marketing, and office supplies.

Regardless of the pricing strategy used, the retail price of the products should more than cover the cost of obtaining the goods plus the expenses related to operating the business. A retailer simply cannot succeed in business if they continue to sell their products below cost. Marijuana is no different.

RETAIL PRICING STRATEGIES

Once you understand what your products actually cost, you should look at how your competition is pricing their products. Retailers will also need to examine their channels of distribution and research what the market is willing to pay. Checking out your competitors' price points should be easy. Here are some ways to research your competitors' pricing:

- Local trade magazines
- Weedmaps
- Leafly
- Dispensary websites
- Visiting dispensaries
- Distributor references (Your distributor should be able to influence your pricing)

Many pricing strategies exist, and each is used based on a particular a set of circumstances. Here are a few of the more popular pricing strategies to consider:

PRICING YOUR DISPENSARY FLOWER

The way you will break down your marijuana will be in grams. Ounce, half ounce, quarter are all terms that you have heard and are widely used in the dispensary. It's your job to understand what those terms mean in grams. Below is a breakdown of suggested product size amounts. Pricing those amounts will be subject to many variables as noted above.

GRAM BREAKDOWN	
TERM	**GRAM**
Gram	Gram
Eighth	3.5 grams
Quarter	7 grams
Half ounce	14 grams
Ounce	28 grams

VENDOR PRICING

Your vendors will have many options for pricing their merchandise. Use the rule of thumb below for edibles. For concentrates, your margin of profit should be even higher. To optimize your profit, use the "trim" that has been cut off your manicured plants and process it if you have the right license to produce it. If not, find a lab that can.

Here are some samples of products that have a higher percentage of profit:

- **Concentrates** - marijuana extracted THC
- **Ear wax** - gram prices range from $6 to $10 to produce and sell to the end user for $35-$40
- **Shatter** - gram prices range from $10 to $15 to produce and sell to the end user for $40-$60
- **Oil** - gram prices range from $10 to $15 to produce and sell to the end user for $40-$50

Prices do vary, depending on the supply and demand conditions locally.

THE ETHICS OF MARKUP

Even though there is no hard and fast rule for pricing merchandise, most retailers use a 50% markup, known in the trade as keystone. What this means is doubling your cost to establish the retail price. Because markup is figured as a percentage of the sales price, doubling the cost means a 50% markup. For example, if your cost on an item is $1, your selling price will be $2. Fifty percent of $2 is $1, which is your markup. We want to be clear in this case. This is strictly for buying merchandise from a manufacturer, farmer, or distributer. The mark-up is 50 percent above what you pay for the merchandise. The overhead of the dispensary operation, utilities, marketing and overall costs associated with running your business is not figured in the profit of any of these items purchased to resell.

This definition of markup was probably developed to avoid using a term that admits to a 100% increase. Most consumers would be appalled that you are selling something for double what you paid for it. They would be inclined to ask why you don't carry a gun and wear a mask for selling retail at such a high price. Most consumers have had no exposure to the myriad costs associated with retailing and they are used to thinking in terms of net profit margins they have heard in the media. For example, an article in the business section of a newspaper might report that Mega-Mart had sales of $500 million and earned a net profit of 4%. An uninitiated reader might conclude that Mega-Mart marks up its goods only 4%. In reality, net profit is calculated after overhead expenses have been subtracted from gross profit (total sales less cost of merchandise).

When growing your own merchandise, there is a benefit—yes, there is more profit over the long haul—but there are many things to consider when figuring out your overall price point. The outlay of setting up your operation is colossal. The overhead of your operation, payroll, and now the ever-changing taxes imposed on everything you grow must all be factored into your overall price point.

Sales and Inventory

SALES AND KEEPING TRACK OF INVENTORY will be the lifeblood of your dispensary and grow facility. In fact, it is the lifeblood of any business that sells products to the public. Knowing exactly how much of any one product your grow facility produces and the dispensary sells will impact the amount of tax you will owe the state, and at the end of each year how much you will owe the federal government. In the State of Colorado, medical marijuana is not taxed the same as marijuana for personal use, and having a system that separates them is mandatory. If you are doing a large number of medical sales, tracking each patient's prescription and how often they are allowed to refill is also necessary. Colorado requires that you have a Marijuana Inventory Tracking System (MITS).

If your state requires that your business pay monthly or quarterly taxes, you will need a software system that will keep track of the amount owed and the due date. Trying to keep track of this on, say, Quickbooks, may be an exercise in futility. You will need specific software designed to perform these tasks for a dispensary/grow facility business.

How in the world are you going to accomplish this? Purchase the right software that will perform this task, called a Point of Sale system (POS). There are several varieties of POS software you can purchase. Do your homework and make sure whatever system you choose will cover all of your state and federal requirements.

The other side of a POS system is that it will also alert you to any theft going on in your dispensary or grow facility. Keeping proper inventory is essential for tracking employee theft. These intricate POS systems will immediately alert you the minute inventory levels are out of skew. Purchasing your inventory is not going to be cheap, and you will need to have a tool that can control every product your dispensary features. A POS system will also help you manage every aspect of your grow facility. Here are two companies which offer POS systems to use as examples:

MJ Freeway has developed online tools like Point of Sale (POS), inventory, sales, grow management, patient validation, and more, all specifically built for the complicated medical/personal use marijuana industry.

MJFreeway offers all of these features within a powerful online business platform, with plans for everything from a startup dispensary or delivery service to a multi-location dispensary and grow facility. This flexibility allows you to choose which one is right for you, without having to pay for the features you don't need. Check out MJFreeway software packages to find the right one for you.

MJFreeway has custom online tools that are built specifically for the needs of centers, collectives, co-ops, dispensaries, and growers in the medical marijuana industry. Their goal is to bring legitimacy to this industry, while allowing you to keep your business and patient information safe and private. The following systems describe each function:

- **GramTracker®** - Follows every gram from seed to sale, including shake, evaporated product, wet weights, or even spillage—leaving only theft to stand out.
- **MixTracker™** - Easily manage the entire manufacturing process for marijuana products such as edibles, concentrates, and extracts.
- **GrowTracker®** - Manage your grow operation: plant ingredients, harvest scheduling, strain performance, ratios and more.
- **Features** - They have included everything you might need to run your business smoothly from point of sale to patient validation, as well as tools to easily comply with state regulations.
- **Video Demos** - A series of videos demonstrating how all of the powerful tools of MJ Freeway can work for you.

BioTrackTHC was designed to not only offer you a turn-key medical marijuana POS software system to meet state regulations, but to actually enhance every aspect of your medical marijuana business. Their MMJ dispensary POS software allows for easy grow house location tracking, inventory, patient management, point-of-sale system and easy accounting reporting. As the market leader in MMJ POS software, BioTrackTHC uses cutting edge technology and offers the most robust medical marijuana dispensary software in the industry to help you run your business more efficiently and profitably while staying compliant—BioTrackTHC.com

Retail with Detail

OWNING A RETAIL MARIJUANA BUSINESS requires that you keep track of every item sold, purchased through a manufacturer or distributor for resale, or grown in your facility. All marijuana retail businesses have a software system required by the state (and new states to legalize pot will undoubtedly have similar requirements). The State of Colorado requires all dispensaries as of January 1, 2014 to use the inventory tracking software called the MITS (Marijuana Inventory Tracking System). If you are not compliant and refuse to use the required systems put in place by your state, they can shut down your business and/or fine you heavily, and you may lose all of your required licenses to do business.

Remember, this is a BUSINESS and must be run like one. You must be organized, detailed, law-abiding, and diligent. You must deal with employees, suppliers, and customers. You must keep records—meticulous ones—and ensure you are reporting all the required information to government agencies.

Web Presence and Social Media

NOW THAT WE'RE FIRMLY PLANTED in the twenty-first century, it's hard to imagine a business operating successfully without a website. Understanding how effective social media can help your dispensary is absolutely crucial to your marketing strategy.

Once you're ready to start your company, select either a domain name or your website URL. Before you formalize the legal moniker of your dispensary, you'll want to make sure (through a site like GoDaddy.com) that that domain name is available.

When you've secured your domain name, you can set up a basic webpage for free. If you've chosen to forgo a professional, you can find a variety of free templates online. These templates typically offer a step-by-step walkthrough that even the least Internet savvy person can follow. I recommend any of the following sites:

www.wix.com

www.intuit.com

www.freewebsitetemplates.com

www.sites.google.com

You'll also want to consider how people will access your website. For instance, are most of your patients using smartphones? If so, you'll need to know that Flash-based sites are not viewable on iPhones. Androids, on the other hand, are Flash compatible, so the patients who use them will have no trouble accessing your site.

The most important element of your website is the sign-in area. Make it a prominent part of your main page, as it's the best way to collect email addresses. This contact information will be critical as far as sending "e-blasts" to your database regarding specials of the week and blowout sales on those products that aren't selling quite quickly enough.

Once your business is off the ground, you can upgrade your website and make it interactive with your dispensary software program. Patients can book appointments online, interact with you, and send feedback on what they love about your business and what they'd like to see improved. You might also create a section for the products you're promoting this week (the ones you have a surplus of, perhaps, at an excellent price!) and links to Flickr or Instagram for sharing photos of your lively budtenders. Create a calendar of events that will draw people into your store and make them want to keep checking your site for new and greater promotions.

Ideally, your site will be a great vehicle for bringing in business. That's why it's crucial to update it often and respond to feedback in a timely manner—it's the best way to start developing a loyal client base.

A common concern among business owners is figuring out a way to get their site on the main page of Google results. The average searcher only scrolls through the first two pages of suggested links before clicking a page or else giving up. Clearly being at or near the top of a search engine optimization (SEO) is important. In most cases, a company's search position is a major factor. For dispensaries, however, being at forefront of an SEO is less critical. Your website is for your clientele and a more localized area than a chain company. Your clientele will find you by local advertising, personal promoting, and, most crucially, word of mouth. That's not to say that SEO results aren't important, and you should absolutely list your dispensary in as many online directories as possible, including Google and Yahoo map services. From a search standpoint, this will equate to a major payoff.

If you decide it's worth the effort to bring your dispensary to the top of the SEO, you have two types of websites to choose between. First, the traditional website: it sits there until someone clicks on it. You can climb the SEO ladder by paying Google (or any search engine) to let you appear at the top of the links, a position you'd pay for per click you receive. If Google charges you $1 per click, and you receive 10,000 clicks in a month, you'd have to pay $10,000. For the average dispensary this is not a cost-effective approach.

The other kind of website is designed through WordPress, online software that allows you to create a newsletter or blog. WordPress allows your site to be fluid, ever-changing, with constant activity. Before you hire a web designer, it's a good idea to interview several and find out how they feel about traditional versus WordPress. As often as the concepts behind Internet exposure evolve, you'll want to hear from experts in the field to evaluate who can do the best job for your individual business. Still, be sure to do a little research on your own, checking especially for SEO myths and scams. Choosing a company that relies on poor tactics to improve your page rank will likely hurt you in the long run.

Once you have your website up and running, what other online methods help bring exposure to your dispensary? In recent years Facebook, believe it or not, has become a top-notch vehicle. The social media site is often considered a place for primarily personal interactions, but it can also be extremely successful for businesses. You might also consider shooting short videos featuring different products and uploading them to your own YouTube channel.

Having an active, interesting Twitter account is another way you can help your dispensary go viral. In 140 characters or less, you can describe your weekly special, what's going on in your dispensary, something funny that will make your patients laugh and show them your brand has a sense of humor. You can send out tiny URLs that link to interesting articles, videos, or other content that will appeal to your followers, as well as track the number of clicks they receive.

You can also increase awareness about your dispensary by maintaining a blog. Each time you post to your blog—or to any of your social media outlets—the information goes into the "Internet universe" to be catalogued for future use. By regularly adding new content, you will increase your odds of being found online. Be sure to talk about the products you carry, especially the ones you're promoting. When a potential client searches online for one of those products, you'll want your dispensary showing up in the results!

WHICH ONE TO USE?

The chart below illustrates the demographics of each social media outlet. In recent years, the biggest age group on Facebook (with over 500 million users) has been forty-five to fifty-four year olds. On average, people spend forty minutes per day on the site, as opposed to one to three minutes for the typical website. This, clearly, is an avenue for your business that you don't want to miss out on.

FACEBOOK, PERSONAL PAGE
- Can import your contact list and allow you to search for Facebook friends
- Up to 5000 friends
- Privacy controls
- Allows sharing of photos and video
- Can group your friends into lists
- Less customizable, though custom tabs, applications, and cover photos can allow for a more personalized look that reflects your brand

FACEBOOK, BUSINESS PAGE
- No limit on number of fans
- Patients don't have to join to see information
- Can control interaction with fans (i.e., wall posts)
- Allows sharing of photos and video
- Bulk messages to fans show up in their news feed, not the often-overlooked inbox
- Statistics on demographics of fans and interactions
- Can personalize applications (through e-commerce, custom tabs, etc.)
- Page administrators are private, so you can either hire outside help to keep your page running or share the duties with a couple of your staff

YOUTUBE
- Video sharing site
- Can make videos public, private, unlisted, or available to only specific users
- Provides embedded HTML codes for adding videos to other websites
- Can create an automatic feed of newly uploaded videos to your website
- Can customize your YouTube channel page to your dispensary's brand

BLOGS
- Blogs are a lot like online diaries, only with less talk about breakups and a lot more about your industry and your dispensary
- Great for sharing information in a less formal way
- An outlet that's continuing to grow in popularity
- Great for SEO
- Provide an opportunity to showcase your credibility as a dispensary owner and operator
- Can blog about business, inspirations, family, causes, or anything you'd like
- Can be tied into your website
- Aside from your homepage, is likely to become the most-visited page on your website

LINKEDIN
- Used primarily for business purposes
- More professional users
- Resembles an online résumé
- Can import your contacts and search for current LinkedIn users

- Can integrate your Twitter updates to post automatically to your LinkedIn update
- Can search by individual's name, company, title, location, etc.
- "Answers" application allows you to position yourself as an expert in the field
- "Polls" application allows you to create polls and share them both on and off LinkedIn
- Can join groups to ask and answer questions

TWITTER

- A "micro-blogging" website
- Users are limited to 140 characters per update
- Allows for personalization of Twitter page for branding
- Can group the people you follow into lists
- Can direct message (i.e. private message) individuals
- Used to quickly update followers or send links to relevant information on external sites
- By adding a hashtag(#) before a word, you create a keyword that's searchable within Twitter—for example, #awesomedispensary
- By adding an at sign (@,) before someone's username, you can reply to him or her publicly—for example, @less_awesome_dispensary
- Twitter courtesy is to "retweet" information that others post and to follow those who follow you

OTHER TOOLS TO CONSIDER

- TweetDeck: simultaneously updates your Facebook and Twitter feeds
- Twitterfeed: feeds your blog into Facebook and Twitter
- Hootsuite: allows you to schedule posts across multiple social media channels

RECOMMENDED PRACTICES FOR SOCIAL NETWORKS

- Combine your various social media efforts with your website
- Repurpose your blog into your social media
- Drive traffic to your website via social media and capture user details
- Include social media icons on your website that will link back to your social media pages

SECTION X

LEGAL

Cannabis Laws:
The State of the States

IF EVERY WORD IN EVERY LAW OF EVERY STATE in which medical marijuana is legal were included in this section, the chapter would run to a thousand pages, or more. Instead, the state-law highlights are presented here. The synopsis of each state's law provided here, though brief, is highly informative and will point you in the right direction if you are inclined to learn more.

Considering the state of the states' medical marijuana laws is akin to placing a frame around confetti after it has gone airborne. The regulations are all over the place. The laws are not uniform . . . at all.

Ever.

However, there are common characteristics you should consider, themes if you will, which occur as a matter of course in each state's medical marijuana statutory scheme. In no particular order those are, but not limited to . . .

Is the state offering for-profit opportunities to open medical marijuana dispensaries and cultivation sites, or only non-profit opportunities? If it is non-profit, will you have to comply with Internal Revenue Code §501(c)(3)? Are dispensaries and cultivation centers permitted to combine or must they be separate facilities and separate businesses? What if your state plans to keep the industry from falling into private hands at all?

FACT

Marijuana is legal and is not even classified as a drug in North Korea.

What is the controlling law, and which department within each state administers the program?

How do you apply for a medical marijuana dispensary license, with whom and how much will it cost you?

If you are unsuccessful in your application, you get your application money back ... right? Wrong.

What if the state mandates that you drug test your employees? In New Mexico that's exactly what happens.

Can local zoning laws affect your medical marijuana facility?

Can felons apply for medical marijuana facility licenses? What if you have a misdemeanor drug conviction?

How many potential medical marijuana patients are located in your state and who has the final word on where to locate your business?

———

ALABAMA

By unanimous vote, on or about March 20, 2014, the Alabama legislature passed a bill, Carly's Law, legalizing medical marijuana. Governor Robert Bentley is on record as stating that he would sign the bill if given the chance. As of April 2014, the governor has not signed the bill. If signed, the law would permit certain medical patients to legally possess CBD, cannabidiol, a marijuana extract oil low in THC, tetrahydrocannibinol. CBD has shown promise treating a variety of medical conditions including seizures.

ALASKA

Unlike other states which permit a patient to purchase his or her medical cannabis from an authorized medical cannabis dispensary, Alaska, in its enabling law, Alaska Statutes Title 17, Chapter 37, makes zero provisions for commercial distribution of any type or any quantity of medical cannabis.

Sale under any circumstances of up to an ounce of cannabis in Alaska is a misdemeanor and becomes a felony if more than one ounce is involved in the transaction. Alaska avoids entanglement between its criminal cannabis statutes and its medical cannabis statutes by providing for a relationship between the cannabis patient and his or her official caregiver, a relationship that involves dispensing medical cannabis without compensation. Provided this relationship blossoms in accord with statutory requirements, both caregiver and patient are immune from criminal prosecution.

Any individual may become a cannabis patient provided they present with at least one from a short list of specific medical diagnosis and comply with the registration requirements set forth in Alaska Statute §17.37.010. The caregiver can be any person who qualifies and registers as one under Alaska Statute §17.37.010.

Alaska Statute §17.37.040 permits the patient or the caregiver to posses up to an ounce of cannabis. However, neither the patient nor the caregiver may possess more than one ounce of cannabis either individually or collectively. Alaska Statute §17.37.040 also permits the patient or the caregiver to possess up to six marijuana plants. Not more than three of these plants are permitted to be flowering.

Alaska's medical marijuana statutory scheme is specifically designed to discourage the operation of commercial grow operations and dispensaries. Given that compensated transfers of cannabis and possession of more than twenty-five plants are both felonies, there is no way for an individual to recover his or her investment. Separately, and were commercial grow operation and dispensaries legal, there does not appear much in the way of a marketplace for the prospective investor as less than five hundred medical marijuana patients were enrolled in Alaska's medical marijuana program as of 2011 even though the program was commenced in 1998.

ARIZONA

Medical marijuana became legal in Arizona in November of 2010. The law, the Arizona Medical Marijuana Act, found in Arizona Revised Statutes Title 36, Chapter 28.1, required the Arizona Department of Health Services to organize and govern a dispensary network that could sell medical marijuana to qualified patients and caregivers. In December of 2012, Arizona conducted a lottery and awarded ninety-seven medical marijuana dispensary licenses. As of December 2013, seventy-seven of those had passed state inspections and actually opened for business.

Ultimately, the number of medical marijuana dispensaries allowed to open in Arizona is tied to the number of registered pharmacies in the state. The Department of Health and Services may not issue more than one medical marijuana dispensary registration certificate for every ten pharmacies that have registered under Arizona Revised Statutes §32-1929. Basically, for every ten Walgreens, Arizona will permit one medical marijuana dispensary. The single exception to this is that the Department of Health and Services will ensure that there is at least one medical marijuana dispensary in every county in which an application for same has been approved. Apparently, this exception is intended to cover those counties in which there are no registered pharmacies. Licensed Arizona medical marijuana dispensaries are sole-source cultivators for patients and caregivers who reside within twenty-five miles of their operation. Patients and caregivers residing outside the twenty-five mile radius may, in small quantities and under specified conditions, cultivate their own medical marijuana.

Arizona permits only non-profit medical marijuana dispensaries. What precisely, non-profit means to an investor is not clear. Somewhere between Internal Revenue Code §501(c)(3) and the Arizona Non-Profit Corporation Act (Arizona Revised Statutes §10-2001, *et seq*) the answer to that question lies and is beyond the scope of this discussion. Arizona does permit dispensary operators to recoupe reasonable expenses. However, it is unclear whether or not, or if permitted, in what manner individuals who contribute capital may recover on their investment.

Otherwise, the specifics of registration and certification of a non-profit medical marijuana dispensary can be found in Arizona Revised Statute §36-2804. Required are a non-refundable application fee of $5,000.00 along with a detailed application filed with the Arizona Department of Health Services and an operation procedure plan. All sales are subject to a state sales tax of 6.6%.

Prospective owners are also required to attest to the fact they are in compliance with city, town and county zoning restrictions. Principal officers and board members must be over twenty-one years of age, not convicted of certain felonies or been part of another Arizona dispensary which has had its registration certificate revoked.

CALIFORNIA

California legalized medical marijuana almost twenty years ago. The enabling law is cited as the Compassionate Use Act of 1996 and can be found in California's Health and Safety Code at §11362.5. Subsequently, Senate Bill 420, The Medical Marijuana Program Act, passed and established a statewide identification card system for medical marijuana patients. Medical use of cannabis in California is open-ended and may be recommended and used for any illness for which marijuana provides relief. In addition to identifying small amounts of cannabis which patients and caregivers may possess, cultivate and transport (later altered by the California Supreme Court to any reasonable amount), SB420 also established a limited right for collective and cooperative cultivation of medical cannabis.

Medical marijuana patients are permitted to band together and cultivate cannabis in a collective. See California Health and Safety Code §11362.775. By one estimate, there are more than one thousand medical cannabis dispensaries in Los Angeles alone. The exact number of grow operations there is likely incalculable. Where these collectives are legal, they are highly regulated.

California insists that any collective or cooperative be organized and operated in a manner that ensures the security of the crop and safeguards against diversion for non-medical purposes. The collective must file articles of incorporation and register under the Corporation or Food and Agricultural

Code. Co-ops may not be organized to make a profit for themselves or for their members. A co-op should not purchase cannabis from, nor should it sell cannabis to a non-member.

Where collective or cooperative medical marijuana grow operations are legal (and the list of municipalities banning them altogether continues to flourish), business licenses, sales tax permits and seller's permits are required. In keeping with California's non-diversion policy, co-ops and collectives are strongly encouraged to obtain and keep on file membership application and verification forms for each participating member. Distribution and sales of medical cannabis to non-members is unlawful.

California recognizes only co-ops and collectives. Investigations, arrests and convictions of individuals who attempt to cultivate cannabis outside of the medical statutory scheme are many and ongoing. Similarly, it is unlawful in California to operate any type of dispensary that is not associated with a properly organized and maintained co-op or collective. Attempts at subverting the statutory scheme though the establishment or the patronization of "Cannabis Clubs" whereby an individual designates the storeowner as his or her primary caregiver and receives marijuana in exchange for a cash donation, for example, are presumptively unlawful.

The California State Board of Equalization collected more than 60 million in taxes from dispensaries in 2012. Separately, the state levies a 7.5% tax on every sale, and cities grab up to another 1.5%.

COLORADO

Colorado legalized medical marijuana in 2000. The law is enshrined in Colorado's Constitution, Colorado Revised Statutes and Colorado's Board of Health Regulations. Colorado's Department of Revenue Marijuana Enforcement Division (MED) implements the Colorado Medical Marijuana Code, i.e., Colorado Revised Statutes §12-43-3.101, et seq.

Colorado's medical marijuana industry is for-profit, and dispensaries in Colorado are not limited in the number of medical marijuana patients they may sell to.

Colorado licenses and regulates Medical Marijuana Centers (dispensaries), Medical Marijuana Optional Premises Cultivation Facilities (grow operations) and Infused Products Manufacturing (edibles, tinctures, lotions and oils). Local municipalities may further regulate medical marijuana businesses. Local municipalities may also ban medical marijuana businesses. Unless the patient is certified as indigent, dispensaries must collect city and state taxes.

In order to participate in Colorado's medical marijuana industry a Registered Vendor Application (DR8533) must be submitted to MED. Application fees are $1,250.00 for infused product manufacturing and grow operations. Application fees for medical marijuana centers vary from $7,500.00 to $18,000.00 depending upon how many patients the center will dispense to. Business licenses must also be obtained.

Video recording, signage, package manifests, delivery routes, registration of employees and payment of state taxes are among the other regulations which must be complied with.

Colorado's medical marijuana industry is well-organized, well-regulated and well-enforced. It is the standard by which all other states in which medical marijuana is permitted will be measured.

CONNECTICUT

On April 3rd 2014, Connecticut awarded its first six licenses to medical marijuana dispensaries. From a field of twenty-seven applicants the businesses competed on the basis of location, site plan, business plan and financial information. It was reported that several of the successful applicants had a background in healthcare. Connecticut awarded cultivation licenses to four growers in January. As of April 3rd, Connecticut had two thousand registered medical marijuana patients.

Connecticut, according to at least one report, is the first state to engage the "Pharmaceutical/Medical" model for a medical marijuana program. The Connecticut Department of Consumer Protection explains that this model begins with physician certification then moves to production facilities operating as pharmaceutical manufacturers and ends with dispensing by a licensed pharmacist.

Specific laws governing Connecticut's dispensaries can be found in the regulations of the Department of Consumer Protection at Chapter 420f (Palliative Use of Marijuana). §21a-408h deals with dispensaries, licensure, regulations and fees. §21a-408i deals with producers, licensure, regulations and fees.

DELAWARE

Delaware legalized medical marijuana in 2011 and became almost immediately entangled with the U.S. Department of Justice over the implementation of the program.

Ultimately, federal concerns were laid to rest and Delaware is on schedule to begin dispensary licensure in April 2014, to authorize cultivation of medical cannabis in July and to begin dispensing in September. According to one report, Delaware presently has less than one hundred registered medical marijuana patients.

Delaware's medical marijuana law is found in Title 16, Chapter 49A of the Delaware Code. Delaware's dispensaries are referred to as "Compassion Centers". Initially, Delaware will maintain a single "pilot" compassion center somewhere in the state.

The center will commence cultivating cannabis in July 2014 and will be limited to no more than 150 plants and 1,500 ounces of inventoried cannabis.

Delaware maintains a website for the dispensary application process. Though the application deadline closed on April 8th 2014, you can look for the next available opportunity to bid for a compassion center at www.bids.delaware.gov, or write to william.ingram@state.de.us.

Delaware considers the following indicia as relevant when awarding a license to operate a medical marijuana compassion center: documentation of not-for-profit status, location and compliance with local zoning restrictions, character and experience of officers and board members, operations and business plans and capitalization, among other concerns.

DISTRICT OF COLUMBIA

In our nation's capital, things move slow. Voters approved medical cannabis in 1998, but it took until July 29, 2013 for Alonzo, an HIV patient, to become the city's first medical cannabis client. Since then things *have* made progress, but just barely. Rabbi Kahn, proprietor of the Takoma Wellness Center, one of less than a handful of medical marijuana dispensaries in DC, is on record as stating that the licensing application he filled out was 350 pages long. At the time the dispensaries opened only one cultivation operation had been approved. Price per ounce of medical marijuana in DC is roughly $400.00, double the price of Colorado medical cannabis. Effective December 2013, only 111 medical patients were being served in DC, and this number from a city with 600,000 residents. Numerous articles on the subject indicate the non-profit dispensaries at the heart of DC's medical marijuana program are not generating enough revenue to cover their expenses. All sales are subject to 6% tax.

The controlling law can be found in the District of Columbia's Municipal Regulations at Title 22, Subtitle C. It is the nation's most restrictive medical marijuana law. To begin with, DC recognizes only five conditions supporting the ethical use of medical marijuana: HIV, AIDS, Cancer, Glaucoma and MS.

There must also exist a bona fide relationship between physician and medical marijuana patient. Presumably, the physician recommending medical cannabis would be the same physician treating the underlying symptoms for which medical cannabis is sought. A casual or short term relationship between doctor and patient will not do. The medical marijuana patient and his or her attending physician must submit an application and a corroborating recommendation, respectively, to the Department of Health for review prior to the patient's successful registration in DC's medical marijuana program.

HAWAII

In Hawaii the acquisition, possession, cultivation, use, distribution or transportation of marijuana for medicinal use is specifically protected. Hawaii defines distribution as the transfer of marijuana and paraphernalia from the primary caregiver to the qualifying patient. Hawaii defines a primary caregiver as "a person other than the qualifying patient and the qualifying patient's physician, who is at least eighteen years of age or older who has agreed to undertake responsibility for managing the well-being of the qualifying patient with respect to the medical use of marijuana." See Hawaii Revised Statutes Title 19 §329-121.

Medical marijuana may be cultivated at the patient's home or at a location owned by the primary caregiver, provided the primary caregiver has registered that location with the Hawaii Department of Public Safety. Quantities per patient are limited to three mature plants, four immature plants and one ounce of useable cannabis for each mature plant.

For-profit dispensing of medical marijuana by a primary caregiver is not permitted at this time. Caregiving for multiple patients is not permitted at this time.

ILLINOIS

Illinois' medical marijuana program, the Compassionate Use of Medical Cannabis Pilot Program Act, Chapter 410 Illinois Compiled States §130, became effective January 1st 2014. Illinois is going to foster a for-profit medical marijuana industry. However, that industry, as a pilot program, is scheduled to sunset and in fact, could come to an end as early as December 31st 2017. The industry will continue to live only if Illinois re-authorizes the enabling law.

Following a merit-based application process, Illinois will award up to sixty marijuana dispensary licenses and twenty-one cultivation center licenses across the state. Cultivation centers will be able to grow cannabis as well as manufacture a host of other cannabis-infused products. Like other states, the Illinois medical marijuana licensure process is thorough.

Required by the Illinois Department of Financial and Professional Regulation, at a minimum, is a non-refundable application fee, corporate particulars like name and address of the proposed organization, identities and addresses of principal officers and board members, proposed corporate by-laws focusing on medical marijuana non-diversion procedures and policies, fingerprints and background checks.

Illinois is also greedy. To be considered for a dispensary license, an applicant must tender a $5,000.00 non-refundable application fee to the Department of Public Health. An applicant must be able to show $400,000.00 in liquid assets. An applicant must also have $50,000.00 in escrow. A successful applicant must also tender an additional $30,000.00 to the Department of Professional Regulation in order to receive its licenses. A 7% excise tax and a 1% sales tax are intended for all medical marijuana transactions.

To be considered for a cultivation license, an applicant must tender a $25,000.00 non-refundable application fee to the Department of Health. An applicant must also have $2,000,000.00 in an escrow account. A successful applicant must also tender an additional $200,000.00 to the Department of Professional Regulation in order to receive its license. On the bright side, a single entity may apply for up to three cultivation center licenses.

MAINE

Maine began its medical marijuana program in 1999. Maine may well be the most accommodating state in which to open a medical marijuana dispensary. The controlling law can be found in Title 22 Maine Revised Statutes Chapter 558 §2383-B. The controlling authority for the administration of Maine's medical marijuana program is the Maine Department of Health and Human Services. Maine permits a broad spectrum of patients to participate in its medical marijuana program, including those individuals who suffer from PTSD. Maine only permits non-profit dispensaries. However, each dispensary may cultivate and may act as the patient's primary caregiver. There is no limit on the number of patients that a dispensary may care for.

As the law in Maine is currently written, the Department is required to register and issue a registration certificate within 30 days to any eligible person or entity who completes an application in accord with the provisions of the law. The number of plants a dispensary may cultivate is dependant upon the number of patients who have designated that dispensary as their primary caregiver.

While Maine dispensaries must be operated as non-profits, there is no requirement that the dispensary conduct itself as a 501(c)(3). At present, there is no requirement that the dispensary even incorporate. There are, however, limitations.

A dispensary may not be located within 500 feet of a school. There must be a board of directors, none of whom may be a convicted felon. Security is paramount and all cultivation must take place in an enclosed, locked facility. Dispensaries may not purchase marijuana. Local jurisdictions may limit the number of dispensaries and adopt appropriate zoning regulations. All sales are subject to a 5.5% tax.

MARYLAND

Maryland's medical marijuana program will become law on June 1, 2014. It is anticipated that Maryland will begin issuing medical marijuana dispensary licenses sometime in early to mid-2016. The program is to be administered by Maryland's Department of Health and Mental Hygiene. Application guidelines for academic medical centers to operate medical marijuana programs can be found at Title 11 Maryland Code Annotated §13-3304. Application guidelines for the cultivation of medical marijuana can be found at Title 11 Maryland Code Annotated §13-3308.

Maryland defines academic medical centers, the state's single source for medical marijuana dispensing, as "hospitals that perform U.S. Health and Human Services-approved research and have medical residency programs," a definition which cuts just about every entrepreneur out of the medical marijuana dispensary picture. However, Maryland's application guidelines for medical marijuana cultivation do not at first glance appear as restrictive.

Precious little information can be gleaned from reading the controlling statute other than grow operations will be in-state and will sell only to approved dispensaries. Maryland will permit up to five grow operations for every licensed dispensary.

MASSACHUSETTS

The state's medical marijuana law became effective January 1, 2013. All dispensaries are non-profit and are referred to as medical marijuana treatment centers. The enabling legislation can be found in Chapter 39 of the General Laws of Massachusetts. The state has capped the number of medical marijuana treatment centers at seventy. In January 2014, the state health department awarded the first twenty their licenses. The application and review process for the remaining fifty is ongoing. It will likely be mid-summer before any of them open their doors for business.

Like other states, Massachusetts uses a point scoring system to determine who among a field of many applicants should ultimately be awarded a license to open a marijuana treatment center. In addition to considering business plans, finances and the backgrounds of the entrepreneurs, the state's scoring system rewards companies which have support for their treatment centers and grow operations from the communities in which they plan to locate. Considerations also included ownership of buildings rather than lease of buildings.

Though Massachusetts publishes a list of diseases which qualify a patient for medical marijuana use; the list is not exhaustive. The state also provides the medical practitioner with the discretion to determine which diseases can be treated with cannabis. In this manner psychiatric disorders make it on to the list. Massachusetts does not limit the number of patients a treatment center may serve.

MICHIGAN

Michigan's medical marijuana law, found at Michigan Compiled Laws §333.26424, makes no provisions for commercial dispensaries or cultivation. A patient may cultivate his or her own cannabis or delegate that duty to his or her primary caregiver. The caregiver may assume responsibility for up to five registered patients and may possess up to twelve plants for each patient for a total of seventy-two plants. Michigan has a fluid list of medical conditions which qualify a patient for use of medical marijuana and recently added PTSD to that list.

Pursuant to *Michigan v. McQueen*, primary caregivers cannot allow patients to transfer cannabis to each other under the program or their business can be declared a public nuisance subject to injunction.

Michigan permits primary caregivers to recoup the costs associated with providing care to the registered medical marijuana patient. Whatever that cost is, the State of Michigan will not intervene and the patient is directed to obtain private counsel to resolve any dispute which may arise. A primary caregiver cannot have been convicted of any felony ten years prior to seeking a license. No person convicted of a crime of violence or of a drug crime may ever become a primary caregiver.

MONTANA

The controlling law for the Montana Marijuana Act can be found at Title 50 Montana Code Annotated §46-301, *et seq*. §46-308 covers cannabis-provider types, their limitations and permitted activities. As of September 2013, just over 7,000 patients were enrolled in the program.

Montana permits providers to cultivate cannabis or otherwise assist a medical marijuana patient with cannabis-infused products. The provider is required to be a Montana resident and submit their name and address and fingerprints to the Department of Public Health and Human Services. Marijuana may only be cultivated at a single location and that location must either be owned by the provider or if leased, the landlord must acknowledge in writing that said premises will be used to grow cannabis. Neither the patient nor the provider may cultivate cooperatively with other patients or providers.

The provider must pay a $50 annual fee and cannot have been convicted of any felony, any drug crime or of fraudulent misrepresentation. Additionally, the provider cannot register with the Department if he or she is delinquent on state taxes, a judgment, child support or student loans. The provider may assist up to three registered medical marijuana patients. If the provider is also a registered patient, he or she must count him or herself as one of the three.

Providers *may not* accept anything of value, including monetary remuneration for any products or services provided to the registered medical marijuana patient.

NEVADA

Nevada's medical marijuana law can be found at Nevada Revised Statutes §453A.010, *et seq*. The program is administered by the state Health Division. Effective April 1, 2014, Nevada permits a regulated medical marijuana industry. Production and distribution of medical marijuana is governed by §453A.320 through §453A.344. Requirements concerning operation of medical marijuana establishments is governed by §453A.350 through §453A.370.

Nevada, like other states, uses a scoring system based upon many different factors to determine who among applicants will operate within the industry. Nevada assigns dispensaries licenses, which may be for-profit, on the basis of county population. Counties with populations over 700,000 may have 40 licensed medical marijuana businesses, for example. According to Senate Bill 374, signed into law on June 13th 2013, this translates into a maximum number of 66 licensed dispensaries at this time.

Nevada sets the schedule of fees for medical marijuana dispensaries, medical marijuana cultivation facilities, for infused product manufacturers, testing laboratories and their staffs. Initial fees range from $3,000.00 for a cultivator to $30,000.00 for a dispensary. Renewal fees are much less. In addition to Nevada's 6.85% sales tax, the state will add a 2% excise tax on both wholesale and retail medical marijuana transactions.

NEW HAMPSHIRE

The state's enabling legislation, Chapter 126 New Hampshire Statutes, permits up to four non-profit alternative treatment centers in the state. The particulars governing the process of establishing these alternative treatment centers are set forth in New Hampshire Statues Chapter 126-W:7 IV(a). The program will be administered by the Department of Health and Human Services. New Hampshire, like other states, will determine treatment center licensees on the basis of a points-scored, merit-based application. New Hampshire alternative treatment centers will cultivate and dispense medical cannabis.

Among the requirements of the successful applicant shall be a board of directors composed in part of individuals who do not have a financial interest in the enterprise but among whom are one physician, one advance practice registered nurse or state-licensed pharmacist and one individual eligible to register as a New Hampshire medical marijuana patient. Other standard considerations such as proposed location and zoning restrictions, expertise in running a business, security and inventory control must be included in the application.

At the time the application is being considered, the Department will solicit input from various members of the community in which the center is to be located.

NEW JERSEY

The state's medical marijuana law, the New Jersey Compassionate Use Medical Marijuana Act, can be found at New Jersey Statutes §24:61-1. The program was commenced in September 2013. The application process and regulations governing New Jersey's alternative treatment centers can be found at §24:61-7. The program is administered by the state's Department of Health and Senior Services. Alternative treatment centers shall be able to cultivate and dispense medical cannabis.

New Jersey has committed to the establishment of a "sufficient number" of alternative treatment centers. Based on uncertain needs though, the precise number of treatment centers is yet unknown. However, New Jersey has committed to the licensure of two each non-profit treatment centers in the North, Central and South sectors of the state. And while each non-profit must comport itself with all applicable New Jersey state laws governing non-profits, the state will not require those non-profits to be organized as one under Internal Revenue Code §501(c)(3). After those centers are open for business, New Jersey will permit for-profit treatment centers to operate in the state.

New Jersey charges $20,000.00 for an alternative treatment center application fee, $2,000.00 of which is non-refundable. As of October 2013, only one treatment center was open. Some 1,200 medical marijuana patients were registered with New Jersey by the last quarter of 2013. New Jersey charges a 7% tax on all sales of medical marijuana.

New Jersey, like other states, requires a criminal background check on any individual seeking to operate an alternative treatment center. Unlike other states, New Jersey will not disqualify an applicant with a felonious background if that applicant can by clear and convincing evidence demonstrate to the Commissioner of Health and Senior Services that he or she has been rehabilitated.

NEW MEXICO

The state's medical marijuana program has been in effect since 2007. It is referred to as the Lynn and

Erin Compassionate Use Act and can be found at Title 26 New Mexico Statutes §2B-2. The program is administered by the New Mexico Department of Health.

There are twenty-three licensed non-profit producers in New Mexico. Each producer is authorized to grow up to 150 total mature plants and seedlings for distribution to patients and their caregivers. At this time no other producer licenses are being considered. According to one source, the Department of Health is monitoring the availability of medical cannabis and will notify the public when the need for additional non-profit producers is identified.

New Mexico non-profit cannabis producers must adhere to strict, state employment guidelines. Those guidelines are specific and leave nothing to the imagination.

New Mexico charges a non-refundable $1,000.00 application fee for producers. Licensing fees depend upon how long the enterprise has been in business: first year . . . $5,000.00, second year . . . $10,000.00, third year . . . $20,000.00, three years and more . . . $30,000.00. As of August 2013, a little fewer than 10,000 patients were enrolled in New Mexico's medical marijuana program and of that number, approximately one third were growing their own. New Mexico collects a tax of between 5.125% to 8.8675% on all sales of medical cannabis. The rates vary depending upon municipality.

OREGON

Since 1998 Oregon's medical marijuana program was strictly homegrown, limited in scope to cultivation by patients and/or their caregivers. However, on August 14th 2013, Governor John Kitzhaber signed HB 3460 and created a program allowing state licensing and regulation of medical marijuana facilities. The governing law can be found at Oregon Revised Statutes §475.300 through §475.346. The program is administered by Oregon's Health Authority and the state's Department of Public health. As of late 2013, Oregon had enrolled almost 60,000 patients and 30,000 caregivers in its medical marijuana program.

The registration system, rules and fees to operate an Oregon marijuana grow site can be found at §475.304. While many of the costs associated with operating a marijuana grow site may be reimbursable at the time of delivery, labor costs associated with running a marijuana grow site may not be reimbursed when delivery is made to a patient or a patient's caregiver. §475.304 is silent regarding how many plants a grow site may contain.

Medical marijuana facility registration, qualifications, inspections, revocations, rules and fees are set forth in §475.314. Oregon law states only that a medical marijuana facility must be registered as a "business" with the Office of the Secretary of State. It is not clear whether or not this business may operate for profit. Statewide zoning restrictions apply to medical marijuana facilities. Once an individual submits a completed facility application and the facility meets the necessary requirements and the applicant passes a criminal background check, Oregon law states that a "proof of registration," i.e., a green light to start the business, *shall* be issued. Medical marijuana facilities may reimburse grow sites for all costs which are "normal and customary."

RHODE ISLAND

Rhode Island is the only state to override a governor's veto and establish a medical marijuana program. The laws governing Rhode Island's medical marijuana program can be found in Rhode Island General

Laws at Chapter 21-28.6. The program is administered by the Rhode Island Department of Health. Dispensary combination grow centers are referred to as compassion centers, and by statute are limited statewide to a maximum number of three.

Compassion centers are obtained by way of application. The controlling law is set forth in Chapter 21-28.6-12. As of April 2014, two rounds in the compassion center application process have occurred. The application fee is $250.00. Out of thirty-three applications, Rhode Island approved three compassion centers and issued registration certificates. As of April 2014, two have opened. As of September 2013, there were approximately 6,000 medical marijuana patients and 3,500 registered caregivers in Rhode Island.

VERMONT

The law governing the therapeutic use of cannabis can be found in Title 18 Vermont Statutes Annotated Chapter 86. Statewide, Vermont will establish four non-profit medical marijuana dispensaries. Dispensary licensure is administered by Vermont's Department of Public Safety. Vermont dispensaries are authorized to dispense and cultivate as well as manufacture cannabis-infused products. Vermont opened its first two dispensaries in 2011. As of late 2013, Vermont had less than 900 enrollees in its medical marijuana program.

Each applicant interested in competing for the opportunity to run a Vermont medical marijuana dispensary must pay a $2,500.00 application fee. If the application is approved, the successful applicant must also pay an annual registration fee of $20,000.00 the first year and $30,000.00 in each subsequent year. For each registered patient, a Vermont medical marijuana dispensary may cultivate two mature plants, seven immature plants and possess up to two ounces of usable marijuana. Vermont medical marijuana patients may not "walk in" to their dispensary, but must instead have an appointment. Cannabis possessed by a dispensary in excess of its patients' needs must be destroyed.

Vermont insists upon a bona fide relationship between recommending physician and medical marijuana patient. Again, a casual relationship between doctor and patient will not suffice. Medical cannabis cannot be the patient's first medical choice for relief from his or her symptoms, but rather, the last resort and his or her doctor must attest to this.

WASHINGTON

The law governing the state's medical cannabis program can be found at Washington Revised Statutes Chapter 69.51a. The program is administered by the Washington State Department of Health. No provisions for commercial dispensaries or commercial grow sites are made by this law.

A medical cannabis cultivation and dispensing relationship is authorized only between a patient and his or caregiver. Either party may, but is not required to register by state law. The qualifying patient or his or her caregiver may possess up to fifteen cannabis plants and up to two ounces of useable marijuana. Cannabis patients may also form cooperative cultivation associations. These are referred to as collective gardens. No more than ten qualifying patients may participate in a collective garden at any one time. A collective garden may contain fifteen plants per patient, but cannot under any circumstance contain more than forty-five plants.

Washington provides local communities with the right to regulate the production of cannabis in terms of zoning and licensure, as long as the zoning and licensure regulations do not prohibit altogether said production of cannabis.

Childproofing Regulations

EVERY YEAR, THOUSANDS OF INGESTIONS ARE REPORTED to poison control centers, the majority involving infants under a year old swallowing cigarettes, liquid detergents, and pills left on parents' nightstands. If small children ingest unpalatable poisons in small or large numbers, they will undoubtedly be even more likely to ingest flavored marijuana edibles or marijuana products specifically designed to taste good. These items can include brownies, gummy bears, hard candies, chocolates, and more importantly the marijuana itself. Any of these items can be mistaken for candy by children, or even adults, if left out in the open or in an area frequented by children.

In a young, burgeoning industry like this one, it's crucial that your business follows every regulation. Who knows when an enforcement agency might send in a secret shopper? Your employees should be aware of every major standard, especially when it comes to packaging. In Colorado, the rules set by Amendment 64 mean that you can't simply slip your product into a sandwich bag and let it walk out the door. Anything you sell—whether herb or edible—must first be placed in a childproof jar, then into an opaque, re-closable plastic bag. Neither should feature a cartoon character or similar images that might appeal to children.

The label on any jar containing marijuana must be clearly visible, its text must be in English and no smaller than one-sixteenth of an inch, and it must contain the license number of both the facility (and facilities) where the marijuana was grown and the store where you're selling it. It should also include the Identity Statement and Standardized Symbol of your dispensary, the harvest batch number of the product, the date of sale, the net weight (to the tenth of a gram), the Universal Symbol (no smaller than a quarter inch by a quarter inch), a list of any nonorganic pesticides used during cultivation, and the following warnings:

1. There may be health risks associated with the consumption of this product.

2. This product is intended for use by adults 21 years and older. Keep out of the reach of children.

3. This product is unlawful outside the State of Colorado.

4. There may be additional health risks associated with the consumption of this product for women who are pregnant, breastfeeding, or planning on becoming pregnant.

5. Do not drive or operate heavy machinery while using marijuana.

Labels placed on edibles must also include an ingredient list (including any potential allergens), a statement regarding refrigeration, a serving size statement, and an expiration date. You may also choose to affix a label with information on the product's compatibility with dietary restrictions and a nutritional fact panel (based on the number of THC servings contained).

Of course, you must keep in mind that the specifics of each label will vary based on the type of product you're selling. And as more and more of the country moves toward legalization, you'll need to look into the regulations being set by your own state. It's likely that many of them will be based on the groundbreaking Amendment 64, but you don't want to make a careless mistake that gets your dispensary into trouble.

You'll also need to research the companies that supply childproof jars and bags, the cost of which you'll have to factor into your budget. Ordered in bulk, particularly from countries like China, the price is minimal. However, you might also see this as an opportunity for continued marketing. By spending a little more for high-quality, personalized jars and bags (with your company logo and website, for instance), you can raise awareness to your brand and demonstrate that your dispensary is a cut above. There are a number of U.S. based businesses that specialize in packaging, many of them striving to be price competitive with their overseas counterparts. Among the largest and best known distributors is Kush Bottles, which worked with Colorado legislators to create childproofing legislation.

Whatever you decide, be sure to do your research and make the best decision for your company, both creatively and financially.

SECTION XI

DREAM BIG

Main Street to Wall Street

SO WHY DOES IT MAKE SENSE TO INVEST in the *Marijuana* business. What is the long-term attraction other than the fact that, well let's just say you enjoy what you're doing. You have been intrigued with marijuana since high school and your college days, but the lure of this business is now much different? Are you thinking love, lust or just the money? We're talking about the green stuff—not the product!—the money. And if you plant your cards right, there could be a lot of it.

There are many different hurdles to get into this business. This book reviews in detail how to to open and successfully run a marijuana business. You may be wondering where is this "BIG" money going to come from when the time comes to sell? The money that takes the everyday Joe Businessman to the Forbes List. What is the Forbes List?

The Forbes List is a series of published rankings that showcase influential public figures and companies. Lists include rankings of the top 100 celebrities, the most powerful women, the largest private companies, the richest Americans and the world's billionaires. These lists are regular features in Forbes magazine, which is produced and published by the Forbes Media company. Its primary audience is business professionals and entrepreneurs.

Can you be part of this elite group? Well maybe. That's entirely up to you. Your journey can start today. Well, assuming you establish a brand, farm mass quantities of recognized quality product and grow your business on a regional scale. Either you continue to consider yourself a "going concern," and continue the entrepreneurial dream, or you start to develop aspirations that will more than ensure your long-term financial security. You get bought out. Not by your neighbor, friend, family member or stoner with rich parents. We are talking big time here. WALL STREET!

The mechanics of Wall Street involvement are two-fold. First, there's the buyer. Who would buy you? The likely players in this space would be your major players in the alcohol and tobacco industry. These guys are not going to get into a business like marijuana while it's nascent. Too many legal and regulatory barriers while legality is still in question in most of the country and the world. But you see those barriers slowly come down. This gives you the opportunity to step in where they cannot. The first-mover advantage cannot be understated in entrepreneurial ventures. Let's say you live in Oregon, or California, Colorado, Vermont or New Hampshire, states with either currently lax cannabis laws or libertarian leanings that make them prime candidates to follow Colorado and Washington. You set up shop when this happens. Operations, distribution, product development. There will be cannabis expos and conferences where you'll network with your competitors and colleagues in other states. You'll become partners with these people, your revenues will accelerate, and your products will diversify and costs will go down.

This is when the bigwigs will really start to take notice. They have declining revenues in cigarettes, and those are likely to never return. Their shareholders will be clamoring for great excess returns, greater alpha, and yes the most important thing—money, dosh, dough, bread, coin. You get what we're saying here? Once the tide fully turns on the marijuana industry, you can bet bottom dollar these guys are going to want in on the business. And they are prime candidates to take your regional, networked, growing business to the next level due to their scale, legal prowess and understanding of these types of industries. Once it's no longer a "dirty" business, the Phillip Morris' and JG Reynolds' of the world are going to want to jump all over this industry and this is where you get to capitalize on your first mover advantage I described earlier. They already are taking notice and dollars to donuts they are well attuned to what is happening across the country and have a plan in place to move when the time is right.

But why would you sell (keep in mind you don't actually have to sell, per se, you can become majority shareholder and maintain your rights to run the firm as chairman or CEO)? You're doing well, life is good. But it could be better. This is where we introduce the concept of the multiplier. Depending on your industry, Wall Street will assign a multiplier to either your top line (revenue), operating profit (EBITDA), or bottom line (net income). For growth stage firms, this is usually applied to the top line, which is better for you. The big time players can clean up your operations and achieve scale in a way you definitely cannot on your own. Grow operations, big time attorneys in place, accountants, human resource departments and banking relationships are all part of their systems. Thus they are not worried about your SG&A costs, or your long-term logistical capabilities. This will all become part of their larger lattice structure in time. Let's say, and this is arbitrary, they offer you 8x revenue, which is standard for asset intensive industries, like oil and gas. That makes it a low number for a business like marijuana, but it's a safe play. Assuming a net income—again arbitrary—of 5% top line, you just got offered 200 times your take home. OMG. Who would have thought opening a marijuana business would give you such opportunities. Trust me, the wheels are turning and Wall Street already has their eyes on many of the Main Street establishments that are operating today. Not only dispensaries and grow facilities but edible consumables, e-cigarettes and the likes of any other product they can develop into part of their new found business.

There will be competition for the top performers as well. This is really where Wall Street comes into play. Investment bankers get a cut of your sale and a piece of the equity, and this is done so that they align their interests with not only yours but your buyer. The firms that will be interested will all depend on your size. Don't expect Goldman Sachs to come calling for any deal with less than 250 million, but you can easily bring in the mid-tier banks like Credit Suisse or some of the boutique specialty shops that will specialize in this new industry. The value of your business will be dependent on how many partners you have in your area, other states or regions, your sales and your infrastructure. But in the end it's mostly about your revenue and how much growth you can achieve. Like I said, any potential buyer will be able to trim the fat and turn your firm into a lean, mean and green fighting machine. Wall Street M&A teams facilitate these deals because they have access to all potential buyers, are independent evaluators of value, and seek the best return for both sides as well as themselves. In a scenario such as this, everyone wins. But you can choose how you want the sale to go down.

Let's say you don't want to sell. Maybe you want to go public. You'll still get Wall Street's attention, but in this case you'll talk to the underwriters, not the M&A team. And your value will be determined by the masses after the deal is priced by the bank. Your equity could skyrocket, you can still be in control of your company, and you can sit on top of the world. Day-to-day employees of a firm like Twitter made 1 or 2 million dollars in equity EACH on the day the firm went public. An industry like cannabis has all the underpinnings of the explosive growth environment of these successful and flashy tech company IPOs. Trust me, everyone wants to be valued like a tech company. That's when the 8x I mentioned above becomes 10x or 15x.

There is an incredible amount of available growth in this industry. It's up to you to individually take advantage of a frontier market. There is literally NO COMPETITION in this space that's legal. Once the walls come down, and the rest of the country follows suit, you can carve out your niche and be off to the races. A successful entrepreneurial venture will have so much long-term value to the major corporate entities as well as worldwide equity markets. How you'd like to play it is your choice. You can build an empire, then sell it to a bigger empire and call it a life. You can sell a minority stake or a majority stake, and stay on with your firm and watch it grow into something only a big name firm could offer. Or you can go public, fill your coffers with cash and become a marijuana magnate with your spoils. You can achieve the scale of a major corporation in time.

Many businesses stay small and that's okay. But for the chosen few who think big, magic can happen. "Move over Mr. Forbes, we have a new person looking to get on your list!" Who would have thought any of this possible?

Pot of Gold

TAKE A CHANCE! YOUR LIFE INVOLVES CHANCE. The person who goes farthest is generally the one who is passionate and willing to do whatever it takes to be part of something unimaginable!

Most people dream the impossible dream. They have the ideas and resources but just can't seem to get motivated enough or have the gumption to actually take the necessary steps to get involved with something novel and different that could make them rich and change their lives forever.

Many dream of being part of a brand new industry or creating a new business model to launch, inventing fresh ideas and introducing new concepts as a potential startup business. Notice the word "potential." If you've read this book, you know the potential in the marijuana business is UNLIMITED as far as growth. Learning this industry now will give you the opportunity to thrive for many years, whether it's ownership, management or employment.

People tend to assume that if they work hard and save money, one day they will end up wealthy. This is wishful thinking. They are more likely to end up with some modest but useful savings, hopefully stay healthy, and have enough money to retire and live out their golden years.

If you want to accumulate serious wealth, you will have to join the movement into the new prohibition: marijuana. No, it will not be easy, but with every risk there is reward. You now have the tools to construct your plan. If you follow the steps given in this book, you may find yourself a wealthy business person in a few short years. It's up to you to be part of the movement into the newest, most lucrative business in the United States today.

In closing, here is a reminder of the new areas of business that will be created from the creation of marijuana dispensaries and gardens. Many don't realize other potential business opportunities that will arise.

- Employment
- Distribution of products
- Construction
- Commercial leasing
- Financial lending
- Manufacturing
- Research and Development

The list goes on . . .

FIND YOUR POT OF GOLD.

10 Facts About Marijuana

1

Roughly 750,000 people are arrested for marijuana each year, the vast majority of them for simple possession, with racial minorities over-represented.

2

Most marijuana users never use any other illicit drug.

3

Increasing admissions for treatment are a reflection of the criminal justice system's predominant role, rather than increasing rates of clinical dependence.

4

Marijuana potency is not related to risk of dependence or health impacts.

5

Marijuana can be good for mental health.

6

Marijuana can be protective against the formation of cancer.

7

Marijuana has been proven helpful for treating the symptoms of a variety of medical conditions. The body's endocannabinoid system may explain why.

8

Rates of marijuana use among young people tend to DECREASE when a state adopts medical marijuana.

9

Marijuana does not cause long-term cognitive impairment in adult users.

10

There is no compelling evidence that marijuana contributes substantially to traffic accidents and fatalities.

ACKNOWLEDGEMENT

A special thanks to Stigs.

THE AUTHOR

JEFF GRISSLER, a consultant and entrepreneur, is a two-time Amazon bestselling author and has been published in many trade magazines around the world. Jeff is setting a new business standard in the fast growing marijuana industry as we see it today. A gifted businessman, he prides himself on his networking ability to bring people together to share new ideas, explore business opportunities, partnerships and marketing techniques.

His cunning ability to explore new businesses first-hand led him to get involved with the fastest growing business in the world today: Marijuana. As a businessman, he understands the landscape and what owners can expect and guides them to financial success.

Jeff Grissler

Consulting for all your medical and recreational marijuana business needs.

Site planning and location

Landlord negotiations

Business plans

Funding procurement

Safety

Hiring employees

Municipality requirements

State requirements

Dispensary plans

Grow facility layouts and equipment

Farming requirments and setup

Jeff Grissler (646) 675-0575
jeffreadysetgo@gmail.com

CPSIA information can be obtained
at www.ICGtesting.com
Printed in the USA
LVOW02s2333270117

522431LV00020BA/88/P